86-

THIS
WAY
UP

THIS WAY UP

Torah Essays on Spiritual Growth

REBBETZIN TZIPORAH HELLER

FELDHEIM PUBLISHERS
JERUSALEM　NEW YORK

ISBN 1-58330-416-9

First published 2000

Copyright © 2000, 2004 by Tziporah Heller
www.tziporahheller.com

All rights reserved.
No part of this publication may be translated,
reproduced, stored in a retrieval system or transmitted,
in any form or by any means, electronic, mechanical,
photocopying, recording or otherwise, without
prior permission in writing from the publishers.

FELDHEIM PUBLISHERS
POB 43163 / Jerusalem, Israel

208 Airport Executive Park
Nanuet, NY 10954

www.feldheim.com

Printed in Israel

NEVE · YERUSHALAYIM
נוה . ירושלים

בס"ד

TANENBAUM COLLEGE

PRESIDENT
Bernard Hochstein

CHAIRMAN OF THE BOARD
Howard P. Ronson

DEAN
Rabbi Dr. Dovid Refson

DIRECTOR GENERAL
Avrohom Stefansky

NEVE
Rabbi Moshe Chalkowski

MECHINA
Rabbi Eliezer Liff

SHALHEVET
Rabbi David Kass

ISRAELI DIVISION
Rabbi Chaim Metzger

FRENCH DIVISION
Rabbi Gerard Ackermann

RUSSIAN/CIS DIVISION
Rabbi Shlomo Nachat

BNOS CHAVA
Rabbi Dovid Abramov
Rabbi Nosson Geisler

MICHLELET ESTHER
Rabbi Boruch Smith
Rabbi Ari Winter

NEVE TEHILA
Rabbi Yair Kramer

ME'OHR BAIS YAAKOV
Rabbi Zecharya Greenwald

ZAIDNER INSTITUTE/
MAALOT YERUSHALAYIM
Phyllis Geisler

MAALOT ISRAEL
Chana Finkel

MORESHET INSTITUTE
Rabbi David Kass

BACHELOR'S DEGREE IN
SOCIAL WORK
Chaya Wexler

MASTER'S DEGREE IN
FAMILY COUNSELING
Dr. Yisrael Levitz

MASTER'S DEGREE IN SPEECH-
LANGUAGE PATHOLOGY
Jerry Koller

REGISTRAR
Dr. Avraham Schwartzbaum

ASSOCIATE REGISTRAR
David Starr-Glass

ASSOCIATE DIRECTOR
Chaya Wexler

It is truly a pleasure to write a few words on behalf of Rebbetzin Tziporah Heller. Rarely does the opportunity arise to express in writing ones recognition of how great is the work of a fellow teacher.

It can be truly be said that Rebbetzin Tziporah is one of the greatest (if not the greatest) women teachers in the whole world. Rebbetzin Heller possesses, and shares with all, a vast wealth of knowledge in Torah, also in the secular fields, and an in-depth knowledge of all areas of human behavior. The above, coupled with an extraordinary sense of humor and a perspective that covers every detail, enables her to give lectures, classes and discussions that have no equal.

This book will surely be of tremendous interest and inspiration; may Hashem bring it to be read near and far. The hope of the author is that those who study this book will apply its wisdom and ideas to themselves and progress in their עבודת השם. This will be a קידוש שם שמים, which is what the author sees as her whole purpose in life. May it be the will of Hashem that Mrs. Tziporah Heller, together with her great husband, see much nachas from their children and from all their many works.

A כתיבה וחתימה טובה to them and to all who acquire this book.

משה מרדכי שלקובסקי

מנהל
ט"ז אלול תשס"ס

P.O. Box 43016, Beit Yitzchak Street, Har Nof, Jerusalem, Israel. Tel. (02) 654-4555. Fax (02) 651-9376
25 Broadway, New York, NY 10004, Tel. (212) 422-1110. Fax (212) 785-0898
ת.ד. 43016 רח' בית יצחק, הר נוף, ירושלים, ישראל. טלפון (02) 654-4555. פקס 9376-651 (02)

acknowledgments

One of my dearest friends asked me how it is possible to write an article on the weekly Torah portion week after week. I have no doubt that no matter how many years the Creator bestows upon me, I will not begin to scratch the surface.

What the newspaper *Hamodia* has given me is the opportunity to observe the depth and breadth of the Torah from a closer place than I would have approached on my own. The light that is concealed in every moment of living is there for us to examine once we open ourselves to observing the vision of reality that God has provided for us. Every era has its challenges, as does every day. What we were certain of yesterday is frequently today's useless and tired cliché. Each week's *parashah* gives us the opportunity to re-examine the premises that govern our lives, to move forward with them and truly "live with the times."

I wish to take this opportunity to thank those who made it possible for me to have access to the Torah, my teachers (especially Rebbetzin Chaya Korf, and far later, Rav Freifeld *ztz"l*, who I knew briefly enough to let him change me forever), and the rabbis at Neve Yerushalayim who gave me the opportunity to teach. The Brisker Rav was known to say that if you can't explain something, you don't understand it. Encountering the intellectual scrutiny and spiritual honesty of my students is one of the greatest treasures that God has given me. Without the trust and encouragement of Rabbis Refson and Chalkowski, I would never have had to examine what I know and believe.

My husband has read these articles as they were written. His erudition and clarity of thought is a hidden presence on each page. Everyone who reads the book is a beneficiary of his integrity.

Further acknowledgment is owed to Mrs. Aviva Rappaport, who is both the kind friend that the Mishnah tells us to acquire, and the perfect evaluator who unstintingly applies her skills and eloquence to my articles and to so much of the English edition of *Hamodia*.

The finished product would never be what it is without the editorial assistance of Mrs. Suri Brand and the editorial and production staff of Feldheim Publishers.

introduction

With all that has been said and written about the Torah community's need for improvement in meeting the challenges of our time, one fact can easily be listed to our credit: the popularity of Rebbetzin Tzipporah Heller's teachings.

We are busy and stressed, coping with daily responsibilities, and at times overwhelmed by the very real difficulties facing us. We juggle home and family, community and work, often feeling that we are one step – or five minutes – away from seeing the whole edifice collapse. And while we may cherish nostalgia and romanticize times gone by, none of us really longs for the days when a move to another country meant not seeing one's family again.

What we do long for is spiritual sustenance.

This is where Rebbetzin Heller comes in. She asks us to open ourselves to the Truth with a capital T, the God-given Truth as transmitted by our Sages, and then she asks us – outright, with no mincing of words – to commit ourselves to that Truth.

She never claims it will be an easy task, human nature being what it is, but she does introduce us to people who have done it. Her gift for connecting with other people brings them to share their stories and struggles with her, and through her, with us. By humanizing the lofty ideals that we know are our real goal in life, she makes them accessible. In this sense, she helps us shoulder the load of our individual and collective burdens.

For over half a century, *Hamodia* has been the voice of Torah Jewry. Guided by Torah giants in every generation, the newspaper has a long tradition of providing a distinguished platform for outstanding writers and thinkers whose words of inspiration have far-ranging impact on the public mind. It was in continuation of this mission of public service that the English-language edition of *Hamodia* invited Rebbetzin Heller to contribute a regular column. Those articles, based on *Parashas Ha-shavua*, form the core of this book.

In the two-and-a-half years since its first issue of Purim 5758/1998, the newspaper has grown both in content and readership. With three editions published– Israel, the United States and England – and worldwide distribution, it unites its readers into a global community. The fan letters received for Rebbetzin Heller's articles and the results of *Hamodia*'s readership survey confirming the column's enormous popularity come as no surprise. They reflect the public's desire for quality writing that uplifts, inspires, stimulates thought and leads to more successful living.

May Rebbetzin Heller's words, which always come from the heart, continue to enter our hearts for many more years to come.

Aviva Rappaport
Hamodia Editorial Dept.

contents

Rebuilding ourselves, rebuilding the world, 1
Becoming your true self, 7
Playing by the rules, 13
Are you fooling yourself?, 19
Fit for a king, 24
The invisible ones, 30
"I'm getting there!", 36
Anatomy of a search, 41
Stopping the clock, 47
Staying afloat, 53
Created in his image, 57
Growing old gratefully, 62
Who are we fooling?, 66
Climbing the ladder, 72
Faded dreams, 77
The gift of joy, 82
The joy of renewal, 88
Confronting rivalry, 94
We can reflect the light, 99
The freedom to be ourselves, 105
Regaining sensitivity, 110
Silencing the voice of pharaoh, 116
The tenth song, 121
The third partner, 127
An encounter with absolute truth, 132
The soul of the world, 138
The power within us, 143

Why I don't hate pesach cleaning, 148
The joy of finding the source, 153
Breaking through the barriers, 158
Does too much freedom restrict us?, 163
Recycling our kedushah, 168
Crossing the bridge, 173
The source of humility, 178
A glimpse of infinity, 183
The light of awareness, 188
Seeing the goodness, 193
The unbreakable bond, 199
Meet Kimchis, 205
Eretz Yisrael: a beautiful gift, 211
The tragedy of envy, 216
Reflections on enigmas, 221
Changing curses to blessings, 226
What makes a hero?, 231
Regaining our ability to remain unchanging, 236

CHAPTER ONE
rebuilding ourselves, rebuilding the world

MOURNING SOMETHING YOU never had is both painful and confusing. The three-week period which begins with the seventeenth of Tammuz and culminates with the twenty-five hour fast of Tishah B'Av on the ninth of Av requires an emotional stretch that at times seems beyond the capacity of those of us born close to two thousand years later. I have vivid memories of sitting at the feet of my counselor at camp, listening to the *kinos* being read and wanting desperately to be touched, to truly feel the loss the destruction of our Holy Temple has engendered. At the time, I attributed the coldness that I could not hide even from my own immaturity to the foreign vocabulary. The poetry of the dirges was far beyond my depth of sensitivity or my very limited Hebrew. As I grew more mature, I knew the lack was within me.

My attempts to envision the horror of the desolation that replaced the *Beis HaMikdash* were hampered by one significant factor. My picture of the *Beis HaMikdash* was flat, lifeless, and disconnected from my sense of reality. I could describe it, but all of the dimensions with which I was familiar were those of the surface. I could not fathom that which was within, its source of life and significance. I didn't know what to do with Tishah B'Av. The long, languid afternoon would pass. Holocaust books with their gruesome content and terrifying photos would capture my inner horizon, yet the connection between our agony and its root escaped me.

I didn't know what it was that I had never had.

The *Beis HaMikdash* was never an edifice purely of stone and wood. When Titus and his Roman legions destroyed it, he misunderstood this actuality. He saw the *Beis HaMikdash* as a building like any other, with the addition of its having profound religious significance to the Jews. He both believed and disbelieved in Hashem; he gave Him sufficient credence to endeavor to compete with Him, but he disbelieved enough to think that competition was rational. "Foolish mortal! You have ground flour that was already ground. You have burned a building that was already burned."

It is easier to define what the *Beis HaMikdash* never was than it is to grasp the scope of what it was. Its essence is an inherent part of the creation. It is one of the five objects our Sages define as Hashem's *kinyan* — an acquisition possessed by Him and no other. It was predestined to be a place of meeting between both worlds. We are tied down to the world we experience through the five senses, yet we experience the other world as well. It comes to us through our longing and our yearning. We express its presence in our hearts through our search for meaning. When the world was less clouded by history and failure, its essence was more accessible. Let us examine the *Beis HaMikdash* through the eyes of Kayin and Hevel — Cain and Abel.

The Battle over Heaven and Earth

Kayin and Hevel understood the essence of the *Beis HaMikdash*. In fact, they understood it far better than we do. It was the source of their controversy, and we know that their clash ended with bloodshed. We also know that the underlying issue was envy. However, we do not have textual information concerning the actual issue that sparked their quarrel.

Our Sages suggest a number of possibilities. One possibility is that Kayin and Hevel had divided the world according to each one's perception of what life is for. Kayin saw life as a struggle for material dominance; he therefore claimed the earth as his own. Hevel saw life as an exercise in transcendence over the limitations of the physical; he therefore claimed the heavens as exclusively his. Kayin demanded that Hevel refrain from stepping on "his" earth. Hevel demanded that Kayin stop breathing "his" air.

While the possibility of such a quarrel actually taking place will seem real enough to mothers of teenagers, its meaning is far deeper than the kind of pettiness that can come to mind when learning of this division of "property." What was the significance of their altercation and how does it change our picture of reality?

Like Kayin and Hevel, the materialistic aspect of our being and the spiritual aspect engage in unending, irrational quarreling. The body is drawn to acquisition and passivity; the spirit is drawn to growth and contribution. There are few areas in which both share joy.

When borders are spelled out clearly, there is no reason for disagreement to arise. For instance, if two neighbors agree to enclose an area and erect a fence, there is no reason to discuss whose side is bigger. But when the borders are less defined, quarreling becomes almost inevitable. If the body were to content itself with the exclusively materialistic side of reality, then it would have no "quarrel" with the soul. However, the body also wants the elusive pleasure of meaning. Thus, for instance, our status symbols take on psychological significance in addition to providing us with material pleasure. At times we even confuse the psychological pleasure that acquisition gives us with genuine self-esteem. Like Kayin, we want to be master of the earth while also breathing in the "spirit" of meaning. Like Hevel, at times we want the authentic joy of *deveikus*, of being close to God, but we must live with the realities of this world and keep our feet on the ground.

In the case of Kayin and Hevel, we are told that the actual catalyst for the confrontation was the issue of ownership of the *Beis HaMikdash* or, alternatively, who would marry the "extra" female who was born with them. Both marriage and the *Beis HaMikdash* share a common feature. Both have physical components that reflect a far deeper, transcendent spiritual bond. The *Beis HaMikdash* was the bridge between this world and the world above it. Its physical loss reflects a loss of *deveikus*, a loss of meaning.

The Bridge between Heaven and Earth

The world is not perfect. We tend to focus on the tangible manifestations of its imperfection. We can't help but be aware of the illnesses and tragedies of every possible dimension that surround us.

However, they are but symptoms of a genus of imperfection of more profound proportions. The cause of all material and physical torment is our inability to express our higher and deeper selves without a catalyst to bring it forward.

The truth is, though, that the world can never be a place of joy if it is approached on exclusively materialistic terms. All physical gratification is ephemeral. The feeling of emptiness we encounter when we "have everything" is so difficult to live with that we often look for "still more" to assuage the restlessness that comes from the fleeting moments when we catch a glimpse of the abyss. What we are really lacking is the delight that comes from bonding with Hashem, with feeling the connection of mind, heart, and deed with the world of *netzach*, the world of eternity.

If we "settle," if we doom ourselves to accepting that which is hollow as though it had content, then there is no place in our lives for mourning the Temple. The *Beis HaMikdash* was where both worlds were unified. It was the one place in which the illumination of eternity eclipsed the vacuous concealment of material desire while giving the material world a voice that was resounding and joyous.

Bridging Our Individual Exiles

Recognizing the choking constriction caused by living with our spirits in exile has another effect: it makes us far more compassionate toward each other. You and I live in our personal exiles; at times we are barely on speaking terms with the person within us that we could be.

Every Jew we encounter wants what we want, yearns for what we yearn, is blocked by that which blocks us. Their blockages may at times be so dense that they have lost all hope. We come upon their personal exiles in many guises: lack of self-esteem, lack of honesty, escapism, and rebellion against the spark of good within them that reminds them of who they could be. At times we categorize them and thereby create an igloo of ice in which we can take shelter. They are safely redefined as "them," and we are "us."

The more we take ourselves out of the exile of superficiality we use as our shelter, the less separateness we will feel from our fellow Jew. What separates us is not our souls; it is our bodies and the configurations of identity that are created by external factors. Age, ethnic background, education, and financial status can only define the external side of identity. Internally we are all groping for meaning and connection.

We are obligated by the Torah not only to be aware of this connection that unites us, but to act on it. This takes place through the mitzvah of loving your neighbor as you do yourself. Love is an elusive feeling. Deep empathy and devotion is the only "address" that awareness of our oneness can take us to, but without the structure of halachah of practical Torah law, we would have no channel for its expression.

What are the laws of this mitzvah to love one another? We must be as aware of them and as careful in their performance as any other Jewish law. The Rambam enumerates three laws that apply:

1. *We are obligated to speak well of our fellow Jew.* Obviously we must use our common sense and not create situations in which *lashon hara*, slander, will follow our favorable comments about others. This can be achieved, for instance, by not speaking about the person by name. (Often the name is irrelevant to the story we want to tell. For instance, when I used to ride the bus to work, there was a bus driver who assisted a handicapped young man on and off the bus daily. I was always moved by the driver's gentility and sensitivity, which was all the more striking in view of his being a rather macho type, the kind I would otherwise have filed away in the ever-growing file of "them." I do not know his name and feel no need to know it, yet repeating his deed recreates a certain spiritual bonding.)
Another guideline is to use a great deal of discretion. The effect of speaking well of others is that we suddenly feel them to be on "our team" and genuine empathy is developed.

2. *We are obligated to be as concerned for the material needs of our fellow Jew as we are for our own. Tzedakah*, charity, is a separate mitzvah; what is implied here is not only contributing, but caring. This includes wanting to see others succeed without jealousy and pettiness. It means rejoicing in the good fortune of others. It means preventing them from sustaining loss when

possible. It also means never letting financial differences act as a wedge between Jews.

3. *We are obligated to validate and acknowledge others.* Not only must we rise above petty slights, but we must seek opportunities to rebuild each other. We can restore the sense of significance and inner greatness to people who have ceased to see it in themselves.

When we reach out to others and rediscover not only the hidden goodness in them but the hidden goodness in ourselves, the effect has a greater impact than we would anticipate. The Shechinah, the Divine Presence, can rest only on a vessel that is whole. By restoring wholeness to the Jewish people, we restore the Shechinah to the world.

The rebuilding of the *Beis HaMikdash* seems so distant. The despair its destruction left in its wake encompasses everything we see. It is there in the dazzle of escapism, and it is there in the kind of banal tragedy we hear of daily. If we would reach out to each other and rebuild each other, we would simultaneously rebuild ourselves and the world.

If we allow ourselves to fall into complacency, we are not only not part of the solution, but we are the essence of the problem. We must relearn to hope. We must stop "settling" and open ourselves like the eye of a needle, so that Hashem will open Himself to us like a great hall.

CHAPTER TWO
becoming your true self

"Early in the morning" is a relative term. In Jerusalem, 7:30 A.M. is peak rush hour. Each household fortunate enough to have a juvenile majority finds the adrenaline flowing throughout its collective veins. The buses are crowded with uniformed girls and boys whose dress and manner demonstrate the power of the dreams their parents have for their futures. The scene is awesome in its spiritual luminance. More prosaically, the numbers of passengers on the 7:15 through 8:00 route provide the bus drivers with enough stress to last them throughout the day, if not longer.

The morning in which I observed *yiras Shamayim* in one of its purest forms was not outwardly remarkable. A boy of about seven got on the bus along with a dozen or so of his variously-sized contemporaries. There was pushing as they entered the already brimming vehicle. He stretched his thin arm toward the driver. It was blocked by the presence of larger boys who squirmed unsuccessfully to allow for freer movement. The driver turned toward the group that encircled him; his frustration from lack of space combined with the insufficient oxygen was evident. In a tone that left little room for misunderstanding, he established by edict a new social reality: we passengers must retreat to the dense and almost invisible back of the bus and allow him an island of potential sanity.

The human wave moved to the rear. The same thin arm found itself holding one of the poles. I heard the sound of weeping. It was initially repressed sobs, but soon the loud cries that characterize the unselfconsciousness of mid-childhood filled the air.

"*Mah yesh?* — What's wrong?" From all sides, the caring family of heimishe travelers inquired, breaking out of the passivity into which they had retreated. "*Lo rotzeh lehiyot ganav,*" he whispered almost inaudibly. "I don't want to be a thief." "*Lo hispakti leshalem lenahag* — I didn't get to pay the driver." As I listened to the words tumble out, I wished that my own fear of iniquity matched his.

What Gives a Mitzvah Special Significance?

Parashas Ekev begins with an admonishment to us: we must be conscientious in our observance of the mitzvos, including the ones that seem insignificant, that we tend to "crush under our heels" (one of the meanings of *ekev* is "heel"). The reward for mitzvah observance is our attaining that which we want more intensely than anything else — causing Hashem to love us.

In every relationship, we seek validation of our essential goodness. With passing acquaintances, it is enough if they treat us as someone with decency and integrity. With people who are significant in our lives, we want to see our ability to care and to sacrifice reflected back at us. Likewise, we are ceaselessly looking for the hidden Face of Hashem; we constantly long for His love. This reward of God's love seems immeasurably great compared to the mitzvos for which it is granted. We must try to understand what the Torah is telling us. How could the mitzvos that seem least significant make us deserving of such enormous reward?

What gives a specific mitzvah significance? In *Pirkei Avos*, we are told that we must value a minor mitzvah as much as we value a major mitzvah. The Ran asks how the reward can be identical for major and minor mitzvos. If we assume that some mitzvos can be accurately described as "minor," why should the reward be identical for mitzvos described as "major"?

He replies that while the reward or punishment may determine the status of a mitzvah externally, we must also reckon with the internal change that takes place within us as we observe Hashem's commandments.

For a person who lives primarily within the parameters of his own heart and mind, the mitzvah to visit a sick person, for instance, may require enormous internal elasticity. The easy, calming smile, the intuitive sense of what must be said and how, may not be part of that person's internal repertoire. The changes that take place when he reacts in a manner far from his natural inclination are inestimable. There are always "outs" — the effortless dismissal of this mitzvah as being one that he can somehow afford to skip is of course the easiest. Yes, someone else may do it, or the patient will probably survive without the visit. But it is the degree of metamorphosis that takes place, which is too subtle for us to estimate, that is the barometer of the degree of compensation to be given in the World of Truth, the realm of being, that is above our estimates.

The very same mitzvah may be performed with far more style and refinement by a person who has the ability to almost become the person with whom he finds himself. While the patient's needs may be better served by the more spontaneous and natural approach, that is no mirror of the amount of change elicited. *Yiras Shamayim*, fear of God, is the decisive inspiration for self-change. Even we don't notice it as we find ourselves making decisions in the midst of conflicting thoughts and barely remembered recollections. Its presence or absence is the one empowering factor we can develop within ourselves. Through its usage, we can redefine our lives.

Three Levels of Yiras Shamayim

There are varying levels of *yiras Shamayim*. The least complex is fear of retribution. The inherent limitations of this level are genuine. At times, the fear is not of Hashem at all, but just of pain; Hashem is completely absent from the picture.

Worse still, at times the line separating dread from abhorrence is crossed. To the person who crosses this line there is the possibility that consciously or subconsciously he will regard Hashem as heartless and lose his ability and desire for a meaningful relationship with Him. There are few human tragedies that are as utterly hopeless. Nonetheless, recognizing that every deed we do has repercussions that will affect us eternally is a tool. Its proper usage is within a framework of rich and profound connection with Hashem. When it is expressed as part of a total relationship, its primary expression is *yiras cheit*, fear of commiting a sin.

True *yiras cheit* is a result of treasuring a connection to Hashem to the degree that nothing is as valuable as the connection itself. Commiting a sin might sever the connection or at least weaken it. The venue for the development of that connection is (believe it or not) the barely noticed decisons we make without thought of connection.

The day-to-day choices that surround us have many facets. There are choices that are consequential in defining the degree of submission we are willing to make, moment to moment, to Hashem's will. The decision to be honest with oneself, to buy a new Halachah book on, say separating milk from meat, is at times reflective of this kind of submission of one's will to Hashem.

There are other choices that require us to define who we want to be moment by moment. As we speak to our families, to our friends and neighbors, we are very much involved in choice-making. The words tumble out instantaneously. Whether they display the part of us that is infinite or the part of us that is transitory is determined not only by who we are at that moment, but by the choices we have made from the moment of our birth until the moment of action. Our general relationship with Hashem will come forward as soon as the door is open.

The third level of *yiras Shamayim* is neither fear of consequences nor fear of damaging one's capacity for connection with Hashem. It's a sensitivity to our own frailty and dependency and simultaneously an awareness of Hashem's enormity and boundlessness. Unlike love of Hashem that thrives on closeness, this awe of Hashem requires an awareness of distance. The Maharal explains that this is the reason why "all is in the hands of Heaven except for fear of Heaven." To understand why, we need to see the difference between love of God and awe of Him.

Taking an Honest Look

Passion cannot exist without knowing the other person. Similarly, our love of Hashem is dependent on His revealing Himself to us, through His opening the curtains of concealment. This takes place by letting us see His caring and His intimate connection to every event that takes place in our lives. The choice to respond is ours; however, there must be an awakening from Above to which we respond. In this sense, our ability to love Hashem is a gift He gave us by His revelation.

Awe of Hashem comes not from our feeling the intimacy of connection, but from the distance that is created by our honesty. We are finite; He is eternal. We live lives that are delineated by our errors; He is perfect. *Yiras Hashem* is, therefore, not a gift, nor can it be. It is the one thing that we ourselves can choose. We can either look or firmly decide to keep our eyes closed.

We put so much effort into trying to control areas of life that are completely outside the realm of our choices. Our financial, physical, and familial situations are not controlled by our efforts. The connection between the efforts we put forth and the results that occur are, at most, tenuous. For free choice to flourish, the Hand that gives is hidden. It is, however, not our hand. Our responses to the situations He provides is the one area over which our choices are meaningful. If we have enough honesty to break through the illusions of human dominion and let our choices be guided by the awe that invariably comes from integrity, we will have achieved *yiras Shamayim*.

The Reishis Chochmah presents us with several choices of where we may put our inner eye. The first is whether or not to see Hashem's light. We all know what spiritual light is, although it is not often in our vocabulary. The purity of an infant's gaze, the luminescence of the children at the bus stop, each one a diamond on his or her own frame of invisible black velvet. We can see it in the infinity of the sea and the sky. While what grabs our attention is only Hashem's creations, what we can choose to let them reveal is the greatness of their Root. Or we could choose to see nothing.

The second choice is whether or not to notice Hashem's wisdom. We can study biology and never question Who directs traffic in the bloodstream. We can study history and never get past seeing the events as being isolated from meaning. When we answer questions beginning with the word *why* without Hashem being part of the answer, then a choice has been made.

Ultimate Yiras Shamayim

We sometimes lose track of where our choices have taken us. In

Nesivos Shalom, the author divides human reality into three parts: the mind, which is the repository of a person's opinions, beliefs, and outlooks; the heart, which is the repository of human longings and will; and the lower limbs, which are the repository of desire. A person is truly whole when the journey has been made by which the ideas and longings have found expression in the actions of the body.

Keeping the mitzvos that are the ones most likely to be "crushed by the heel" is the ultimate expression of the *yiras Shamayim* that begins in the mind and heart. The more a mitzvah penetrates beyond the surface and reaches the core of one's soul, the greater the reward.

While for every person the challenges are unique, what we share in common as Jews is the inner knowledge that we want more for ourselves. We are torn at times, but like the child on the bus, we all hear the voice within us that says, "*Lo rotzeh lehiyot ganav* — I don't want to be a thief." I want to be able to present myself at the end of the journey undiminished. I want to be able to say that I have used what Hashem has given me honestly. This is what we all want.

Let us be worthy not only of learning to respond to life with *yiras Shamayim*, but to interact with our families in a way that will give us the merit of parenting children such as the one I saw on the bus.

CHAPTER THREE
playing by the rules

A WINDING ROAD leads up to Meron from the roadside village that annually springs into being overnight on Lag BaOmer, the day of Rabbi Shimon bar Yochai's passing, when he gave us the kabbalistic secrets known as the Zohar. On that day, this village is by all accounts rich with life, unique and unqualifiedly unforgettable. From the sound of the medley of accents to the visual feast of what seems to be every possible representative of our people, it is rich and inspiring. No two faces are alike, and no two descriptions of Lag BaOmer will correspond unequivocally. That which is shared by all, no doubt, is a sense of unity and wonder as we go beyond the mundane side of our roles. There is arguably no other place in the world where one can find half a dozen hucksters with whom one can haggle for the latest (?!) edition of the Zohar.

It was here, in the midst of throngs of our extended family, that I witnessed the birth of a new superstition. A woman of indeterminate age was asking for charity. She gave all of those who opened their hands (and wallets) a piece of red string. It clearly gave her the feeling of having given something in return and thus made her onerous task less demeaning. As I approached, though, she ran out of red string. The kiosk at the top of the hill was able to provide her with green string.

As the sun was setting, I, among thousands of others, searched for a bus that would take me back to Jerusalem. After settling in (together with a scattering of family members and friends), I found myself engaged in conversation with my seatmate. It has always been a matter of curiosity to me that the sort of questions rarely broached by those nearest and dearest are the open territory of seatmates. I am not referring only to the obvious topics ("Who did you marry and why?" "How much money do you make?" "Is it legal?"), but to the confidences they want to share (illnesses, family tragedies). Therefore I was not very surprised to be asked whether I know the significance of green string. It was apparent that the question was rhetorical, and before I could begin to hold forth, I was provided with an answer. "Green, the color of life and renewal is a *segulah*, an aid, for babies and children, while adults should wear red...."

In *Shoftim*, the Torah tells us, "*Tamim tehiyeh im Hashem Elokecha* — Be *tamim* with Hashem your God" (*Devarim* 18:13). We must maintain a relationship of *temimus*, simplicity, with Hashem. This requires us to let go of the types of escapist complexity and sophistry we turn to in order to escape the intensity of the relationship that we, as Jews, have with Him.

It is easy to mistake simplicity for anti-intellectualism. The difference is that any intellectual search that has integrity is one in which human limitation is factored in. Let us look for a moment at the simplicity of faith displayed by Avraham when it became clear to him that Sedom and Amorah were doomed.

Avraham's Faith: Simplicity and Love of Hashem

Avraham's love of Hashem was one in which there was no confusion of *ikar* and *tafel*, of that which is most significant and that which is of secondary significance. Because he saw Hashem as the Source of all reality, he realized that Hashem is the ultimate Cause, with everything else in the universe being an effect. This recognition gave him a love and connection to every person, a love we can barely fathom. The common bond of our being "related" by virtue of a spark of eternity found within the soul of each human made in the image of one Creator was to him as vivid as physical reality is to us.

Avraham realized that the destruction of Sedom would awaken revulsion in the hearts of the people of his time. It would weaken their belief in God's mercy and he could not forsee that any benefit could result from this. Massive destruction such as that which Hashem told him was imminent would be too much for their level of choice. They wanted a relationship with God that was conditional on His being interpretable to them. They were so closely identified with the people of Sedom that they would not see its destruction as anything less than a random natural calamity. That would be an incomparable tragedy for mankind. Avraham's years of endeavoring to make an imprint would be wiped away in moments. He loved Hashem too much to bear seeing Him despised.

Yet when Hashem pronounced the decree as being unchangeable, Avraham said, "I am dust and ashes." He recognized that as a human being his limitations are as real a part of him as is his transcendence.

Segulos, Magic, and Mekubalim — Part of the Problem or Part of the Solution?

We are often unwilling to put ourselves directly in Hashem's hands. We look for *segulos*, and blame our difficulties in life on mysterious factors that can somehow be alleviated without *teshuvah*, repentance. At times we look for the counsel of *mekubalim*, those well-versed in Kabbalah, not for insight into how we can move ourselves forward in the direction of self-improvement, but for magic words that will somehow make everything different.

The Rambam counts the mitzvah of attaining simplicity in one's relationship with Hashem as a positive commandment. He explains that what this entails is unification of our hearts with Hashem alone. Practically, this means believing that only Hashem knows the ultimate truth and what the future holds. We were allowed to seek to know His will through the prophets in their time or the *urim v'tumim*, worn by the *Kohen gadol*, high priest, in the Holy Temple, since they enlightened us to His will. We must not, however, turn to other means of either learning or controlling the "big picture." When we hear predictions of the future from earthly sources, we must realize that there are never earthly guarantees of outcomes. Hashem is committed to determining outcomes in order to draw us closer to Him.

Why Do They Seem To Work?

While the Rambam doubts that the average "magician" is anything more than a charlatan, others argue the possibility of a given practitioner having a degree of insight. How does it work?

As with everything else we observe, the vehicle by which Hashem created the potential for our having free choice is by His concealing His light. When we see an apple tree, we can either be awestruck by the compassion and life force being revealed, or we can say "McIntosh" and let the moment take us no further. Hashem veils the vast and endless light of His creativity and presence by hiding it behind innumerable mediums. For instance, the apple tree came from a seed, and the seed was planted by a farmer. We can stop our process of searching by seeing the source of the tree as being either the seed or the farmer. Or we can look deeper and find the true Source.

All of the laws of nature follow this pattern, as do the spiritual forces with which Hashem imbues them. Thus, for instance, at least in earlier times, the stars revealed the spiritual realities that govern physical outcomes. *Segulos* are like any form of medication. The powers they have (when they are genuine) are still only manifestations of the ultimate power: that of Hashem.

While this manner of making efforts on one's own behalf is permitted, it is fraught with the same challenges as any other efforts we make on our own behalf. The difference between an authentic *segulah* and penicillin is its territory. Penicillin operates within the realm of purely physical cause and effect. Laws concerning the world's physical nature don't exist in a vacuum. They are always subservient to Hashem's will. *Segulos* may work within the realm of purely physical cause and effect (as the Gra points out, a definite effect of crumbs on the floor, a well-known portent for poverty, is the feeling of disintegration and lack).

Alternatively their territory may be spiritual (such as grounding a spiritual force by doing a physical action like putting wine in one's pockets after Havdalah). The outcome is equally as much in Hashem's hands as is the outcome of taking penicillin. The action itself, even if untainted by the egotism that would render it unholy, has no independent effect.

A true tzaddik, a genuinely righteous person, is compared to *playing by the rules* 17

Yaakov's ladder. In Yaakov's dream, a ladder touched the earth and its top reached into the Heavens. Likewise, a tzaddik's feet are on the earth of this world, yet his mind can penetrate the heavens. He is not deceived by the multiplicity of creation and relates every object and experience that touch his life to its authentic root. Through his prayers, he can draw down the forces Hashem created, to benefit both the world as a whole and to benefit specific individuals. This is the positive consequence of the usage of his free choice. We are familiar with this phenomenon from our Sages' statement, "*Tzaddik gozer v'HaKadosh Baruch Hu mekayem* — A tzaddik decrees and Hashem brings about the decree."

When this process is corrupted by even a seemingly trivial inclusion of ego, the entire procedure is redefined. Instead of leading one closer to Hashem, it leads to self-empowerment or to a subtle form of nature worship. This is true whether the "nature" being worshiped is the external, physical side of nature (the apple tree itself) or its spiritual cause (life force or anything other than Hashem Himself).

The issue is not only whether the various *segulos* work or not, but where they take us. It is therefore not hard to conjure up a vision of two people doing the same thing (such as putting wine in one's pockets after Havdalah) and being affected differently. One may be "playing the game by the rules" exactly as he would when taking conventional medication. He is completely aware of Hashem granting the act its power. The other may be focused on the act itself, to the extent of reading Hashem out of the picture. The potential for making the correct choice lies at the heart of both of them. Hashem will lead either one to where he wishes to be taken.

The Maharal notes the fact that the Torah uses the feminine noun *mechashefah*, witch, when forbidding the practice of magic (*Shemos* 22:17). He explains that the side of feminine nature that yearns to be connected and defined by Hashem, *emunah*, faith, can be corrupted when misused. Awareness and desire for meaning can be so intense that the desire to take "shortcuts" and become the ladder without ascending the rungs seems an option.

Perhaps this is why I found the inclusion of the green thread to the repertoire of superstitious practices so excruciating. It is a degradation of the most sacred aspect of woman's nature. We can do better than this.

Back to Simplicity

What being *tamim* means in essence can be understood only by the words of the verse itself. The verse says: "*Tamim tehiyeh im Hashem Elokecha* — Be *tamim* with Hashem your God." *Temimus*, simplicity, means being in a state in which Hashem's presence is so real that there is neither room nor desire for anything else. Its natural manifestation is the single-mindedness that brings one to prayer and repentance. We can lay our hearts bare to Hashem and approach Him directly. We can release ourselves from the constraints of perceived unworthiness and get past the need for "shortcuts." We can be *tamim*. We spend so much of our inner strength in attempting ascent. We hope that Hashem will answer our desire for *temimus* by saving us from self-deception.

The winding path that leads to Meron is full on Lag BaOmer. Each person's footsteps echo those of thousands who have passed before him. Each heart wants more than can be offered by countless sacrifices to others. We want connection and closeness. We will never find it as we stand in line for palm readers, stargazers, and "wise" men whose wisdom leads us only to them and not to closeness to Hashem's will. Let us have the insight to recognize Hashem's hand in every manifestation of His creativity.

Throw away the green thread!

CHAPTER FOUR
are you fooling yourself?

A FAMILY FRIEND came to Israel in a way that is almost unprecedented.

Jesse was born to a family that could be described as either traditional or Orthodox, depending on the elasticity of one's lexicon. Candles were a definite part of the scheme of things. Buying at the almost-definitely kosher butcher was *de rigueur*, even though the same cuts were at least 10 percent more expensive there than they were at the local A&P. Pesach included reading the Haggadah, as well as a family get-together. The kids belonged to religious youth groups and went to kosher camps.

The amount of personal self-sacrifice this required is inestimable to those of us who have had the benefit of growing up in the kind of home where saying one eats only kosher is similar to saying one doesn't practice cannibalism. Jesse's family was by far the most observant non-rabbinical family in a hundred-mile radius of their Southern domicile.

One of the most meaningful and deepest experiences of Jesse's youth was his camaraderie with the sea. When he looked at its infinity, what he saw was something of what Rav Chaim Vital saw when his mentor, the Ari, *z"l*, took him to swim in the Kinneret in order to open his heart to the nature of endlessness. The magnetism that the Gulf of Mexico held could not be put into words; it came from a place within him where words are limiting rather than defining.

The accident took place during university vacation. The sailboat Jesse was on capsized. In far less time than he would have anticipated from the safe haven of solid earth, he found himself breathless and exhausted, swallowing mouthfuls of sea water.

This can't be real competed in his mind with *This is really all there is. This is the end.*

As his inner and outer eyes met, he took one more glance at the infinite stretch of water and said, "God, save me. I'll go to Israel and study Your Torah." The words had barely moved from his mind to his mouth when the rope thrown from a vessel approaching whispered its presence to him.

He did not come to Israel until half a decade had passed.

When I asked him how this could possibly have happened, he told the truth. He never made a conscious decision not to keep his vow. His enormous sensitivity and integrity would never allow him that luxury. What he told me was that subconsciously, as soon as he was safe and dry, he made a simple addition to his original declaration. The addition was both subtle and silent.

It took him close to five years to see through the clouds of self-deception that shrouded the words of the addition almost completely. The addition was "as soon as I can."

Decisions We Never Made

No one decides to live a life in which nothing of consequence happens. No one votes against self-transformation. No one has either the capacity or the desire to do so. There are various obstacles that prevent us from keeping the vow we all made before our birth.

What vow?

Our Sages tell us that before a child is born, it must take an oath. The oath has various clauses. The one that is relevant to our discussion is "Be righteous; do not be wicked. Even if the whole world tells you that you are righteous, you must seem wicked in your own eyes" (*Niddah*).

The need to define ourselves as righteous is therefore inherent. When people make terrible mistakes in life, the easiest way to live with them is to redefine righteousness. We lack the ability to face the unmitigated truth about ourselves on one hand, and on the other hand we have to contend with the second clause of the oath. Even if we live lives that are so exemplary that the whole world tells us we are righteous, we still must resist believing in our own goodness. In fact, this feeling of lack and incompleteness is what causes us to hold on to life so tenaciously. It could, when misdi-

are you fooling yourself?

rected, lead us to despair.

What are the obstacles that confront us? Why do we corrupt the very oaths that could lead us to lives of truth and meaning? In *Nesiv HaTeshuvah*, the Maharal discusses several of them.

I'm Not the Thirty-Seventh Tzaddik!

One obstacle is fear of being too good.

We tend to confuse normality with mediocrity. I recently felt I was being drawn into battle with myself. Of course, the nature of inner struggles is that neither side discloses its authentic identity. Both voices, at least initially, sound like they are my most genuine self. Both sides wave the banners of truth and compassion.

This particular conflict started innocently, as they all do. I received a pamphlet on the topic of proper dress that was distributed at a women's learning event. I discovered upon scrutiny that the standards have gone up since the last time I read a similar pamphlet. My initial response was *How dare they*! I would now have to either face being relegated to being less than perfect or move upward. The defenses came into play instantaneously. So much of this is subjective; so much is beyond the letter of the law. Could such focus on superficialities lead to anything except the type of loss of identity that is the result of confusing surface with essence?

The truth finally made its appearance. With whom am I doing battle? The two sides seem to be me against me. One side is the idealization of who I am and what I am at this moment. The other side is who I could be if I were less anxious about change.

I had to ask questions that I don't often ask: Is there no room for upward mobility in an area that I would not have intuitively selected? Does the fact that superficiality is a very real part of the challenge of *tznius*, of being modest, imply that as a result there is a blanket exemption from growth?

The realization that I was apprehensive of development in uncharted territory (after all, according to the old pamphlet, I was doing fine) is what saved me. Or, more frankly, what saved me this time. *Teshuvah* belongs to everyone; it can define every experience and cannot coexist with complacency.

How We Choose without Choosing

There are three ways we block ourselves from our better selves. The first one is the fact that we are so mesmerized by the material world to the point that we stop searching for anything more. One of the words for "fool" is *pesi*. Its literal meaning is "one who is seduced." The ability to be enraptured by the world's beauty and variety and to be deceived by its richness is no doubt one of the reasons we are at times so spiritually dead. We deny ourselves life and bury the pain of meaninglessness under more layers of consumerism.

The second is the power of escapism. We can live vicariously. We can escape from lives in which the sweetness of genuine achievement is absent by many means.

We are all familiar with the power of stories of the tzaddikim. When we hear stories such as those, the part of us that longs for lives like their lives is touched. We are even at times inspired to move closer to the sacred and hidden part of ourselves. Conversely, when we escape by dulling our senses (by sleeping, playing games to distract ourselves, or mentally playing games to avoid introspection), we experience momentary peace and at times the sweetness of feeling accomplished without necessarily doing anything of meaning.

A number a years ago, a fad called Rubik's cube was in vogue. It involved bringing geometrically designed revolving squares on a cube into a specific design. I was rather good at it, and, while demonstrating my prowess at the aforementioned to my colleagues during a work break, I was distressed to hear one of them ask me how much time I had invested in the attainment of this skill.

The third blockage is the allure of doing that which is depraved. There is a dark side to us in which the empowerment of destruction is enormously attractive. Since children are more transparent than adults (and in far less control), we observe this on occasion more readily with them. We see the smile on the five-year-old's face when he takes away the infant's toy. We see the barely disguised pleasure little girls sometimes display when excluding someone from their group. Children are innocent. They make no choice against their better selves; their better selves are in the process of development. When adults respond to life in this manner, it reflects the tragedy of the corruption of spiritual energy.

If It's So Easy, How Come It's So Hard?

Hashem wants to free us from the entrapments we have set up for ourselves. When our blockages are strongest, He will send us messages that can force us into acknowledging who we really are and how foolish our little games are. For Jesse, the message was his nearly fatal encounter with the sea. We all have encounters with our frailty and mortality.

The ultimate decision of how we want to live our lives must come from ourselves. Hashem's supreme act of goodness is His willingness to be fair and to give us the ability to change. No achievement can match self-change, and no treasure is as valuable.

By giving us the opportunity to do *teshuvah*, to repent, what Hashem has done is to give each person not just the capacity to sanctify the world and bring it to Him as an offering, but to sanctify himself. This comes as a result of our being willing to elevate our very souls and effect change on the deepest levels of our identity. In order for this to happen, there must be a basic belief in our own capacity for goodness.

We sometimes confuse honesty with despair. When we break through the defenses of escapism, self-empowerment and love of everything transient, we sometimes think that there is nothing underneath it all. However, we are never a mere collection of failures. Our ability to see through our failings and find ourselves at the deepest level is that which makes us whole.

Hashem is connected to us through our souls. That connection, unlike His glory, isn't a garment He wears to make Himself known to us, but His very essence. It is that connection that draws us back to Him no matter how much distance and time there is between us.

That is what brought Jesse to Jerusalem after five years of oblivion. May Hashem awaken it in all of us.

CHAPTER FIVE
fit for a king

ONCE THERE WAS a king. The king had a servant to whom he entrusted a precious vessel. The vessel was somehow damaged. The servant's awe of the king was so great that he did not know what to do, where to turn. He found a wise man and sought his counsel. The wise man told him that he may not bring the shattered vessel before the king; it was not befitting. The servant decided it would be better to seek advice from one of the king's closest friends. The servant thought a person such as that would be more likely to have a deep knowledge of how the king would respond and would also know what course of action the king would take.

When he appeared before the king's trusted companion, he asked his advice and received the following reply: "I know the king's greatness and exaltation. A vessel such as this may not be placed before him. You must destroy the vessel completely."

The servant still did not know what to do and finally decided to go to an expert craftsman, hoping that perhaps he would be able to repair the broken vessel. He went to the craftsman, who told him that even if he succeeded in repairing it, it would still look damaged. Its appearance would remain marred; it would never be appropriate to take to the king.

The servant said to himself, *I cannot act as though nothing has happened; I cannot absolve myself from responsibility. I will go before the king. Let him do to me as he sees fit.*

The king said, "I will use the broken vessel. Those with whom you consulted responded as they did for the sake of my glory. I, however, choose to use the vessel as it is."

Fear of Hashem and Fear of Confronting One's Failures

Hashem unveils His presence to those who are able to see. The awesome splendor of nature, the intimacy of Divine Providence, are visible to anyone who has not blocked his vision.

When we seek to go beyond the blinders of ego, materialism, and escapism, we are still at times blocked. What causes our blindness is not what we *don't* see, but what we *do* see. When we let ourselves hear our deepest selves, the voices of inner wisdom of spiritual yearning, we are sometimes overwhelmed. We feel that "the vessel cannot be placed before the King." So overwhelming, in fact, are these feelings of spiritual inadequacy, that we don't know what to do. We see our brokenness, and, in sharp contrast we perceive the power and goodness of Hashem. At moments of stark revelation, we tend to retreat. How can we possibly live with what we have become? The more honest we are, the less accessible *teshuvah* feels.

The truth is that what Hashem presents to the world can be compared to a garment. As it says, "*Hod v'hadar lavashta* — You have clothed Yourself with glory and splendor" (*Tehillim* 104:1). When we wear clothes, it is to define our relationship with the world as a whole. The clothing a human selects is, therefore, enormously indicative of the person who chose them. It is irrational to say, "Don't judge me by my clothes." Who chose the clothes? If this is the message the person himself wants others to hear, don't blame them for listening to it. Nonetheless, the garment is not the person; it is a message *about* the person.

Similarly, by observing Hashem's interactions with the world, we can sensitize ourselves to hearing His message. We can come to recognize that we are creations of a wise, subtle, insightful, and infinite Creator. This does not tell us the true nature of His essence anymore than a garment can tell an observer the true nature of its wearer.

However, what *teshuvah*, repentance, is cannot be defined as a message that Hashem gives us. It is a statement of His very nature: never-ending compassion.

The ultimate insult one person can give another is lowering one's expectations of him. The attitude "I would never expect any better from you" is not one of compassion. It is the most profound form of disdain. Hashem does not give up on us. His exacting judgment, which we must face on Rosh HaShanah, is real. We must not allow ourselves to be defeated by the dread this knowledge inspires.

Hashem judges us, not because He wishes to punish us and see us get what we deserve, but because He believes in our ability to transcend our blockages. Even the most severe punishments ever meted out to humanity, such as Adam's expulsion from the Garden of Eden, were given to enable personal rebuilding of that which was broken in Adam and in the world.

Teshuvah is the key to our rebuilding ourselves. We must trust Hashem's compassion and not be afraid to approach Him honestly. Elul is the time of year when the spiritual nature of the season moves us toward Him and Him toward us.

Seeing Ourselves as We Are

Examining where our lives have taken us is the first step. The purpose of this is not to generate self-hatred or despair, but to seek correction and ways of moving beyond our present situations. We must be willing to look, not only at the specific actions that may be less than perfect, but at the character traits that motivated errors in moral judgment. When we content ourselves with superficial self-examination, our efforts are doomed.

I am a fairly unsuccessful gardener. The verdant plants I bring home from the nursery live very uneventful (and unusually short) lives. Part of the reason is that my own urban childhood brought me to maturity without the ability to look at two green shoots and know which one is a weed. When the shoots grow tall enough to make it clear (even to me) which is which, I tend to cut the weed rather than uproot it. The regermination of aggressive and unwanted weeds is an eternal, unpleasant surprise.

Similarly, when searching for the "real" self, one must ask the basic question: why? Why do I do this? Why do I want this? Which basic trait is somehow contorted? Until these questions are honestly answered, the root of the weed is left untouched. There is still little awareness of which *middah*, trait, needs to be corrected. The "plant," therefore, is very likely to flourish again. The same deed (or its very similar first cousin) is likely to be a prominent part of one's soul-searching next year.

What To Do with the Flaws

Middos don't disappear. One of the most irrational decisions that can be made is the rejection of one's essential personality. Finding new and appropriate channels for the traits that are the least desireable is a challenge. Denying their existence, or attempting to eliminate them, is escaping the challenge that is part of one's very being, for finding a positive outlet for them often has the effect of uprooting the negative aspect of the *middah*.

To understand the mechanics of change, let us look for a moment at one of the most striking examples of self-change I have ever seen.

Irene's parents never wanted a child. Perhaps they wanted a trophy to show others, very much as they collect art and hang it on the walls of their exquisite home. Irene never felt wanted. This was not a matter of unrealistic expectations; it was a realistic acceptance of her status. When her parents' marriage dissolved, the custody battle revolved around who would be "stuck" with the child. She was raised from the age of eight by various hired women.

By the time Irene was an adult, her insecurity was a very strong component of her personality. We all know the forms insecurity takes. No friend was loyal enough, and therefore she constantly "tested" them until they almost always failed to meet her expectations. No situation was stable enough, and she moved from lifestyle to lifestyle.

I, too, was a member of the society of failed friends. I liked her and admired her enormously; she is a woman of rare brilliance and refinement. However, I was unable to give her the kind of unconditional support she needed and therefore demanded.

We drifted apart. I heard of her occasionally. She is an artist, and her works are displayed periodically in various galleries. One Elul I wrote her a letter in which I asked forgiveness for having allowed our friendship to disintegrate.

As Hashem would have it, I met her on the bus the very day I put the letter in my purse. As I handed her the letter, I did not know what her response would be. Would she trust my sincerity or would she see this as a sort of cushion upon which I could lean to alleviate any guilt I might be feeling before the High Holidays arrive? She smiled at me warmly, gave me her address and phone number, and invited me to her home.

In the course of my visit to her somewhat isolated house on a remote Israeli settlement, I found myself feeling as though the body of the person to whom I was speaking was Irene, but the person inside the body must be someone entirely different. The warmth, security, and genuine interest she showed in me and my life were completely out of character.

As the sun began to set over the desert, I felt comfortable enough to ask her how she had accomplished such a major achievement. She knew exactly what I meant. She had decided to uproot the negative side of her insecurity completely. In order to do this, she wrote a brief account of everything good she experienced every day. She opened her closet and showed me a collection of tens of school notebooks. Each one was full, and each one was a statement of its owner's longing to free herself from the limitations that enveloped her. This changed her view of the Creator and His world.

Simultaneously, she decided to use her insight to zero in on other people's fears and insecurities and make herself a friend to many people who would never approach someone less sensitive to their fears. I felt that I was in the presence of one of the authentic heroines of our generation.

Mitzvos: Their Place in the Cure

The Maharal speaks about the difference between *mitzvos aseh*, positive commandments, in which the Torah tells us how to direct our energies, and *mitzvos lo sa'aseh*, various actions the Torah tells us to refrain from in order not to diminish ourselves. Both are necessary for us to retain the integrity of our characters. Therefore, when one notices that a certain *middah* is the root of behavior that is self-destructive, reestablishing a commitment to the mitzvos that are most difficult is a first step. When this is done with the consciousness that what is at stake is not a specific mitzvah, but also a redefinition of how one's traits can be used, there is a world of difference.

We must use every day that is left to see ourselves as we are. We must see our histories, our choices, our potential, our habits and hereditary tendencies. We must not be afraid to see the flaws; rather, we must take our broken vessels to the King and let ourselves be healed.

CHAPTER SIX
the invisible ones

WE SEE THEM all the time. They are in the fast-food emporia, the malls, and the stores. They are at times invisible to us. They frequent places we don't frequent, because the places themselves are in either symbolic or actual opposition to our collective self-portrait. They face confrontations with themselves that we do not face. They often fail. It is painful to see them because they are our children.

The easiest response (one reserved, of course, only to those unaffected) is not to see. It is as effective as the stratagem adopted by my three year old, who hid her eyes in order to render herself invisible in a game of hide-and-seek.

The widespread scourge has become sufficiently public — by it's very nature — that only the most oblivious among us can remain unmoved. Many have drifted away for reasons within themselves or within their environment. There are certainly no pat answers that will bring about an immediate change in the lives of the hundreds of families that are affected. There is no apparent single cause and therefore no easy solution. The most potent weapons are prayer and repentance.

Prayer: Personal Responsibility for Collective Problems

We pray daily. The clear implication of making daily supplications to Hashem is that we are judged anew every day. The way in which we are judged is as individuals. *Chazal* say that on Rosh HaShanah, however, "*olam nidon,*" the entire world is judged.

Each year is a specific unit within the spectrum of creation. The possibility of accomplishing defined goals that Hashem set forth when creating the world can be done only within the framework of the time He preordained. Each year has its own possibilities that were never touched before and will never recur. The challenges of the times catalyze the potential within each person.

The response that could be elicited by granting us the opportunity to live in the era of the first *Beis HaMikdash*, for instance, when we would see people of such enormous spiritual stature that the Vilna Gaon said he could not imagine what it would be like to be a simple householder at that time, would be unique. Equally unique, but of course completely dissimilar, would be the challenge of living at the time of the Enlightenment, when what today we can easily see as illusion was far less clear.

Every year we begin a new mission. The mission of the previous year is no longer operative. Thus, the Nesivos Shalom says, we can understand the Rambam, who correlates the way we are judged yearly at Rosh HaShanah to the way we are judged at death. Both are times of closure; both force us into a new reality. Our prayers at this time cannot be emotionally separate from the prayers of these children's families (and perhaps even those in the hearts of the children themselves). This is one of the great challenges of our times.

Teshuvah: Weapon Number Two

The need for searching our own hearts and questioning our own moral rectitude is essential in Elul, the month before Rosh HaShanah characterized by repentance. We cannot hide from what we see (and what we don't) when Hashem Himself is open to us. Our ability to respond to others with compassion, without condescending or separating our lives from them, is fundamental.

The *teshuvah* that is done by each and every one of us will affect the entire Jewish people. No one can do *teshuvah* for another. No one inhabits anyone else's world, his *olam katan*. The effect of our individual *teshuvah* can create a situation of Hashem turning His face not only toward us, but toward people who are as yet unready to turn to Him. In the month of Elul, every deed we do can be invested with two additional components: *teshuvah* and *geulah*, redemption.

Picture yourself giving *tzedakah*. While writing the check, try to move beyond the surface. Let's say the *tzedakah* is a donation to a yeshivah. Picture the students gaining access to the word of Hashem. You have now brought the world a step closer to the time when His Presence will cover the world as the sea covers the seabed.

Envision yourself saying a *berachah* on a piece of cake. This is not only a mitzvah in itself, but it is possible to invest it with sufficient depth that it can be the beginning of rectifying the countless times in one's life in which Hashem's goodness was unacknowledged. This, in turn, can open gates that are still closed, not only for oneself but for others as well.

The War against Complacency

It is so hard to stay awake spiritually. Our complacency isn't just aimed toward others, but it even dulls the natural consciousness of responsibility for ourselves. We must regard complacency as the enemy. We must not fight today's battle with yesterday's weapons. We must be creative and honest in dealing both with the outer and inner world.

We live in times not only of unprecedented material prosperity but also of unprecedented permissiveness. Success and pleasure have become synonymous, even within the limited circle of those who believe that having less will bring less clutter (both materially and emotionally) and therefore more pleasure. The possibility of there being a higher goal than immediate pleasure is not even an issue under discussion. When ideals are nurtured, it is almost always as a means toward actualization rather than a goal of inherent value.

We, as Jews, have the goal of *malchus Shamayim*, Hashem's kingdom, as our collective vision. The world in which we live has individual empowerment as a goal. The two are not only incompatible but antithetical. As the Rambam says, we are all affected by the society in which we live. He presents this as human nature rather than human frailty. We must therefore see these times as a catalyst by which we will come to a deeper and more genuine level of *kabbalas ol malchus Shamayim*, accepting the yoke of Hashem's kingdom.

Instilling the Right Goal in Our Children

In the case of the rebellious son described in *Ki Seitzei*, who turns aside from the moral instruction of his parents and commits deeds of such ridiculously extreme self-indulgence, the Torah demands the death penalty. The case at hand is couched with so many qualifications — the specific age of the child, the type of evidence that would be admissible — that in fact it never happened. One of the things that could be learned from this episode is that indulgence can lead to ruination.

When we integrate the values of our society, it is only natural for us to want our children to be happy as a goal in itself. A child's vision of happiness is often far from a spiritual or altruistic one. When we encourage the child to idealize self-gratification as an objective, we guarantee his future unhappiness.

As he grows, his needs and those of others will invariably clash. He will find himself not only frustrated but also angry. The rules of the game have changed. No matter what he does, he cannot always get what he wants. Behavior that is endearing at the age of four is not at all charming at age sixteen. The need for connection, the most basic human need of all, will be repressed. Rejection will be invariably encountered as his clashes with those who are both the victims of the rage born of frustration and his tormentors become more frequent and intense. Happiness will be not only a goal that has become elusive but one that is doomed.

In the society in which we live the above scenario is almost inevitable, not only with our children but also with ourselves. Too often we lose our sensitivity toward *malchus Shamayim* and condemn ourselves to lives of discontent and repressed rage. The solution is not the sort that is sold to us via the culture in which we live. We are told again and again that if we really try anything is attainable. The solution is redefining our relationship to *malchus Shamayim*.

Four Changes

Letting Hashem's mastery define us does not allow exceptions to the rule. One cannot be a partial servant. According to Jewish law everything owned by a slave is the property of his master. We must let Hashem's rule be manifest, not only by what we do, but also by what we think and feel. We must give Him admission to the deepest recesses of our hearts and offer Him the gift of our minds. This is the only way in which we can truly accept His Kingship.

In his *Sefer HaMitzvos*, the Rambam begins his list of mitzvos by presenting us first with the four commandments that demand the allegiance of our minds and emotions. The first on his list is faith in Hashem. This means seeing everything as being caused by Him and therefore everything in existence as having a purpose known to Him. When a person lives with this awareness, there is no more space left for blaming others or rejecting challenge. The implications in the way we live our lives are enormously far-reaching.

The second is seeing God's unity and living in those terms. If we see everything as a part of Him (including ourselves and others we encounter), there is far less space for rejection. Since everything and everyone is a result of His will, we will respond on His terms, not our own. Our goals will then change from immediate gratification to climbing upward on the mountain Hashem has set before us. In the same way in which words can only be diminutive to describe the exhilaration of reaching the top of Mount Everest, the joy of ascent has no parallel in the superficial gratification of self-indulgence.

The third is loving Hashem. This is accomplished by observing His hand in nature and in the daily flow of our lives. It is also attained by allowing the mitzvos to touch us more deeply than they often do. By gaining greater awareness of their awesome power, our connection to Hashem is deepened. When our relationship to Hashem is more intimate and real, it is an inevitable consequence that we will seek to open others to Him. In the same way in which it is human nature to want others to love those who are beloved to us, it is the nature of those who love Hashem to live lives that will make Him beloved by His creations.

The fourth is fearing Hashem. This includes not only recognizing the mastery that only He has, and the enormity of accountability we have to face, but holding Him in genuine awe.

Our interdependence is absolute. Any awakening that takes

the invisible ones

place in this world creates a more than parallel awakening from Above. A meritorious deed, for instance, affects a person immediately (by sensitizing him and opening his heart). The effect does not end with him. Hashem magnifies its power, which is hidden to the human eye, to the point where it can affect not only countless people but countless generations as well.

The yearning for personal redemption that is in every heart can, when brought to fruition, affect the fate of every Jew. If we open in our hearts an entrance the size of the eye of a needle, Hashem will open the hearts of all of *Klal Yisrael*.

May our own pursuit of illumination bring light, not only to our families, but to the visible and invisible children who are stumbling in the dark.

CHAPTER SEVEN
"I'm getting there!"

WE ALL KNOW people who have made dramatic changes in their lives. One of the most significant differences between the times in which we live and those which the over-forty group remember is the number of people returning to Judaism. Thirty years ago a *ba'al teshuvah* was regarded as a cross between an exotic, newly discovered species of animal and a suspicious stranger of questionable credibility. There was simultaneous attraction and repulsion.

For some individuals, little has changed in the way they perceive the most astonishing spiritual turnabout to occur in the modern era. For many of us, *ba'alei teshuvah* are a source of inspiration. However, there is still a pervasive feeling that our lives and theirs are somehow unbridgeably different.

For most people, the entire phenomenon has become commonplace enough to render the average *ba'al teshuvah* worthy of far less investment of our limited supply of emotion. We have thereby reduced the process of self-change in its most dramatic configuration into the prosaic. The undistinguished formlessness that occurs when anything is reduced to being seen as ordinary is a great loss to us. The reduction of a spiritual journey to a cliché (from X to Meah Shearim — fill in the X: Broadway, Harvard, the State Department, or the Olympics) is often superficial and therefore diminishing. The failure to think about how that sort of journey is made minimizes our perception of what we can expect of ourselves.

Can the Already Observant Become Ba'alei Teshuvah?

A distinguished rabbi in Yeshivas Ohr Somayach delivered an eloquent and erudite lecture to his audience of neophytes to Jewish learning. At its conclusion, one of the students asked him, "Are you a *ba'al teshuvah?*"

"Not yet," he replied. "But I'm getting there...."

What he meant, of course, was that his own journey toward the maximization of what he could be was not finished. He did not see his own lack of spiritual completion as less significant, and therefore less worthy of striving toward, than that of the young man who questioned him. He meant this unequivocally and honestly.

We have to learn to take ourselves seriously. The stream of time flows onward at a pace that is simultaneously gradual and rapid. The days sometimes move on sluggishly, but the years go by so swiftly that we are astonished by their passage. This is true not only for us, but for those whom we refer to as *ba'alei teshuvah*. What they have done is break the patterns they have established. What we must determine for ourselves is whether we care enough about ourselves to do the same. If the answer is that we at least want to want, we must look more seriously at the mechanics of pattern-breaking.

The Maharal tells us that the act of confessing to Hashem creates an inner dynamic by which we give ourselves over to Him. There is no gift that is more authentic than the gift of oneself and no gift more lovingly received. It is for this reason that the Rambam counts *vidui*, confession, as the most important part of the process of *teshuvah*.

We feel at times that the act of confession is coming too late. The consequences of our deeds are irreparable, whether one uses the extreme example of having committed a murder or the far less extreme (and far more commonplace) example of saying words that are so hurtful because of their truth that no apology can ever completely heal the wound we have opened. We then say (in words or in defensive feelings) that since we are responsible for the outcome we can never be forgiven because nothing can really be changed.

While we may never be able to reverse the end result of our choices, we ourselves can change. The consequence of self-change that is genuine is that we are judged on how we have evolved rather than how we once were. Through this process, we are no longer held down to the past; the reality is the present.

In this sense, *teshuvah* is a miracle; it reverses the ever forward flow of time.

Reuven and Yehudah are our models of self-transformation. They both performed acts that in essence were irreversible. Their *teshuvah* is nonetheless considered exemplary in its wholeness. It is for this reason that when Moshe blessed their descendants at the end of his life, there was no other tribe placed between them. Shimon and Levi should have been placed between them if the blessings were given in the order of their birth. However, Reuven and Yehudah were joined by their common realization that Hashem is One and one can return to Him. In direct proportion to their clear realization that there is no place where His light does not penetrate was their realization that they can give themselves over to Him.

The awareness that *ein od milvado*, there is nothing other than Him, is in a similar vein the deeper meaning of the thanksgiving we express in the Shemoneh Esreh prayer. It is not a coincidence that the thanksgiving prayer begins with the words *modim anachnu*, which not only mean "we thank" but also "we confess." Both gratitude and confession come from the same root — the recognition that Hashem is the source of all reality.

When Reuven and Yehudah confessed their misdeeds (which certainly would not be called sins using the vocabulary we use to describe our own deeds and the standards of behavior to which we are accustomed), they let it be a springboard for self-transformation. Instead of the self-acceptance of being "only human" that would be the easiest out of all, they recreated awareness from the midst of distance and shortcoming. Taking responsibility, and therefore not allowing their frailties to define them but rather their closeness to Hashem, was what made their *teshuvah* work. Achievement is attained by the act of moving forward. The choice is not ultimately between responsibility and feeling good, but between complacency and achievement.

What Makes Us Human?

The Talmud tells us that there are four means by which punitive edicts Hashem decreed against a person can be averted: changing one's deeds, prayer, charity, and changing one's name.

To understand this better, we must realize that a *gezeirah*, a divine edict, always corresponds to the personal reality of its recipient. The word *gezeirah* is linguistically similar to the word *gizrah*, which means "pattern." The *gezeirah* is "designer-made" to fit the spiritual need for rectification of a person or a generation. A person might think a *gezeirah* can never be changed, since it is tailor-made to his needs. While this assumption is realistic, it leaves out one significant factor — the person can change so completely that the *gezeirah* no longer fits. The way in which such radical movement happens is through the act of changing the components of our sense of identity.

There are four ways by which we define ourselves. One way is by our physical self-image. When we are asked, "Who are you?" the simplest answer is " I am five feet, seven inches...." When a person changes his deeds, the entire picture of his physical self changes simultaneously. Thus one way of averting a severe decree is to redefine one's entire spectrum of physical functions.

Another dimension of self-definition is through one's soul. While our physical body is the simplest aspect of oneself to access, it never acts totally on its own. The underlying longing for meaning and connection or, conversely, for dominance and power is far closer than one's physical self-image. Prayer redirects the deepest side of us so completely that it can, in effect, change a decree for the same reason that change of action can do so — the person is no longer the same person.

A third way by which we categorize ourselves is material status and possessions. We often answer the question "Who are you?" by telling the asker what we do for a living. We do so because this is usually the piece of information desired by the questioner. We invest an enormous proportion of our time and energy (not only physical but also intellectual and emotional) in the course of earning a livelihood. Because of that, we see our money and, to a lesser degree, the possessions money can buy, as reflections of who we are on many levels. When we give charity, the act of placing the needs of another human being above our needs can be self-transforming enough to avert severe judgment.

The fourth and final component of our self-definition is far more subtle than the other three. In the same way that a house is more than a collection of the various pieces of furniture and appliances within it, the self is more than any specific component. Changing one's name means changing the words one uses in one's internal dialogue to describe the total self. This inner movement toward redefinition is in fact the most characteristic of what being a *ba'al teshuvah* is about.

Teshuvah is this redefinition — making one's definition of self reflect the reality of being Hashem's servant. This means redefining success and failure in ways that may be as radical as those used by the former movie star or athlete who adopts Torah Judaism.

Shofar blowing is the only mitzvah that requires us to use our capacity to breathe. When God created Adam, the means by which He invested the first man with a spiritual soul was by breathing. The source of breath is deep within the body of he who breathes. In a similar manner, the spiritual soul is an actual "breath" of Hashem from above.

While one effect of the shofar is to redefine ourselves as Hashem's subjects by "coronating" Him (in ancient times, *shofros* were blown when the kings of Israel were appointed), it also brings us back to the deepest level of self-definition. We are a breath of Hashem. We can never erase the mystic memory of our source. We can never totally separate our identity from His. We can never entirely stop longing to be *ba'alei teshuvah*.

CHAPTER EIGHT
anatomy of a search

I WILL NEVER forget the time I discovered that while innovation has its place, it should not be implemented when walking home from the Kotel.

A number of years ago we lived about a twenty minutes' walk from the Wall. It was one of my foremost delights to let the walk take forty minutes or more to allow for the slower pace of my young children. The long summer afternoons gave us time for embroidering stories around the events of our lives as well as those of imaginary characters. We intertwined our walk with Chassidic tales.

As we entered the Arab market at the massive Damascus Gate in those pre-intifada days, the sights and smells of another era accosted us with intense, unforgettable power. We were simultaneously attracted and repelled by the combination of impurity and mystery. The haze would immediately dissipate with startling clarity as we approached the Kotel. The fusing of physical and spiritual light was accompanied by our wordless inner sense of illumination.

My mother, z"l, was living next door to us at this time. Her immigration to Israel took place at the age of seventy-five. She left a life back in Flatbush that was characterized by the orderliness and solitude brought about by both her life's circumstances and her nature. Her meticulous and silent home was an almost theatrical contrast to my chaotic abode. At that time, my eldest child was ten and the youngest an infant. My husband was a rebbe at a *ba'al teshuvah* yeshivah that was close enough to make ours the second home of quite a number of the *bachurim*.

My mother thrived on the constant unfolding of what must have seemed to her an unending situation comedy. Her apartment next door was a wonderful refuge. It was there that my children learned to appreciate the serenity of soundlessness and to experience the dignity of a formal dinner.

When Mother announced that she would enjoy partaking in our walks to the Kotel, it was not a surprise. Her delight in participating in life made the decision almost foregone.

The way there was uneventful. As we began our trek homeward, an idea occurred to me. It seemed to me that going through the gate nearest the Kotel would get us home even sooner than the old way would have. While I had no reason to resist new ideas in a general sense, my critical faculty should have warned me to be more suspicious of anything that required me to trust my sense of direction.

Whether the day was as hot as I recall it, I am not sure. To my best recollection, it was the sort of day one can almost feel when looking at pictures of refugees trekking through the desert. After a half-hour of getting to know the Wadi Joz suburb, an East Jerusalem Arab neighborhood with many garages and vacant lots, I had to admit that this was a major mistake. The tomb of Shimon HaTzaddik was a landmark. It told me that we were at least twenty minutes from home.

What makes this story remarkable is what *didn't* happen. Mother didn't say a word. The fact that this was the sort of mistake she was extremely unlikely to make, one with which she could not easily empathize, made her stoic acceptance of the situation far more meaningful.

Adventure was never high on her list of favorite experiences. Our trips were planned well in advance, as was every other aspect of my family's life. There was ample opportunity for her to tell me in various and completely justified ways that I had let her down. The scorching heat and sordid neighborhood could easily have been sources of running commentary. They were, instead, the catalyst of her moving beyond her *middos*.

True and False Self-Preservation

We tend to resist moving beyond our *middos* comfort zone. The almost paranoiac fear of being taken advantage of is one of the most pervasive dreads of twentieth-century secular society. The hidden suspicion that lending a neighbor an egg may (Heaven forfend) lead to lending a cup of sugar, and from there the possibilities are unlimited, has led to a certain reluctance for some people to develop relationships with their neighbors. Needless to say, it is certainly an uphill battle for any couple to maintain a reasonable level of *shalom bayis* (let alone the love, brotherhood, peace, and companionship we wish them at their *sheva berachos*) when apprehension and fear of being taken advantage of replace trust in the marriage. The same suspicion results in taking measures to avoid being "too good." The fear of being "too self-protective" is heard with far less frequency.

What are we actually afraid of? After all, we can always lend the egg and stop at the fragile and priceless family heirlooms. It is possible to go as far assuming that an error on the side of giving may result in being brought closer to each other, which is what we want most deeply inside. At worst, the possibility of responding self-protectively can always be reserved for the far less likely situation of genuinely unhealthy imbalance (which in marriage would, of course, need the serious counsel of an experienced spiritual guide rather than a self-prescribed double dose of inflexibility).

The fear is that somehow we will lose ourselves. Our sense of our own significance on a deep and authentic level has been so degraded by our times and our insecurity. The times in which we live are so superficial and consumer-oriented that giving away anything tangible at all leaves one feeling as though he has somehow compromised his value as a person. After all, if his worth as a person can be determined by possessions, he would need a very good reason to part with them. In a similar vein, if his significance to his spouse is measured by how much the other gives rather than how much he gives his spouse, then the smallest compromise is a degradation.

The fact is, of course, that our human worth is determined neither by possessions nor by the ability to dominate. It is resolved day by day as we choose to give the divine spark within us articulation. We can't lose ourselves. The soul within us is eternal. The more we fear losing ourselves, the more we suppress the side of ourselves that is the most authentic and enduring. When we let go of this fear, we can truly be ourselves.

Anatomy of the Character

The Talmud tells us that as a reward for moving beyond the parameters of one's character traits, Hashem forgives all of one's transgressions. To understand this better, let us take a deeper look at how we define ourselves.

Once the surface is scratched, we come to understand that we are far more than the sum total of our possessions. We also realize that we are similarly not defined by the degree to which we can preserve ourselves by retreating from giving. What is left under the surface is the stuff from which our characters are formed: our *middos*.

The *middos* are the means of getting to know the spark of Hashem within us. They are the foundation from which all of our access to the higher part of us stems. In *Tanya*, the author explains the nature of our *middos* by using the paradigm of the physical body. The body is physically composed of the four elements — fire, wind, water, and earth; from them the limbs and organs of the body are formed. They mold the body's potential, both for health and for illness. Similarly, there are four spiritual elements that form the basis of all of one's *middos*. These elements can be used in many ways to create spiritual health or to do the opposite.

Longing for Significance

The nature of fire is to ascend to its source. The core of the *middah* of fire is our longing for significance. Its negative manifestation is arrogance, which is, as we know, far too often the fruit of insecurity in one's sense of significance. Invariably, anger is an inseparable partner of insecurity, as any affront is seen as a statement about one's lack of significance. This leads to an overdeveloped sensitivity to one's own "piece of the pie." Any insult, no matter how minor, is a slur on one's importance. The only way the insatiable need for ascent can be assuaged, even briefly, is by momentary dominance over others. The fear of being "less" than anyone else can lead even to hating those who are in any sense gifted or superior to us.

The positive manifestation of this *middah* is humility. The fire in one's character can be redirected, and one's sense of meaning and significance can be defined by the degree to which one is truly aware of the other people with whom one is interacting. Being there in the fullest sense for the other person validates one's own significance. Learning to see others in this light causes one to replace anger and envy with responsiveness.

Wanting To Be Heard

The *ruach* Hashem blew into Adam, the breath of life itself, is translated by Onkelos as the "spirit of speech." The need to verbally express oneself is one of the deepest human needs. Additionally, since speech uses both the body and soul in equal measure, it is the most honest measure of who we are as humans. The misuse of the *middah* of verbal self-expression is to be undiscerning in what is expressed. Lies, slander, flattery, and verbal self-aggrandizement are ways of feeling that you've expressed yourself without having genuine attachment to anything but illusion.

The rectified usage of this *middah* is using speech to enhance other people's sense of their importance to you. Prayer, study, and encouraging words are examples of this. Instructing others is also the way through which our speech can connect us to Hashem's truth. The authentic self is expressed rather than the self created from illusion.

Addressing Our Needs

Water is nature's major means of nourishing life. It therefore serves as an allegory for our need to nourish ourselves, implanted in us by Hashem. We feel a need to take care of ourselves. When corrupted, this *middah* is manifest in jealousy of the possessions of others (and ultimately the financial outcome of jealousy — theft in its various "rationalized" forms) and the unceasing pursuit of physical pleasure.

The perfected channeling of this *middah* is recognizing that the continual pursuit of transient physical pleasure leads to the starvation of the spiritual side. One has to learn to "treat" oneself to a really interesting Torah lecture, a *shiur*, or a really satisfying kind deed.

A friend of mine who found herself retired from active motherhood (her children grew up) has converted a room in her home to a one-room convalescent home for new mothers. Her delight in decorating it couldn't have been greater if it were the living room in her spacious and tasteful home.

Keeping Still, Keeping Safe

The nature of earth is that it does not move on its own. One must move it. Passivity is a component of the human character. Its negative manifestation is the dread of failure that leads to depression. Lethargy in its various forms is the result of the paralyzing nature of fear of failure and the defensive adoption of passivity. The positive manifestation is accepting the tools Hashem gives a person as his lot in life and endeavoring to change them for others. However, once one acknowledges that the source of one's specific set of circumstances is Hashem, the fear of failure is mitigated by the knowledge that the challenge can be met.

When we make our choices to channel our *middos* with foresight and flexibility, the ultimate discovery is within reach — the discovery of self. The Maharal explains that the effect of this choice of rediscovering that which we share in common with Hashem is powerful enough to grant us the atonement we yearn for in ourselves and for all of *Klal Yisrael*.

CHAPTER NINE
stopping the clock

MY FIVE YEAR OLD RECENTLY celebrated his birthday. He had been "almost five" for what must have seemed to him an eternity. Although he took pleasure in receiving his gifts, the luminosity of his eyes was much brighter when he announced his new age. Soon after the great day, cheder resumed after the summer break. Eliyahu had been promoted from *gan* to *mechinah*.

He returned home with a look of amazement on his face. When I asked him what had happened, he replied, "There's a new little kid sitting on my old chair in *gan*!"

He had been introduced to the never-ending progression of time. Once childhood passes, the vision of progress and movement often passes with it. The days merge without our necessarily mapping out the direction in which our feet take us.

New Beginnings

Parashas Bereishis reveals the destination to which the road we are on will take us. The Ramban guides us through time in his classical commentary, unveiling the pattern created by its passage. He divides the world's history into eras, each one bringing the world closer to the purpose for which Hashem created it, making for Himself a dwelling place in this, the lowest of all worlds.

The Torah hints by the use of the phrase *asher bara Elokim la'asos*, "that Hashem created to do," in the present tense, that the days of Creation are in a continual state of unfolding. The Midrash tells us that Hashem's "day" is a thousand years. The Ramban explains that every day of Creation reflects the spiritual forces that will influence the course of events in each one of the thousand-year periods in the world's history.

The first two thousand years since the world was created are referred to as the Age of Desolation. While there were tzaddikim before Avraham, there were none who called Hashem's Name.

Calling Hashem's Name implies two things. One is the ability to experience Hashem in a way that is sufficiently part of one's sense of reality so that He can be given a name that is genuine. While the idolaters referred to the various spiritual forces they served by name, they had no sense of the unity and transcendence of Hashem. The various names they used to refer to Him reflected their confusion.

The other implication in calling Hashem's Name is the desire to make Hashem known to others. Avraham was not content with knowing Hashem; his love of Hashem brought him to raising the awareness of Him in others.

The first part of the two-thousand-year period was not completely dark. In spite of there being no one of the spiritual stature of Avraham, for whom the entire world was created, the era was nonetheless dominated by the illumination of Adam. This light was not extinguished by the emergence of idolatry until the era of Enosh at the end of this period. This era, the first thousand years, considered the Age of Adam, is paralleled in the Torah with the creation of light.

The second half of the two-thousand-year period was the era of the Flood. One of the most significant lessons of the Flood is that Hashem viewed the entire world as being worthy of salvation in the merit of one person, Noach. The awareness we have of Hashem's mastery over everything imaginable could at times prevent us from valuing our own significance. Recognizing the value of the spiritual journey of one righteous person can change our entire concept of what is implied by the word *important*.

We are corrupted by the current definitions of this word. In reality, almost nothing of what people call important is of significance. Our ability to identify that which has genuine significance is molded by what the Torah teaches us about the events that took place on the second day of Creation.

The Empty Space Inside and Out

The second day of Creation was the day on which Hashem separated the higher waters from the lower waters. This separation of the spiritual source of the world's sustenance from the physical manifestation of the waters that sustain life leaves not only the physical expanse of emptiness that we call sky and space, but also a spiritual parallel.

Rebbe Nachman of Breslav explains that the spiritual form of the "empty space" can be found in the heart of human beings. Each person is an *olam katan*, a small world. All of the features of the great world outside are found in a different form in the inner dimension of being. At times we cannot perceive the connection between Hashem and the world. This "space" in the heart parallels the space between the spiritual source of reality, the *mayim elyonim*, higher waters, and the physical waters that sustain us, the *mayim tachtonim*. And it can be filled with either faith or its opposite.

What gives significance to the life of a tzaddik is his free choice to fill that space with faith. When there is no sense of disconnection from Hashem, every deed a person of faith does is important in the most authentic sense of the word. Thus the act of separation that was created on the second day of Creation was expressed by the great Flood and the separation of Noach from all humankind during the thousand-year era which corresponds to that day.

The Nesivos Shalom points out that we sometimes find ourselves in the world of *sohu*, confusion. This is one of the descriptions the Torah uses for the world before Hashem created light. We lose our sense of destination and fail to see beyond the moment. The light within Adam, our *tzelem Elokim*, that spirit within us which renders us a reflection of God, can guide us. The light of Noach, who brought the *tzelem* into actualization in a world defined by bestiality and denial can guide us. And the realization that he refused to get lost in the emptiness surrounding him can guide us.

Hashem moved the world on to its next phase. The lessons of the Age of Desolation had been learned.

Fruition

The third day of Creation was the one in which Hashem caused the earth to sprout forth vegetation. The greening of the world on this day was paralleled by the events of the third millennium of the world's history.

This period began in Avraham's forty-eighth year. It was at this time, the Torah tells us, that he "called out in Hashem's Name." This was when his own personal flowering and his awareness of Hashem became so central to his identity that he saw Hashem in every aspect of reality. It was a turning point for the world as well.

The Vilna Gaon points out that the limitation of the non-Jewish vision of God is reflected by the totality of their exclusion of Hashem from the material world and, even more so, by the exclusion of the material world from their vision of Hashem. It was this very awareness of Hashem's unity and constancy that Avraham taught to his followers, the "souls that he made in Charan."

While the myriads of disciples were lost to the erosion of time, Avraham's children were taught, not only the abstract knowledge of God, but the living awareness of God through bringing His presence into the material world. The days of *sohu* were over.

The culmination of this era was our receiving the Torah. We were instructed on the very day the second Tablets were given that we must build a sanctuary here in this world, and that if we would, Hashem would live in the heart of each and every one of us.

Entering the Land of Israel opened the possibility of elevating the sparks of holiness inherent to the Creation. The majority of mitzvos are dependent on our having lived in Eretz Yisrael on a level in which every physical action, from eating to working, reveals Hashem to us. Thus this era was the zenith of human development toward encounter with Hashem and our living out His plan of making the world worthy of His habitation.

Time

On the fourth day of Creation the two luminaries, the sun and the moon, were created. As the text tells us, they define for us the passage of time. Defining time is far less simple than measuring the course of its passage. What time is, in essence, is the sequence of changes by which we define reality.

The two great lights symbolize the two Holy Temples. Their effect was to determine the boundaries of what can be achieved in this world. They redefined change and thus redefined time.

The sacrifices offered on the altar took us back to the moments in the Garden of Eden when Hashem assigned Adam the mission of elevating the world and everything in it. The soul-shaking force of the *korbanos*, the offerings, brought the light of Hashem's glory to the world. In the words of the Ramban, "The light of Yisrael was the fire of the altar."

The brilliance of the light diminished the first exile. The light of the Second Temple was more subtle. Its fire blazed with less brightness, but its light remained in our hearts throughout the subsequent exiles.

The darkness of the exiles led to further and further decline. The spark of Adam, the *tzelem*, was buried under heavier and heavier layers of base desire. Humanity had fallen to the fate of fish in the sea. They were caught up in a never-ending struggle for survival in a world in which God was not discovered because there was no longer a search. This is symbolized by the creatures formed on the fifth day — the fish and the birds.

The Pinnacle of Creation

The animals created on the sixth day were of a more sophisticated nature than those of the fifth. The anonymity of the sea is not an accurate symbol for the emerging empires of the millennium in which we now find ourselves.

The final creation of the sixth day was Adam. Corresponding to the creation of Adam, we can look toward the restoration of the *tzelem* to all humanity with the coming of the Messiah.

When we observe the passage of time in our own lives, there is an analogous phenomenon of light and shadow. We experience times of greater clarity and times of almost impenetrable darkness. We must recognize however, that with the recommencment of *sefer Bereishis*, our feet are taking us forward — not to an uncharted future, but to a future that is predictable. We are headed toward a world in which awareness of Hashem will fill even the empty space in our hearts "as water covers the seabed." Every step we take leads us to only one destination: personal and collective *geulah*, redemption from this long exile. Awareness of our responsibility to ourselves and to the world should inspire us to move ourselves forward with grace and hope.

CHAPTER TEN
staying afloat

THE DETAILED DESCRIPTION of the dimensions of Noach's Ark has no doubt been a source of bewilderment to many readers of the *parashah* throughout the years. The Torah gives us information that on the surface is very difficult for us to apply to our own lives.

Everything in the Torah is instructive, part of our deepest selves. The terror the world went through during the year-long ordeal of the flood cannot be put into words. The consequences of man's collective descent brought him to the very edge of total annihilation. The ark, the means by which Hashem saved the world, requires deep contemplation.

In a certain sense, Avraham was very much the "ark of his generation." Avraham was born at a time when Hashem had been forgotten by mankind. The trauma of the Great Flood must have been so horrific that one would expect its imprint to be permanent. In reality, its occurrence was remembered, but its message was forgotten. In Avraham's generation, the possibility for the world to be engulfed once again in spiritual darkness was real. By Avraham redefining the generation's approach to Hashem, as well as the indelible effect he had on the world for all time, he became an "ark."

Let us examine both arks.

The Ark of Noach

The Kli Yakar explains that the text details the construction of the ark, as well as its dimensions, for two reasons. One reason is to show us the greatness of the miracle by which the ark, not at all large by contemporary standards, contained every species of animal. By performing this miracle, Hashem revealed Himself as the Master of nature. By instructing Noach to build an ark which would contain all the world's animals, He was giving Noach's generation the opportunity to search for the meaning of their own blind pursuit of gain.

The second reason is that the various multiples of the number fifteen in the dimensions of the ark delineate the Hebrew letters *yud*, which has the numerical value of ten, and *hey*, which has the value of five. This indicates that the source of the destruction was the loss of any spirituality in the relationship between men and women. The Hebrew word for "man," *ish*, and the Hebrew word for "woman," *ishah*, would spell the word *eish*, fire, but for two letters: *yud* and *hey*.

Ten, the value of the *yud* from *ish*, is the number that ends every number series and is therefore a symbol of wholeness. By pursuing truth (ultimately done through learning Torah), man's spiritual side is manifest. The *hey* from the word *ishah* equals the number five. The world in its most limited state (directions, seasons, elements) is symbolized by the number four, the value of *dalet*. By placing a *yud* inside the *dalet*, one emerges with a picture of the letter *hey*. The way in which women manifest their spiritual side is to elevate the world with all of its limitations. If neither side, man nor woman, reaches its potential for spiritual expression, all that remains are the fires of destruction, the *eish*.

The idolatry and theft that doomed the world to the Flood were caused by the promiscuity that characterized that era. The fifteen *amos* of water that covered the world for a hundred and fifty days, the three hundred *amos* length of the ark, multiplied by its fifty *amos* width were not coincidental. All represented the number fifteen or were multiples of that number, which represents the *yud* and *hey* of spirituality. How many questions could have been asked, how much soul-searching could have been done, during the decades of its construction! The desecration of God's Name was the primary cause of the flood. Once a sense of Godliness was lost, the world sank deeper and deeper until it was no longer redeemable.

Chizkiyahu and David

This phenomenon was not unique to the era of the flood. King Chizkiyahu was rebuked by the prophet for his failure to marry. He was told that both worlds were at stake: the future world (the world of the *yud*) and this world (the world of the *hey*). This is why the decree was so severe. When Chizkiyahu repented and married, he restored the *yud* and *hey* to their rightful places and thus was granted another fifteen years of life.

When David HaMelech dug the foundations of the *Beis HaMikdash*, he came to the waters of the depths. He feared that they would flood the world. The waters of the *tehom*, the hidden waters that lie under the world's surface, are a physical manifestation of the *tehom* that is found on the dark side of every individual. By singing the fifteen *Shir HaMa'alos* (*Tehillim* 120–134), which hint that the Jewish people are guarded against all forms of promiscuity and Hashem's Name is implanted within them, David saved the world from being inundated.

Avraham and Sarah

The Or haChaim tells us that Hashem didn't "reveal" Himself to Avraham, but began speaking to Avraham without any prelude. The reason being that although he had sought Hashem more than any human before him, he would only be worthy of revelation in the deepest sense when he had been tested. Only after the challenges were met successfully would Hashem make His covenant with Avraham. Every aspect of Avraham and Sarah's journey was part of the process of challenge.

There are two basic inner drives that direct our actions: the drive to give and the drive to take. The more a person has developed the capacity to emulate Hashem, the more his giving side will make itself felt. Conversely, the more the taking side dominates his personality, the less Hashem's Presence is expressed through him. Avraham and Sarah reached a level of being in which Godliness was imbued in their every movement and conversation.

The same spirituality and commitment to giving that we see in their hospitality and their teaching characterized their relationship with each other. They brought the *yud* and the *hey* together and reintroduced Hashem's Name to the world.

The difference between the world before the Flood and the world in which we live today is becoming more and more blurred. We find it increasingly difficult to join the *yud* and *hey* together by including Hashem in our everyday lives. Our homes and our schools are the "ark" that can save us in the midst of the flood.

The ark was illuminated by the *tzohar*. There are two views concerning what the *tzohar* actually was; it may have been a window or it may have been a gemstone.

We must live lives into which we welcome Hashem's light. The base desires of today's society impede this light from entering our lives. We must be like Avraham and affect our external environment; we must not lose sight of how to build an ark.

CHAPTER ELEVEN
created in His image

ONE OF THE most frequently asked questions *ba'alei teshuvah* hear is, "How did you come to be involved in Torah Judaism?" I have heard the question asked in ways that could merit the Nobel prize for tactlessness or, alternatively, with great tact and sensitivity.

My own fascination with each and every story is not easy to put into words. While curiosity and love of drama no doubt play a major part, what I feel comes from the fact that each person's journey is always part of my own.

One of the very brightest lights in the world of *kiruv* is an eloquent, charismatic, and extraordinarily sensitive young rabbi. He is open with his students about his emergence from an upper middle class secular background. This admission generally arouses an enormous amount of curiosity. Clearly he was not escaping "from," but going "toward," something.

At a single glance one can see that he is a person for whom all doors would naturally open. It requires no stretch of imagination to see him in judicial black or operating-room green. His story is, therefore, one he finds himself telling on a fairly regular basis. It is unique in its pristine and unexpected simplicity.

About ten years ago, Jerry (not his real name) was a teacher in a Reform Sunday school. In retrospect, the pathetic nature of his teaching others, given the paucity of his own knowledge of anything Jewish, is a source of wry amusement. At the time, nothing could be more natural than that he whose knowledge of Jewish learning included the *alef-beis* and not much else should teach those who didn't even have that connection to their heritage.

One Sunday afternoon, a badly dressed, unfortunate individual passed through the oak-lined lobby of the temple and walked to the room in which the Sunday school met. The "rabbi" heard the footsteps and left his study to see who had arrived. One look was enough. The destitute individual was callously banished.

Jerry left almost as fast as the poor person. The hypocrisy displayed by a religious leader whose entire theology began and ended with one commandment, "Be nice," was appalling.

The Common Denominator

Hashem's Providence brought Jerry to an Orthodox synagogue. He was neither "searching for truth" nor studying. His entrance coincided with that of a down-and-out panhandler.

The rabbi greeted Jerry and immediately switched on the electric urn to begin the process of warming up the beggar, something he realized the man sorely needed. When Jerry asked the rabbi whether he always had such empathy for people, the rabbi responded by explaining the laws of *tzedakah*, charity. The fact that the rabbi's generosity was not a result of his personal sensitivity but a part of the religious code that governed every moment of his life was most meaningful to Jerry. The idea of charity being a binding religious obligation led him to reintroduce himself to Judaism.

While every story of *teshuvah* differs, there is a single common denominator. Somewhere in the course of his journey, the returnee encountered an event that made him aware of the fact that he is created in the image of Hashem and that his life has sufficient significance to be guided by the mitzvos. Hospitality is almost always a part of every story. The recognition that the law requires caring about a person with whom one has no relationship is, in fact, the first step to comprehending the goals in a Torah lifestyle, as opposed to aspiring to being a "good person."

What Is the Secret?

What power is concealed in an act of *chesed*? Why does it move us so deeply?

The Maharal explains that the spiritual force of *chesed*, lovingkindness, stems from its changing the person who does the deed.

We have trouble deciding whether our inner or outer self is the "real" one. Why is our sense of who we are so fragile? The reason is that the earsplitting voice of the body has only one message: "Give me more!" The body, by nature, takes. We don't notice that the "I" doing the talking is the body, not the soul.

The utterance made most resoundingly by the soul is "I must feel that I am giving of myself." When a person does an act of kindness, he confirms his spiritual identity. Each act of expression makes his spiritual identity stronger. Similarly, the recipient of an act of kindness becomes more aware of his own integral value. The fact that he is human, and therefore worthy of being cared about, can totally redefine him. He becomes aware of being *b'tzelem Elokim*, an image of God. While this takes place with any act of kindness, the mitzvah of hospitality deserves special mention. When the guest is a stranger, the only reason for the host bringing him into his home is the recognition that he possesses integral human value.

Avraham: Symbol of Chesed

Parashas Vayeira begins with the narrative of Avraham extending a warm welcome to three rather unusual guests — Arabs who he assumes are worshipers of the dust of the earth but who were actually angels in disguise sent by God to accomplish three missions. We are all familiar with the *mesirus nefesh*, self-sacrifice, involved not only in this particular act of kindness (on the third day after his bris, a day on which the heat was so oppressive that Rashi uses the phrase "[God] removed the sun from its shield" to describe it), but the *mesirus nefesh* of his entire way of life. The Torah is not giving us this information so that we arrive at the conclusion that Avraham was a "nice man," a "good person." It was the acid test of his determination to cleave to Hashem's ways.

The Rambam says the reason the hospitality to the angels is mentioned at all is to explain to us why Hashem made him the promises mentioned later in the *parashah*. Those promises could only be made to a person whose level of *deveikus* could transform him into a fitting vessel to receive these vows.

Later in the *parashah*, the text states that Avraham planted an *eshel*. There is a debate in the Talmud as to whether the word *eshel* means an "orchard" or an "inn." The Maharal explains that both opinions contain profound statements concerning Avraham's nature.

According to those who say that *eshel* is an orchard, the unique characteristics of Avraham are comparable to an orchard. He himself is the first "tree" to be planted, the first to make his strong roots into a force analogous to a strong tree. He in turn was able to plant other "trees." He did this by searching unceasingly for truth. His profound and fundamental understanding of creation left no room for the exclusion of its Creator.

The word *eshel* is composed of the same letters as the word *sha'al*, "he asked" — *alef, shin, lamed*. Avraham could answer any question posed. He would share his wisdom unstintingly. The result of his commitment was his orchard of followers.

The opinion that the meaning of the word *eshel* is "inn" reveals another facet of Avraham's character. The scholars maintaining this opinion hold that the true mainstay of Avraham's character was not his ability to share intellectual truth, but rather to inspire changes in the deeds of others. His disciples were not only men blessed with vast intelligence; they also included ordinary people. These students were introduced to Godliness as well as to God by Avraham and Sarah. Not only were they changed intellectually, but they also changed their day-to-day actions.

The effect Avraham had on those to whom he opened his door was tremendous. The Sefas Emes explains that the closeness the giver feels toward the recipient of his kindness awakens a parallel feeling of closeness in the heart of the recipient. This is similar to the way Hashem, in His desire to draw His creations closer to Him, filled the world with His goodness.

While it is worthy for us to do deeds that bring us closer to Hashem and make us deserving of His love, few of us can walk that path without first feeling beloved by experiencing His constant goodness. We may need an "Avraham" to enter our lives, to give us the sense of our being recipients of Hashem's love. This awareness should make us mindful of how much the people around us also need an "Avraham."

Our attempts to be both an orchard and an inn take us to Jerry from California or even Kim from London. Closer to home, they *created in His image*

may bring us to feel the barren heart of the lonely elderly woman who lives in cold isolation or a child who wonders whether he can be loved. They will always take us to the deepest and most beloved part of themselves and ourselves, the *tzelem Elokim*.

CHAPTER TWELVE
growing old gratefully

During World War II, the U.S. Navy sent planes to Papua New Guinea to defend Australia, should the need arise. In order to prevent the inhabitants of the island (who had not yet discovered either the wheel or the use of stairs) from treating the airmen as undesirable aliens, a plan had to be put together. Each airman was provided with gifts to present the natives. By far the most popular of the various trinkets that were given as insurance against being "taken to dinner" in the literal sense was a hand mirror.

Imagine seeing yourself for the first time!

The inner eye is usually far kinder than the mirror. There are many subconscious adjustments one makes to allow oneself to see an image not too different from the face that stared back in the mirror in one's unwrinkled youth. Of course, the self-deception is far too transparent to last very long. Whenever photos come back from the shop, one finds oneself looking them over to see if they "came out well."

The society in which we live is completely unwilling to contend with the nonnegotiability of aging. Women hang on to the fantasy of being under thirty well into their seventies. Consider the image-evoking names of the *sheitels* we wear. How can we even ask the *sheitel macher*, the wig stylist, for the model we want with a straight face?

In reality, the normal process of aging puts us face to face (literally!) with our own mortality. The finite nature of the body, its invariable decline and ultimate decomposition into the elements from which it was formed, are disturbing reminders of the brevity of our lives. The degree to which our lives are defined by material concerns is the degree to which mortality is a source of horror.

The Talmud tells us that Avraham asked Hashem for the gift of old age. His resemblance to Yitzchak was so striking that when people saw them together, they did not know which was the father and which the son. He was concerned that this would create a situation in which people would not know which one to honor more.

When we hear this, we must ask ourselves two questions: Why do we give respect to the aged? And why, if one's appearance must change, does the act of aging make a person less good-looking? After all, far fewer people are interested in dyeing their hair gray than in buying products that promote their ability to disguise the gray.

The answer is that the act of natural aging should promote an awareness of the fact that one's body is not one's self. Age should be respected, not only for the wisdom that can only be acquired through the passage of years, but for the act of moving to a higher and more transcendent plane.

Thus we find in *Pirkei Avos* that, unlike the paradigm presented by contemporary society, life does not flower at thirty and then relentlessly decline. The need to "hold on" is ignored by the Sages. *Chazal* bring to our attention the realization that insight comes at forty, the ability to give counsel at fifty. The last age presented in the mishnah in *Avos* is the age of one hundred. It is described as being a time in which one is *over u'batel min ha'olam*, when one has "passed over and is negated from [the desires of] the world" (*Pirkei Avos, perek* 5). Far from stating that senility is the invariable end of life, the mishnah is telling us that a person of that venerable age can reach a spiritual level that is above the pettiness and insatiable appetite for material pleasure.

In *Parashas Chayei Sarah*, we are presented with Sarah's death. The narration of her death follows a description of the stages of her life. Rashi says that the verse describing her age, "a hundred years and twenty years and seven years," is telling us that at the age of one hundred she was as innocent as a woman of twenty, and at the age of twenty she was as beautiful as a girl of seven. We would expect her beauty to be compared to that of a twenty year old and her innocence to that of a seven year old.

The Maharal points out that what the text is describing is her perfection. Humans are comprised of body and soul. Perfection of the body is the state of being where the body has not "taken over" the personality to the point of becoming a barrier between a person and Hashem. The beauty of a seven year old bespeaks purity and potential. This was the beauty of Sarah. Everything about her reflected her purity and spiritual light. Perfection of the soul is a state of being where the soul's own power is uncorrupted.

We must now focus on why this is reflected by Sarah's being at the age of one hundred like a woman of twenty. An earthly court judges cases in which the defendant may be as young as twelve or thirteen. The Heavenly court, however, only judges a person from the age of twenty. The reason for this is that at the age of twelve or thirteen a person is able to take responsibility for the material consequences of his choices. The earthly court is given authority to judge the case itself, not the person being judged. No magistrate, regardless of his sagacity, can judge whether the boy standing before him is a tzaddik, a righteous person or a rasha, a wicked person. That assessment may be made only by Hashem.

The Vilna Gaon explains that in our infancy our entire spectrum of reality is filled with our awareness of ourselves and our desires. As we mature, the ability to experience spiritual pleasure through helping others and reaching outward develops. By the time we reach twenty, there is sufficient balance between the two forces that govern us for our choices to be really free.

At the age of one hundred, Sarah's innocence was comparable to the innocence of a twenty year old. This innocence is the fruit of conscientious, free choice. It is not the innocence of a seven year old, who is not aware enough to make choices.

Not only do we devalue aging, we devalue innocence. Even in our circles, describing someone as sophisticated is meant to be complimentary. We tend to associate innocence with ignorance and intellectual limitation. What the *parashah* is bringing to our attention is that innocence can be a choice. We have the ability to say *no* or *yes* to the things contemporary society calls "significant" and "wise." It is from society that we have learned to deny our potentials for growth and to idealize being thirty forever. But we do not have to make our decision apologetically. A decision for innocence can be made with pride.

growing old gratefully

When Sarah died, Avraham knew what a treasure he had lost. Nevertheless, he would not allow himself the luxury of excessive mourning. While his personal loss was unfathomable, his awareness that Sarah had gone on to a higher plane was enough to limit his expressions of grief. He did, however, spare no effort or expense in acquiring her a burial place in Me'aras HaMachpelah in Chevron.

The literal meaning of the word *chevron* is "joining." The nature of Me'aras HaMachpelah is to act as a place of joining between this world and the next one. Unlike Yerushalayim, in which the connection takes place because of its preeminence and superiority, Chevron is built on rocky terrain described in the Gemara as the area of least value in Eretz Yisrael. Its connective power is similar to the connective power of old age. It has within it the power to evoke transcendence. It rises above its physical nature.

Another name for Chevron is Kiryas Arba. It was named both for the four giants who once lived there and the four couples buried there. The physical enormity of the giants parallels the spiritual magnitude of the four couples.

The Maharal explains that the number four is often used as a symbol of the most fundamental realities of both worlds. This world is defined spatially by its four directions and its elements, fire, water, earth, and air. He states that the extension of the higher world to this world is symbolized similarly by the four rivers that flow from the Garden of Eden to this world. The outpouring of Hashem's Providence and intervention wears many "faces." At times we experience the oppression of the four exiles, and on other occasions we use the four expressions of redemption symbolized by the four cups of wine we drink at the Seder. The two names, Chevron and Kiryas Arba, show us that even that which is most tied to this world has its source in Hashem's Providence and can lead us to a connection with the higher world.

It is our choice to be either a giant of body or of spirit, to walk either toward exile or redemption. We can choose to live lives in which we are not held back by the limitations of the physical. We can be like the patriarchs and matriarchs, the *yesheinei Chevron*, "those who sleep in Chevron." They are very much alive, very much unrestricted by mortality.

CHAPTER THIRTEEN
who are we fooling?

MY STAY IN the hospital after the birth of my son had passed, *baruch Hashem*, with the usual enjoyable and blessed lack of momentum. The one outstanding feature was the extraordinary caring attitude of a particular member of the nursing staff. The sounds emerging from the nursery were several decibels lower when she was on duty. This was caused by her willingness to literally rise to the occasion whenever an infant cried for her attention. It was to her that I posed what seemed to me to be a harmless, though perhaps somewhat personal, question. I asked her why she had decided to be a baby nurse.

"They are all good! They don't hurt or defame anyone with their idle chatter."

The sentence was said with such fire that no one in the room knew quite how to respond. Since it was my question that had elicited such passion, I was even more astonished than the rest of the group of young women in the hospital nursery. It had seemed such an innocent inquiry at the time.

While many years have passed since that day, the memory of that moment is still vivid. In the several seconds of silence that met her outburst, I found myself studying her. She was a woman who appeared to be in her mid-thirties. She was preparing a baby for a bath in a large red plastic sink. Her gaze met mine evenly, but without the touch of humor that would have offered me the option of trivializing what she had said.

At the time, the truth of her words moved me so deeply that I suddenly realized that the puzzle of the emergence of human individuality was far more intricate than I had imagined. We all know children from the same family who seem to be almost a different species in adulthood. How does this occur? What makes one person choose a path that leads him to everything meaningful and precious life can offer, while another child, raised in the same environment, chooses a life that could be described as a game of "trivial pursuit," seeking every banal and ultimately self-destructive prize that can be offered by the world of illusion?

The Rambam says that anyone can be a tzaddik as great as Moshe or a rasha as corrupt as Yeravam ben Nevat. Let us gain some insight into the process through the *parashah*.

Negative Pressures Abound

Parashas Toldos is replete with the fascinating narratives of personages whose stature we can barely glimpse. There are limitations imposed on perspective by the passage of time from the one perfect moment of truth we experienced at Mount Sinai. There are other limitations that are the consequence of our limited knowledge and personal subjectivity. Nonetheless, who can fail to be moved by the almost impossible reality of Rivkah's emergence as a righteous person from the midst of a family and society that opposed her on every possible level? We observe the failure of Esav to mean anything other than a "hunter" viewing the entire world as "prey" and the endless demands of his ego. How could he have shared a childhood with Yaakov? How could he have met the power of Yitzchak's gaze or shared a meal with Rivkah?

Let us examine Rivkah's background. The Midrash includes the entire population of Padan Aram as partners with her father, Lavan, in their almost unbelievable moral ambiguity. They lived in a society in which there were laws they defended and ignored with equal aplomb. The Maharal explains the textual emphasis on the negativity of the setting from which she came as testimony to her righteousness. Her love of truth emerges from the picture he shows us.

He points out that people are moved toward negative behavior because of three factors. The first is fear of opposing someone who looms larger than life and suffering the consequences. The second is love of a person who is involved in the wrong behavior and wanting the closeness that is attained by developing the commonality upon which love is often built. The third is the unwillingness to be a loner in a society that is steeped in its own depravity.

Rivkah withstood pressures from every possible angle: from the natural awe a child feels for a father, from the closeness she would feel for a brother whose role in the house was that of a "star," and from every aspect of her surroundings. There was no "outside" in which she could have found refuge; the corruption of the outside was a mirror of that at home. Her only refuge was the integrity of her choices.

The *Orchos Tzaddikim* points out that the soul comes from a place of truth. It is carved from the throne of Hashem's glory, from which He rules the world and from which His word emanates. The soul, therefore, always knows the truth. When we are honest, not only with our words but in our inner dialogue, we strengthen the capacity to maintain connection with Hashem's will. Conversely, inner deception, and even petty departure from the factuality of the world that Hashem has presented to us through His Providence, creates discord between the part of us that wants to know Him and the part of us that doesn't.

Tithing Straw and Salt

The contrast between Esav and Rivkah is reflected by the dominant characteristic in Esav's makeup, his duplicity. His questions were so *"frum"*: How do you tithe straw? How do you tithe salt? Note that he does not question whether or not straw and salt should be tithed; his only question is how this should be accomplished. Of course, neither require tithing.

The Maharal points out that the focus of his questions were pseudo-philosophic. Straw is exempt because its total lack of taste relegates its function to the protection of the grain. It can't be said to have intrinsic value; its value is only in the grain it protects. Similarly, salt cannot be eaten on its own. Its value, too, is not intrinsic; its significance is relative to the effect it has in seasoning food. They are, of course, diametrically opposite — straw has no taste, while the taste of salt is so concentrated as to render it inedible.

What Esav wished others to think was that his inner picture of Hashem's unity was so profound that he saw even objects of no authentic intrinsic value as part of Hashem's indivisibility. Who was he fooling? Was it only Yitzchak? Was it not Esav who wept with earthshaking violence when he realized that the *berachos*, the blessings Yitzchak was supposed to bestow on his firstborn son, would never be his? Had he not ultimately failed at fooling himself?

While it may be difficult to envision ourselves "becoming" Rivkah, or even becoming significantly more similar to her, it is an even greater stretch of the imagination to envision oneself descending to the depths of Esav's corruption. Conversely, it may seem to us at first that Esav is not at all at fault for what he became; after all, it seems the deck was stacked against him from the very beginning.

The text tells us that while Yaakov and Esav were still in their mother's womb, they were embattled. Yaakov was drawn to Shem's house of study, while Esav was drawn to idolatry. This was not a result of Esav being pulled toward bad choices. The Torah tells us that " the inclination of a man is evil from his early youth," not from before his birth. What the text is telling us is that all of us are drawn by nature to that which is similar to ourselves. It is undeniable that Yaakov and Esav were intrinsically different. The one question that is relevant is how they used their natural proclivities.

How Should We Respond?

Esav and David HaMelech are the only characters in Tanach who are described graphically. While we know, for instance, that Sarah was beautiful, we don't have any sort of physical description. What Esav and David shared in common, the Ramban points out, was a fiery nature which is, by its very definition, corruptible. The difference lies in their responses to their natures. David directed his drive to conquest in order for Hashem's will to prevail in the world. Esav directed his drive to conquer for the sake of his own self-validation. The resultant self-worship is the source of the collective egotism that has given birth to the intellectual, cultural, and physical imperialism that defines the West.

The Maharal tells us that the descendants of Yaakov and Esav reflect the parting of their ancestors' ways. The Sage Rabbi Yehudah HaNasi elevated this world for Hashem. He did not deny the beauty and grandeur of the world, yet he never lost track of its Source. His allegiance to truth was the result of there being something of Yaakov within him and his choice to let that part of himself be the most definitive aspect of his character. Yaakov was unique, not just because of his inborn purity, but because of the integrity of his choices. His sense of truth led him to see the world with a clarity that was unparalleled by any since Adam. In his search for truth there was no room for egotism.

Antoninus, the Roman emperor who was Rabbi Yehudah HaNasi's contemporary, also responded to the world with depth. Yet the inherent splendor and harmony of the world which touched his spirit did not lead him closer to Hashem — it led him closer to his own core need for meaning. He, too, was a "hunter" in pursuit of the conquest of both worlds.

The personalities of Yaakov and Esav are to a large degree too "big" for us to grasp in their entirety (as is true to a far lesser degree with regard to Rabbi Yehudah HaNasi and even Antoninus). Yet in today's society we cannot avoid seeing fragments of them wherever we look. When we look carefully at Esav's descendants, what do we see? Their constant pursuit of meaning devoid of truth and harmony, devoid of God, pervades every available avenue of self-expression. Because there is pursuit of meaning and love of harmony, we are at times deceived. They are still busy tithing straw and salt.

Honest Choices

We must never forget who we are; we must be constantly aware of the fact that we are always making choices. We can easily allow the spark of Yaakov to be eclipsed, at least momentarily, by the sort of vague cloudiness that comforts us into oblivion and blinds us to the fact that we are constantly emerging. We, too, know the truth; we must let it touch our choices. We must question what we say and how it is said, what we allow ourselves to bring into our homes and why, what we reject and how we feel when rejecting. Are we "hunting," Esav's favorite pastime? Are we impressing

who are we fooling?

others by tithing salt?

Once we are aware of the fact that we are making choices, we can begin to be honest. We can be the kind of parents who pass the spark of Yaakov to our children and allow them to retain the goodness and sensitivity to truth that is within them from the moment of their birth.

How can we transmit truth? The Sefas Emes says that the garments of the soul — thought, speech, and deed — can, in the case of a tzaddik who serves Hashem in truth, bring something of Gan Eden into this world. This is the scent Yitzchak smelled when Yaakov entered his tent. When we live lives of truth, we affect not only ourselves but, since we take who we are wherever we go, we change the awareness of those around us.

When I was a student in Bnei Brak over thirty years ago, I witnessed a transmission of truth I have never forgotten. My friend arranged for me to be invited to her aunt's house for Shabbos. The feeling was warm and delightfully heimish. In the morning, when her uncle was about to leave for shul, he observed that the women of the house were far from ready. He looked at his wife and said with a warm smile, "Your mother had the keys to the shul." Nothing more had to be said.

When I bring myself back to the moment I stood in the nursery surrounded by innocent newborns, the truth of the nurse's words ringing in my ears, I feel the simultaneous awareness that each of these children are descendants of Yaakov. Each has the capacity to not only know truth, but to live truth.

But they are living very much in a world that is as yet in the hands of Esav. Each will have his or her own decisions to make. They will turn their eyes to us, their mothers, and we must enable them to smell the subtle fragrance of Gan Eden.

CHAPTER FOURTEEN
climbing the ladder

THERE ARE SO many things we don't know. Of course, the worst part of not knowing is the blissful unawareness that we are generalizing. The generalizations that are true enough in their own way are often redefined as truth in the subjective sense. Judgment is often made so instantaneously that we are unaware of the fact that we have not only failed to consider where the other person is coming from, but more basically we forget at times their right to be themselves.

This phenomenon is not new. The differences between us that allow us to instantly reduce others to caricatures are purposeful. Our individualistic tendencies are an inherent part of the essence of the Jewish people. The twelve tribes were far from identical on any level. The fact that they were born under the twelve different astral bodies reflects their individuality.

The Ramban makes a fascinating comment in this regard. We perceive the individuality of the tribes as being a consequence of their each having a different *mazal*, a different way of experiencing Hashem's outpouring of blessing. Each month has a different astrological sign in the zodiac, which reflects its *mazal*. What the Ramban adds is that Hashem created the awesome variance of the *mazalos* in order to generate the emergence of the twelve unique and individual tribes. Hashem created the cosmos to accommodate the need for each tribe to be itself!

We often fail to recognize that the physical side of reality is less real than the spiritual side. We think, for instance, that the reason the Torah tells us not to steal is a response to the fact that we live in a world in which we don't always have what we want. The truth is that Hashem purposely created a world in which we are faced with the challenge of living without the material possessions we yearn for in order to test us. He could have just as easily created a world in which everything is accessible without effort, in which theft would be a moral impossibility.

In the same vein, Hashem could have created twelve tribes who share similar personality traits. That would have created a completely homogeneous Jewish people. If we all had the same *mazal*, not only would we understand each other, but we would also enact our collective mission identically.

Instead, Hashem created twelve different paths that will affect not only the inner composition of each tribe but also their mission. Therefore, the responses they make to life not only can be, but must be, completely distinct. The twelve sons of Yaakov are referred to as "tribes," not "sons." The reason for this, the Maharal says, can be understood by focusing on the nature of the Hebrew word *shevet*. *Shevet* literally means "branch." In the same way that a branch continually draws its life force from the tree, the tribes of Israel continually draw their sense of Hashem's unity from their ancestor Yaakov.

The way they maintain individuality while at the same time draw from a common source can be understood through observing the human body. The Maharal says, in the name of the *Sefer Yetzirah*, that there are twelve main limbs and organs in the human body. The *neshamah*, the soul, unifies them. Nonetheless, each one of them must retain its separate function in order to benefit the body. In the same way that the human body has twelve main features, the world as a whole (which is a macrocosm of the human body) is also divisible geometrically through the twelve possible angles (as of a three-dimensional square). The physical reality (in this case, not just of humans but of the world as a whole) was created to allow for spiritual reality to be expressed. Hence we find references to twelve "agates of the firmament" and twelve permutations of Hashem's Name.

Unity in Diversity

Until the tribes were born, Hashem had chosen one person in each generation to act as the heart and conscience of that generation. With the birth of Yaakov's sons, there were twelve branches stemming from one root, Yaakov, that could take on the mission of sanctifying Hashem's Name in the world. It is, therefore, no coincidence that the number of the tribes plus Yaakov, their source, is thirteen. Thirteen is also the numerical value of the Hebrew word *echad*, "one."

We now understand why each tribe received its own individual *berachah*, blessing (both from Yaakov, at the end of his life, who described their potential, and from Moshe, who described their actualized development). Even more significant in a certain sense is, as the Malbim brings, that they were all included in all the *berachos*. Thus the Torah says, "All the tribes of Israel are twelve," meaning that each and every one of them have components of them all.

Yaakov's wives Rachel and Leah also were very different in character and mission. Each was designated for a specific path in Hashem's service. Rachel's portion, "of beautiful features," is explained by the Zohar as being reflective of her finding expression in *alma d'esgalya*, the revealed world. Leah, on the other hand, who is described as "having soft eyes," found her path through developing spiritual vision of sufficient depth that it gave her the ability to penetrate *alma d'eskasya*, the hidden world.

The tribes that descended from Rachel initiated the physical enactment of bringing the vision of *malchus Shamayim*, the Kingdom of Heaven, into this world. The conquest of Eretz Yisrael by Yehoshua epitomized this goal. Later Mordechai, a descendant of Binyamin the son of Rachel, defeated Haman in his attempt to physically annihilate the Jewish people. We are told that the future defeat of Amalek will also be achieved by a descendant of Binyamin.

The tribes that are descendants of Leah have the mission of bringing about the spiritual redemption of the Jewish people. The final redemption will be brought about by Mashiach ben David, a descendant of Leah.

It is easy to focus on differences. We tend to make almost instantaneous judgments on the basis of how similar or dissimilar we are to each other. Appreciating and validating difference is an entirely different matter. In order to genuinely value individuality, one must learn to see not only the aspect of the person in question that is "tribal" — separate and unique — but also the part of that person that is "Yisrael," connected to the root. Let us look to *Parashas Vayeitzei* and follow Yaakov on his journey from his home to Lavan's house, where he found his wives. We will discover that every aspect of his life speaks to the corresponding part of each one of us.

A Collective Mission

The *parashah* begins with the departure of Yaakov from his parental home in Be'er Sheva. His departure affected the city profoundly. Its inner splendor, its spiritual radiance, and its glory were all diminished. He, however, remained Yaakov.

Toward night, he gathered twelve stones around his head and they united into one. This hints at Yaakov's ability to unify all twelve of his sons. It was then that the Torah revealed to us the ladder vision, and it is from within this vision that the collective mission of the Jewish people can be found. It is this mission that unifies us in our diversity.

The Sefas Emes explains that each person is a ladder. The body has its feet firmly in this world, while the soul reaches the heavens. The angels of Hashem ascend and descend the ladder. They are higher than the body, but the root of the soul is above them. In the course of our lives, we find ourselves struggling to ascend the rungs as we seek to return to the Source from which we all come. When Yaakov recognized the nature of the ladder he saw in his dream, he experienced heartfelt awe, as he observed how far his soul could rise. To ground this awakening, he made vows so that he would never abandon this vision regardless of where his life took him.

Each person has an inherent sense of his or her own significance. The desire to be beloved, to be first and best, comes from the part of us that yearns to climb higher. The specific drives that motivate one person are different from those that motivate another. The goal they are focused on is not.

"Shabbat Shalom"

Recently I had my sofa cleaned. It was not a particularly attractive job from the perspective of the cleaning company. It is neither part of a set, nor dirty enough to legitimize an extra fee. In all honesty, it also wasn't clean enough to be a fast job that would have left the serviceman his afternoon open for other pursuits. Erez of Easy Clean was duly unimpressed.

After toiling over Old Faithful for about an hour and a half, Erez looked at his handiwork with satisfaction and called me in to see the finished job. The sofa was indeed far younger than it had been in my memory. It was the sort of sofa that never seemed really new. Suffice it to say, the only other place I saw the sofa's twin was in the living room of a tzaddik far better known for his piety than for his home decor.

The glow on Erez's face was reflective of more than a job done well. He took pleasure in his own integrity and in the joy that he had brought to the children who cheered him on. As he wrote the receipt and prepared to leave, he took a final look at the sofa, turned to me, and said, "I guess it is too far from any holiday to say 'Good *Yom Tov*.' " Indeed, it was. The day was Monday, not a day specially highlighted on the Jewish calendar.

He looked at the children and then back at me and said, "*Shabbat shalom.*" He turned to the door. We took a final glance at him, at the shorts and T-shirt, the shaven head, and said, "*Shabbat shalom.*" At that moment I knew that, whatever else his name was, it was also Yisrael.

I had made my assumptions about him from the moment he walked in. No doubt in a general sense they were true. The insight I gained is that they were irrelevant. Wishing him every success, I closed the door.

CHAPTER FIFTEEN
faded dreams

WE ALL EXPERIENCE loss. There are territories in our road maps we never expected to see. The extremity of anguish we suffer in times of bereavement is mirrored in miniature in the disappointments we experience when our vision of how our lives would be doesn't dovetail with what actually happened. We suffer from pain and frustration once we realize that our dreams have not come true.

There are myriad ways of classifying such times. What they share in common is the indisputable authenticity of pain. The pain is real whether the unrealized dream is one of relatively insignificant consequence — such as recognizing that the longed-for "dream house" is likely to remain precisely that — or the incomparable wretchedness of recognizing that the "dream children" or "dream marriage" one yearned for are not reflected in one's present circumstances.

Even when the disappointment is minor league, we still must learn how the Torah tells us to address it. The alternative is either repression of the knowledge of what one is lacking, or, worse still, the subtle disbelief in the goodness of Hashem and His world.

Feeling the Blessing

How can we feel blessed in the midst of grief and disappointment?

The Nesivos Shalom points out in the name of the Baal Shem Tov that no two people have ever been created alike since the world's beginning. Each individual has his own rectification to achieve and is given the circumstances by which he can reach his objective. True blessing is the maximization of our potential through accomplishing whatever hidden mission we were given.

It is difficult for us to know what this mission is. What we do know is that *berachah*, blessing, is a consequence of maximal striving. *Mesirus nefesh* literally means giving over one's very soul to Hashem. By its nature, this includes surrendering dreams and expectations. It does not mean "settling for less" but rather gaining more — the abundance of spiritual gratification that can be gained through no other means. This means that we must be creative enough to discover the spark of blessing that lies dormant in any situation with which we must contend. It includes being truthful with oneself about one's internal makeup.

In some ways, it is easier to accept a situation that is clearly not one's "fault," such as an illness, than it is to accept that one must live with one's faults and deal with their presence on a daily basis. We are challenged not only by outer events, but also by our personal imperfections. Rather than embarking on a stratagem of endless defenses, we must learn to find beauty and goodness in the act of struggle within ourselves.

Finding the Beauty

The only alternative is living out the curse. What does being accursed mean? It does not mean being challenged either by inner or outer realities; it means not rising to the challenge. It means living a life in which Hashem is perceived as absent, in which passivity, escapism, and defensiveness are one's constant companion. A life such as this is genuinely unactualized. This is the ultimate curse.

Where does curse come from? Since the sin of Adam, all humans are born with the capacity for "seeing" what is not there and not "seeing" reality as it is. Our imagination, which is the source of aspiration and hope, has another function. It is the catalyst by which we internalize the forces that allow for the confusion of good and evil. In every difficult situation and imperfect character trait there is the potential blessing in an intensely formidable task. The effort expended is in itself a source of blessing as well. What resources do we have to provide us with guidance in achieving this level of honesty?

In *Parashas Vayishlach*, the Torah narrates to us the struggle between Yaakov and the spiritual manifestation of the powers of

faded dreams

Esav. The struggle took place not only externally, but also, as the Malbim explains, within Yaakov himself. The time had come when every aspect of Esav had to be rejected. What defined Esav more than any other characteristic was his identity as a hunter. The gratification that comes with conquest is incomparable to any other human pleasure except one: the elation of genuine accomplishment. What differentiates the two?

Often we find the answer to this question elusive. The Kli Yakar points out that Esav's embrace of Yaakov and Yaakov's struggle against him are described by the words *vayechabkehu* (embrace) and *vayei'avek* (struggle), which are closely related to each other. We feel simultaneously attracted and repulsed by his attempts to blind us. We welcome the elation of challenge, but seek to exclude Hashem from our vision of reality. We attribute our conquests to our own prowess. Or, alternatively, we reject the embrace of ego and retain our integrity. We continue to retain our recognition of Hashem's Providence, and submit our ego to Him.

When we experience loss, the pain of the moment can create the following response: "Yes, Hashem is just. Yes, we grow through challenge. No, I don't want this circumstance. I hate it with every fiber of my being. I will say the right words, because I am afraid of the wrong ones." What the person is saying in this torturous monologue is really, "I don't trust You."

In order to acquire the ability to trust, we must learn to turn our inner eye away from the need to constantly monitor our feelings about what we experience. Rather than asking again and again, "Do I have what I want?" "Do I like what I have?" "Is it what everyone else has?" we must learn to ask new questions: "Where is the spark of good that can be released even in the midst of this blackness?" "How can I find the Godliness in myself now, in this situation?" Through changing the direction of one's gaze and the nature of one's questions, the entire fabric of one's life can unquestionably be altered.

My neighbor is one of those rare individuals blessed with the intuitive ability to ask the right questions. This venerable lady, a matriarch who presides over a multigenerational clan with grace and wisdom, told me of an incident that occurred about sixty years ago.

Hungarian by birth, she immigrated to the United States at an early age. Her early married years were spent in the sort of lower-class neighborhood that, unlike the Lower East Side, for instance, cannot be easily romanticized or gentrified. The young couple resided in one of the projects famous only for the banal nature of its hopelessness. There was a small Orthodox synagogue that provided a clearing in which light could enter the jungle that surrounded them. There was a *shiur* on Shabbos afternoon and at times there were guest speakers.

Her husband came home from shul one Saturday evening elated and uncomfortable. The reason for his feeling two such opposite emotions simultaneously was the appeal that had been made by that week's speaker.

For those of you too young to remember old-fashioned appeals, feel no loss. While fund raising today tends to revolve around dinners in hotels that exude the congenial aura of refined elegance, the locus of fund raising of yesteryear was the local school or synagogue hall (used in the loosest sense of the word). Instead of haute cuisine and high-tech presentations, there was usually a passionate (and at times surprisingly eloquent) rabbi who would endeavor to inspire his captive audience (after all, where could one go between Minchah and Ma'ariv) of hardworking *balebatim* to contribute their hard-earned pitifully small earnings to various causes. At times, their education was too limited to appreciate the need to contribute to their own spiritual welfare, but as a rule they responded with their Jewish hearts and gave what they could.

Mrs. Kagan's husband told her of the rabbi who spoke that day encouraging them to contribute to the founding of a yeshivah in their own area. While there were a few yeshivos in the United States at that time, there were none close by. The very idea of a yeshivah brought tears to his eyes, yet his earnings would allow him the luxury of donating only one dollar. He felt the pain of financial failure. No amount of looking at the peeling paint and antiquated furniture had ever wounded him this deeply.

Mrs. Kagan listened to her husband's words. After Havdalah, rather than allow herself to once more feel choked by their poverty, Mrs. Kagan immediately began planning. She would make a

faded dreams

house party. A date was decided upon. Calls were made to her sisters-in-law. Each would cook her specialty. Chairs were borrowed from her non-Jewish neighbors. Signs were placed near the shul, at the kosher grocery, and every other Jewish meeting place.

Gala Pot-Luck Supper
Twenty-five cents admission
Have a good time!
Proceeds to charity

The royal sum of fifty dollars was raised that evening. When the yeshivah representative came, he told the Kagans proudly that they had just allowed the yeshivah to hire a *mashgiach* and pay him his first salary.

This was the first position of one of the most renowned and erudite Torah scholars of our generation. The entire story poured out when I asked Mrs. Kagan whether this *rav* was a relative. His picture appears in three generations of photographs of her family simchahs. The influence he has had on her family cannot be estimated.

When she decided she could allow herself to honestly acknowledge her financial limitations and feel the pinch, while simultaneously seeing challenge and face it with courage and verve, she was blessed. May we always have the clarity to choose blessing over curse.

CHAPTER SIXTEEN
the gift of joy

IT WAS ONE of those rare, picture-perfect evenings. As we sat on the couch, my children and I found ourselves vicariously living the life of the famous *tzaddik*, Reb Aryeh Levine. The trip back to Yerushalayim of the 1920s was easy enough. We had often made trips as far back as Adam and Chavah. Moving Reb Aryeh back with us to the twentieth century, of course, was a feat that required a considerable amount of talent. It was far easier to relegate him to an era that never really existed — the era of easy piety.

To ensure that the journey back had indeed occurred, a spot check was needed. Turning to my blessedly uncritical audience, I asked with rather theatrical heartiness, "Would you like to be like Reb Aryeh?"

The candor of childhood came forward with full force. "I don't want to be like Reb Aryeh. I want a friend like Reb Aryeh!"

I was forced to acknowledge to myself that the return trip to present-day reality had been only partially successful. What was left behind was the *simchah shel mitzvah*, the pure joy that only a mitzvah brings into this world, that was so much a part of Reb Aryeh's life.

If I could have conveyed the exultation that is experienced only through the giving of oneself, the trip would have been successful. I find myself filling the rather snug-fitting shoes of the student of the Brisker Rav, who once said, "I know what I mean, but I can't explain it." The reply attributed to the Rav is, "If you can't explain it, then you don't understand it." I had to face that I, too, relegate *simchah shel mitzvah* to a place that is far dustier and less accessible than it need be. *Parashas Vayeishev* tells us how we can retrieve it.

the gift of joy

Simchah Brings Reward

One of the most powerful paradoxes in the Torah can be found in the Midrash on *Vayeishev*. What it tells us is that in the midst of what was arguably one of the great failures of history, there was still room for *simchah shel mitzvah*.

What could be more tragic than the brothers misjudging Yosef? We recognize that this apparent moral catastrophe may have been *min haShamayim*, a consequence of Divine Providence. It was Hashem Who caused Yosef to have the dreams. When Yosef interpreted those dreams as illustrating Yosef's inevitable superiority though he was the youngest, his brothers had little choice but to see Yosef as being no more than a usurper of the unity in which lies the power of the Jewish people. To them, the dreams only reflected his actual desire to rule.

Hashem gave Yosef the strongest resemblance to Yaakov. The Malbim points out that the jealousy and subsequent hatred the brothers felt toward Yosef was beyond their control. Hashem expected it of them — and did not comdemn them for the sale itself — given who they were and what was possible for them to achieve. However, they were held accountable for their emotional state at the time of the sale, because they still had a choice in that area. They made themselves unfeeling enough so that it was possible for them to sit down and eat a meal right after the sale.

Reuven recognized that their course of action was miscalculated. He was aware that his brothers were so committed to their decision to put Yosef in the pit full of scorpions and poisonous snakes that there was nothing that could be said that would change their decision-making process. His strategy was to "agree" with them, let them throw Yosef into the pit, and then return for him later. His mission failed dismally.

What in many ways is most remarkable in the narrative is the fact that Reuven did the mitzvah of attempting to save Yosef with great *simchah* and was rewarded for the *simchah* itself despite the fact that superficially nothing was accomplished.

The Midrash tells us that whenever we do a mitzvah, we should do it with a joyous heart. Thus, had Reuven known that the Torah would recount his deed with the words "And Reuven heard and rescued him from their hands and he said, 'Let us not kill him,' " he would have carried Yosef home to his father. Similarly, we are told that if Aharon would have known that Hashem would say about him, "And he will surely go out toward you [Moshe] and see you and his heart will rejoice," he would have gone out with instruments and musicians. Likewise, if Boaz had known that it would be recorded that he gave Ruth a pinch of grain, he would have presented her with fattened veal.

We humans are so complex. We express ourselves through three primary means: thought, speech, and action. In order to provide us with avenues of connection to Hashem on every possible level, there are mitzvos that are done with each of these powers. However, it is not only through the channels mitzvos open for us that we make connections, but also through establishing (or at times rediscovering) the deep satisfaction of connection with Hashem in the midst of challenge. Aharon's formidable task was to maintain *simchah* in his heart in the face of Moshe taking over the leadership that had been his. No one but Hashem could know his level of sincerity. Reuven's sincerity was reflected by the power of his words. Boaz's sincerity was marked by his deed.

Ignoring the Inner Cynic

The holy Alshich, when explaining this Midrash, says that sometimes we don't give free rein to the part of ourselves that takes joy in mitzvos because of our unceasingly persistent belief in the "little critic." Whether or not another person is involved, we hear that voice:

"Who do you think you are, a big tzaddik?"
"Everyone knows we're tainted by our need for social approval. Our mitzvos are not all that genuine."
"Scratch the surface and you will see who they really are, with all their *frumkeit*."

We believe this about others, and we therefore believe this about ourselves. It is this lack of belief in our own authenticity that holds us back.

Reuven had an interest in saving Yosef. If Yosef's dream was prophetic, and all eleven brothers equally would submit to Yosef, Reuven included, then this indicated that Reuven's misdeed in placing his mother's bed in Yaakov's tent would not cause him to be excluded from *Klal Yisrael*. It would be prophetic evidence that his *teshuvah* was accepted, for Reuven was still considered on the same footing as his brothers.

If, however, Yosef died, obviously his dream was mere fantasy. Reuven would then have no solid evidence of his being his brothers' equal and it would only be natural for his brothers to be suspicious of his intervention. If he overtly saved Yosef, he would certainly be suspect in his brothers' eyes. He had to make a choice: he could speak or remain silent. Silence would be far less risky. What motivated him to speak was not fear of error, but *simchah*! His challenge to speak what must be said was met with joy. The joy of knowing that this was the correct thing to do.

Aharon's choice was more subtle. Relinquishing the leadership that had been his acknowledged prerogative for close to a lifetime was a decision few of us could imagine being easy. But the truth is, for Aharon it was. His years of leadership had not left him naive. His warm and loving involvement with his fellow man left him with compassion for their struggles with their faults and weaknesses. He would not feed their limited ability to transcend their own narrow horizons by presenting them with the option of seeing him as an opportunist, faking joy in the midst of jealousy. The instruments and musicians were not ordered, but Hashem testified to the joy that was in Aharon's heart.

Boaz similarly was confronted with a situation in which his showing overt interest in a young single woman could lend itself to misinterpretation. Boaz was a man of great dignity. As the leader of his generation, he had to anticipate what people might choose to say. He had to decide instantaneously what action to take. By giving her a small contribution, but assuring her of safety in and access to his fields, he did not compromise his sensitivity to her poverty. It would have been far simpler for him to "not notice" her. His joy in doing a kindness is what saw him through.

What inspires such joy? How can we let it penetrate through all the obstacles? There are so many diversions along the way. Our bodies make demands for comfort and pleasure. Our fear of somehow not "deserving" to feel joy is still another obstacle. We continually look over our shoulders, blinded to the light the mitzvah itself provides. We don't see it because we are too busy looking the other way.

The source of the joy mitzvos provide is rooted in Hashem's infinity and unity. The Mishnah (*Pirkei Avos, perek* 3) tells us that all our deeds are written in a book. What this means, the Alshich explains, is that whenever we do a mitzvah in this world — the world of action — there is more than one consequence. There is, of course, the observable result. For instance, if one gives charity, the burden of the recipient is lightened. However, there is another result. This result is inevitable whether or not the recipient actually finds his situation was improved. Even if the money is lost or stolen within seconds, the *giver* has changed. The "writing" — the impression his or her deed made in the highest spheres — can never be eradicated. Hashem's glory and light has found a vessel in which it can reside. The vessel is the person himself. If we take off our blinders, we can permit ourselves to feel it.

Revealing the Light

When the Rashash arrived in Israel from Yemen over a century ago, he left much behind, not the least being his reputation. In Yemen he had been one of the brilliant lights in the darkness of their exile; in Eretz Yisrael he was unknown.

He took the position of *shamash* in Midrash Beis-El in the bustling Jewish Quarter. He was the one who maintained the synagogue, who swept it clean at night and opened its doors in the morning. The narrow streets were overflowing with wisdom and piety. It was easy to be anonymous. During the day, he sat in the back of the synagogue and recited *Tehillim*. Whether he heard or understood the lectures was of little interest to anyone. Occasionally, the *shiur* would conclude without resolution of the Talmudic question under discussion. On one such occasion, he wrote his answer on a piece of paper. Late at night, the paper was placed inside the Gemara used by the *rosh yeshivah*. In the course of time, he contributed to the *shiur* in this way a number of times. While the mystery awakened a great deal of speculation, the last person they suspected was the *shamash*.

His secret was revealed by one of the *rosh yeshivah*'s children,

the gift of joy

who got up one night and went out on the porch for some air. There he saw the drama unfold. The next morning, the *rosh yeshivah* read the note out loud. Not for the first time, he asked the anonymous scholar to come forward. This time, however, when no one responded, he stepped down from the lectern. He then announced that the *shamash*, Rav Shalom Sharabi, was now the *rosh yeshivah* and that he was his student.

Who can even begin to see the luminescence that must have been felt by everyone in the room? Who could blind themselves to it, even when the story is retold? This is the light we must learn to see. If we train our own eyes to see it, then we can teach our children to discern it.

We can give them the greatest gift of all, the gift of joy.

CHAPTER SEVENTEEN
the joy of renewal

WHICH BRIDE CANNOT remember the moment of wonder under her *chuppah*, the wedding canopy, when the yearning to build her family was so clearly in her eyes, the ultimate gift the Master of the world could bestow? Even the least sentimental among us cannot fail to be stirred by the sense of eternity of that moment. Yet it doesn't take long for the wonder to fade. The mundane, repetitive details of our daily life create an avalanche of familiarity that suffocates our ability to breathe in the constant miracle we experience. The burden of plenitude can be almost unimaginably wearying. We find ourselves so overwhelmed by the minor struggles of daily life that so clearly say "after," that the blessing of "before," with all its brilliance and luster, fades from memory. The disappearance of gladness, while gradual, has the cumulative effect of creating an inner stoniness that leaves the heart dead. When we look not only at the miracle of Chanukah, but at the time on our calendar that it occurred, we can begin to understand the process of the rebirth of joy.

Personal Rededication

Hashem engraved the designs that give direction to the chaos of the passage of time, and every facet of these designs have the inherent ability to transmit a message to us. The holidays are as far from coincidental in their structure as anything could possibly be. The date of an event that was later established as a Festival, as well as the time of year in which it takes place, provide us with markings that set out for us the direction our journeys must take. Let us look carefully at the date of Chanukah, the twenty-fifth of Kislev, and see it as a marker. The first day of the Festival of Lights surely

the joy of renewal

has a corresponding place within us as the renewal of our own personal *hallel* and *hoda'ah*, our own personal redefinition of gratitude and thanks.

The Maharal points out that the twenty-fifth of Elul was the day on which Hashem began the process of creating the world with the creation of light. The light created at that time was not the light of the sun, which was created on the fourth day; it was the light that is referred to as *or elyon*, exalted, lofty light. This is the light that will ultimately be revealed to the righteous in the future world. At times, it is seen even by us. On Shabbos, for instance, when we strip aside our involvement with the material side of reality and see the day's inner grace, the light we are absorbing is something of the *or elyon*.

The physical light that is hidden by the darkness of winter is the physical parallel of the forces that conceal spiritual light. The beginning of the renewal of light is the twenty-fifth of Kislev. This reflects the possibility of the rebirth of *or elyon*.

The Midrash tells us that spiritual light was created from the place where the *Beis HaMikdash* stood. The *Beis HaMikdash*, the Holy Temple, was a place of spiritual transcendence within the reality of physical matter. We thus have the *or elyon* meeting the emerging physical light of this world. The miracle effected through the Chashmonaim in the *Beis HaMikdash* did not take place at that particular time by fluke. Rather than being a random event, it was the way in which Hashem's Providence guided historical forces to meet and bring about the emergence of both physical and spiritual light.

Letting in the Light

Chanukah is the day, according to *Midrash Rabbah*, that Kayin and Hevel offered their sacrifices. They were both looking for spiritual light, each in his own way. The path of Kayin was misdirected, but his intent was, nonetheless, to experience this light. Thus, the Midrash says, the disagreement that led to their quarrel was about who was to have the *Beis HaMikdash*, the source of light, in his portion.

This is also the day in which the Mishkan, Tabernacle, in the desert (about which God says, "Make Me a sanctuary and I will dwell in you") was finished. The effect of the building of the Mishkan was not for the light of Hashem to dwell in it, but rather for it to dwell in "you" — in each and every one of us.

The Shem MiShmuel tells us that the self-sacrifice that preceded the miracle of Chanukah had an effect of such vast proportions that it was the catalyst for removing barriers to light that had been in place for years.

What is the barrier to light? It is compared to the stone that Yaakov found covering the well. The stoniness of spiritual immobility is the effect of *sohu vavohu*, chaos and emptiness, that preceded the creation of light. Three months separate the twenty-fifth of Elul, the day of the creation of light, and the twenty-fifth of Kislev, the day of renewal of this light. In order for spiritual light to replace the confusion and emptiness that is an inherent part of the immersion in the mundane that we all experience, time is needed. As Rebbe Nachman would say, a person must be patient with himself. Similarly, for the Jews to receive the Torah, time had to elapse from the Exodus from Egypt.

The passage of time, even three months' worth, is not enough on its own to effect the level of change that is needed for the "rock" to be removed and light to enter. The three mitzvos of Chanukah — lighting the menorah, giving praise, and giving thanks — are necessary steps to ground the dimension of *or elyon* that entered the world at this time and make it part of our very being.

Ending Exile's Darkness

When light is absent, we are left with darkness. The fact that we would fall victim to this darkness, both as individuals and as a people, was revealed to us in the Torah. When Hashem made a covenant with Avraham, He revealed the entire future of the Jewish people who were yet to be born. Avraham saw the passage of exiles and the effect of the various ruling nations upon us. The text hints that each exile has its own character. Each is therefore referred to with a phrase that epitomizes its very essence. The word used to describe the Grecian exile, when the miracle of Chanukah occurred, is *choshech*, darkness. Their decrees, more than those of

the joy of renewal

any other people, "brought darkness to our eyes."

The word *choshech* with its three letters *ches, shin, chaf* hints at three different forms of blockage. Each one hints at a specific form of spiritual degradation that is epitomized by the animal force of three animals: the *chamor*, donkey; the *shor*, ox; and the *kelev*, dog. Each begins with a letter from the word *choshech*. Corresponding to these three representations of darkness are three mitzvos which bring back the light — bris milah, circumcision; *kiddush hachodesh*, sanctifying the new moon; and Shabbos. These are the three mitzvos the Greeks decreed the Jewish people could not keep under their rule.

The donkey is used as a symbol of utter materialism. Its very name, *chamor*, is the same word as that for the material, *chomer*. The coarse and vulgar passions that have caused sensuality and pleasure to become synonymous with Western civilization are of course a consequence of the totally material self-definition of the surrounding culture. The mitzvah of bris milah is antithetical to this world view. It represents the removal of coarse sensual pleasure, and it is a sign that we belong to Hashem, that instead of pursuing that pleasure we seek Hashem's light. It is not surprising, then, that a decree forbidding bris milah was a consequence of the Grecian exile long ago and that there is a contemporary social and media-oriented movement against circumcision.

The ox is a symbol of power. The spiritual manifestation of power-grabbing is the path of Esav. The attainment of power as a goal and not as a means is, to put it mildly, by no means an invisible factor in public life today. The inherent humility symbolized in the ritual of *kiddush hachodesh* is irreconcilable with this world view. The renewal of the moon by Hashem's grace is very different from the symbol of the ascending star that typifies the collective dream of fame and power that is the defining statement of the society in which we live.

The dog is often presented as the emblem of chutzpah. It leads its master as a matter of course rather than accepting its master's lead. Lacking any genuine identity of its own, it adopts the characteristics of its master. How often have we seen pairs of dogs and masters walking together and noticed a "family resemblance"? The worst of all responses to canine nature is that not only does the dog think of itself as an equal to its master, but the master regards the dog as a family member.

The Amalekite people embody the essence of denial of the Master of the world. They see themselves as the masters and deify their every idea, doubt, and emotional attachment to self. It is not power that is their exclusive desire; rather, it is the denial of power to Hashem. They are symbolized in *Chazal* by the dog. Shabbos, of course, is our statement of self-definition. By observing Shabbos, we not only redefine ourselves but we also arrive at a new and different way of describing the world's reality. We and everything else we encounter are creations. We are not the masters; God, the Creator, is the Master.

When we prevailed against the Greeks, who forbade us to keep bris milah, *kiddush hachodesh*, and Shabbos, in an attempt to block the light, we not only removed the barriers to light, but in a certain sense used the very same barriers as mediums with which we broadened our own vistas. Each challenge that was successfully met created a new and specific focus on the *or elyon*. Our Sages instituted the observance of the three mitzvos of Chanukah — menorah, praise, and thanks — to act as a means of preserving this light and letting it rest within us, forever changing the nature of our vision.

Every night of Chanukah we add another candle to the menorah. The light of Chanukah inspires the same awareness as Shabbos. We want to live lives in which *penimiyus*, the capacity to know Hashem within His every creation, is definitive.

Hallel, the prayer of praise we recite on this Festival, can move us to a recognition of Hashem's eternal power and give us the inner strength to let go of the Esav within us. Our power plays (which can be almost as dramatic in domestic life as they can be in the political arena) can be seen for what they are: petty and meaningless escapes from the *or elyon*. The mitzvah of Rosh Chodesh has new meaning in this light. We see ourselves as living in a world in which Hashem's light is our guide rather than the insatiable needs of our ego.

The mitzvah of *hoda'ah*, thanks, gives us an appreciation of how small we are. Rather than devoting ourselves to the pursuit of material pleasure, which so often is expressed by the words *I de-*

the joy of renewal

serve, we can look toward the spiritual pleasure that comes from hearing ourselves say, "I am accountable; I am committed." Bris milah represents this commitment. No one tires of commitment. No one wearies of light that is as new as every encounter. No one wearies of knowing Hashem and seeing His light.

May we all be worthy of all our Chanukahs being full of the joy of renewal.

CHAPTER EIGHTEEN
confronting rivalry

THERE WERE ONLY two empty seats on the bus. Given that only two passengers were standing in the aisle, no amount of hot weather, crying infants or general midday irritation seemed likely to ignite any spark of anger.

One of the standing passengers politely asked a favor from a woman sitting near the aisle. "Would you be willing to sit on the other side so that my friend and I could sit together?" was said with the unstated message that a refusal would be both unreasonable and unexpected.

As soon as she sat down, another request came in. This time, the entreaty came from the second "standee," who asked in a tone that made clear that the matter at hand was of dire urgency. "I feel dizzy when I sit over the wheel. Would you mind switching?"

My interest in the exchange was such that the impact being made was exclusively as background noise. The words were no doubt being stored in the same section of my mind where aircraft sound and washing machine rumble coexist in subconscious harmony. Until I heard her reply: "If I keep on giving everyone else my seat, who will look out for me in the end?"

The irrationality of the answer jarred me into awareness. The bus had all its seats; none were missing. The speaker had no reason to think she would need someone to "look out for her," at least not in this context. I turned around sharply to see as well as listen. The face I saw was a pleasant one, and, much to my surprise, smile lines creased the cheeks. Her speech went on for another moment or two with passion and fire. Her theme was self-preservation. Logic was given no leeway. *Sanity* seemed for a moment to be a word with relative rather than absolute definition.

Long after the episode had passed, the fragility of our sense of security stayed with me. We are so afraid of each other; the unspoken covenant we invoke in every interaction is frail. The primitive ethos in which each man views himself involved in a war with his tribe against all others, his family against the rest of the tribe, his brothers against the rest of the family, and he against his brothers is one that reaches places we would like to think are impregnable. What brings about the initial movement that makes everyone we encounter a potential rival? Let us look at *Parashas Vayigash* for some clarity.

Understanding Jealousy

As Rav Dessler points out in *Michtav MeEliyahu*, it is natural (although not necessarily permitted and certainly not desirable) for any human being to feel hatred toward a person who has done him harm. However, there is another category of hatred: that which is born of jealousy. It is this type of hatred that *Chazal* refer to as *sinas chinam*, senseless hatred.

The hatred Esav felt toward his brother Yaakov is a prime example. Unlike the rancor Yishmael felt toward Yitzchak, in the case of Yaakov and Esav the issue was not the inheritance of Eretz Yisrael. As the Maharal points out, Yishmael will ultimately repent. The reason for this is that their hatred is built around issues that are external and thus resolvable. The hatred of Esav, though, is not built around any issue at all. He hates us because of the rivalry he feels; our very presence in the world is perceived as a threat. It is not that we have harmed him in any way, but rather the spiritual redemption of the world depends on us. This creates an unspoken threat to Esav's sense of autonomy and significance.

In a similar vein, Yosef's brothers felt his "separateness" was an accusation against them. The division he revealed to them in the dreams of the eleven brothers being one group and one, Yosef, being the other was enough. The Maharal points out that what they saw was no illusion or misinterpretation; Yosef indeed was as separate from them in his ability to rule as Esav was from Yaakov in his inability to rectify the world.

Had he genuinely harmed them in any way? No. Were there "enough seats on the bus"? Yes, but they were not all equally "important" places. Is it possible to retain equilibrium in the face of real inequality? Is the challenge of contending with spiritual dominance without rivalry within our grasp? Since failure is so likely, what is Hashem, Who loves us more than we love ourselves, demanding of us?

Noblesse Oblige

What separated Yosef from his brothers was his *malchus*, kingship. On the surface, hierarchy seems to be the inevitable social response to the fact that we humans are at times a rather savage bunch. To paraphrase *Pirkei Avos*, if not for the fear of government, men would swallow each other alive. The true purpose of rulership, however, is to act as a catalyst for Hashem's will to be done in this world. This takes place technically — the hearts of kings and princes are in the Hand of Hashem. He uses them to bring about the result He has decreed. And this takes place spiritually as well.

Yosef's rule brought about both effects. Not only did he act as the earthly messenger of Hashem's Providence by catalyzing the situation in which the Jewish people descended to Egypt to emerge as a nation, but *kiddush Hashem*, sanctification of God's Name, was accomplished through him even with the Egyptians. He succeeded in bringing light to the darkest recesses of the spirit.

This deepened understanding of Yosef's difference renders the humiliating confrontation with his brothers far more difficult for us to understand. What awakened their jealousy was spiritual rivalry; what motivated him was *kiddush Hashem*. The author of the famous *mussar* classic, *Chochmah U'Mussar*, points out that by saying, "I am Yosef your brother whom you sold to Egypt," Yosef seemed to be pouring salt on the exposed vulnerabilities of his brothers.

Vulnerability often stems from fear of humiliation. It is our fear of humiliation that makes us defensive and causes us to coat our words with ego and brutality. Once the words have been said and nothing more could be added, there is nothing more to fear. Rather than intending to humiliate them, Yosef had given his brothers the ability to face him — and themselves. At that moment they saw the truth. They were not the same as Yosef, and they would never be.

There was, however, nothing to fear; both he and they were "sitting in the seat" they were meant to sit in.

Submission: Gateway to Majesty

Let us look at the relationship between Yosef and his brothers to gain insight into their respective "places."

The Shem MiShmuel explains as follows: Yosef is the paradigm of *tzaddik yesod olam*, "a righteous person is the foundation of the world." The relationship of a building to its foundation is one of absolute dependence. Similarly, Hashem brought the brothers into a situation of absolute dependence on Yosef. However, in order for them to gain from him, they also had a role to play. They had to submit to him.

Their initial response to Yosef's "difference" was not only manifest by an unwillingness to receive anything from him at all. Any form of "giftedness" was suspect. They were certainly unwilling to relate to him with submission. It was only later, when they found themselves falsely accused of espionage and were forced to bring Binyamin their youngest brother and the only surviving progeny of Rachel (so they thought) to Yosef against their will that they were finally humbled. When Yehudah, who believed that his failure to rescue Binyamin would cost him both worlds, declared his willingness to serve Yosef as a slave, it was the ultimate submission. The other tribes followed Yehudah's lead, and the relationship was redefined.

On the surface, Yosef was the only one who gained by this change in relationship. The rivalry that had pursued him almost to his death finally ended. The other brothers appear to be the "losers," perhaps having sold their fears too cheaply. This image, though, is distorted, for it is actually this quality of submissiveness, the root of humility, that gave Yehudah his crown. It was his mastery of self that gave him the role of Mashiach's ancestor. Thus it was Yosef's dominance that prepared the road for Yehudah to truly be his highest and most developed self.

It is one of life's great ironies that confronting rivalry honestly is the catalyst that can not only eliminate rivalry but can open doors that would otherwise have stayed closed. I recently heard the following story:

Despair is too small a word for the scene at the train station in Holocaust Europe: the crowding, the wrenching separations, the uncertainty of the next moment are impossible to describe. She stood there alone, clutching all her possessions crammed into one large box. As the train rolled into the station, she drew as close to the edge of the platform as she could, knowing that she would only get a seat if she was among the first on the train. When the torrent of what the Nazis had reduced to human freight poured in through the open doors, Dora (not her real name) allowed herself to be carried into the car and found her place. She sat down quickly, placing her box beside her. As the car quickly filled, the torrid air enveloped her.

When Dora looked up, her eyes met those of a man barely able to hold his body up in the crush that surrounded him. No words were necessary and none were said. She picked up her box and put it on her knees. It pressed into her chest with a violence that was uninvited but not unexpected. With each turn she felt it as she breathed in the suffocating air. There was no place to put it. Even had she been willing to part with her only possessions, there was no escape from them. She had known this the first moment their eyes met; there were no surprises.

Decades passed. Rav Y. S. led his *kehillah* in postwar America with courage and fortitude, erudition and compassion. When he recounted the story of the girl who saved his life by giving him a seat on the train, one question always preyed on the minds of the listeners. How did she do it? Where did the inner resources come from at a time when every breath was precious?

A friend of mine asked her. Dora told her own story: She was her sister's rival. Her sister was the diamond, whose beauty was dazzling. Dora grew up feeling like the black velvet that existed only to give focus to the brilliance of the diamond. Her turning point came when she made the decision: "*Ich bin nit fil uber eppes bin ich* — I am not much, but I am something."

Her decision to define herself as "something" was not made out of rivalry or competition. It was made with the genuine realization that being "something" means responding on Hashem's terms to a pair of eyes that meets one's own.

CHAPTER NINETEEN
we can reflect the light

THE CROWD IN the parking-lot-cum-courtyard shared one thing in common: their presence there that day was totally unplanned. The rhythm that synchronized the ebb and flow of daily life had stopped for all of them, leaving the jarring discord of broken plans and minor disorder. It would matter very little. They had gathered to mourn an unexpected death.

As the eulogies poured forth, the awesome burden of adequately doing justice to a lost life weighed heavily on the hearts of the speakers. With the kind of feeling that can only be the child of truth, the words that described the life of the woman who had left us returned to one theme: dedication to the ideal of pursuing the goal of building a house for Hashem. What made her so unique was the intelligence and joy she had brought to that task. When studying her life, one can't avoid at least the subtle whisper of inspiration.

When I returned home, I found myself returning again and again to the realization that during our acquaintance I never allowed that whisper to be heard. Her endearing normality and moment-to-moment celebration of life precluded her being the victim of my tendency to introspection. But there is another factor: death lends us the detachment to see the deceased without the limitation imposed by our egos. When we are here, sharing the same air and the same gravitational field, it is too difficult for us to see anyone as completely separate from ourselves. The final separation is, therefore, at times the first glimpse.

When a person draws close to death, he, too, is able to see the world without the inclusion of self. The last words, the last days, seem to encompass so much more than any others. The words and deeds we recall are the ones that have a dimension of eternity. The vision of one who leaves the world is such, and the partition between worlds at times is so fine, that he shares that vision with others. The tradition of deathbed blessings and guidance is reflective of the spark of eternity that binds both worlds. Let us look at the passing of Yaakov Avinu and allow it to touch the infinity within us.

A Gift from Yaakov

Of all the blessings given by Yaakov to his descendants, the one we are most familiar with is "*Ha-malach ha-goel osi mikol ra yevarech es hane'arim* — May the angel that has redeemed me from all evil bless the lads." The *Midrash Ne'elam* asks about the nature of the angel described in the text and tells us that it is the presence of the Shechinah that never leaves an untainted person. It walks with each of us as long as we can draw it to ourselves through the power of the Torah and mitzvos, which act as a wick to allow the flame of Hashem to burn within our earthly bodies. Yaakov was able to transfer his experiential awareness of this light to us. Thus the mishnah in which we are instructed, "A man shall not walk alone" (*Avos*), takes on a new dimension. We must never allow ourselves to come to a point in life where we feel the unspeakable isolation that can only be felt by one who has lost the presence of the Shechinah.

When we examine our lives, it seems at times that not only do we not experience the quality of Yaakov's awareness and closeness to Hashem, but we feel very little connection to Yaakov. Although we are all aware of the fact that we have been bestowed with the merit of the patriarchs, it seems almost like a gift that was generously given without much of a relationship to the ability of the recipient. It is difficult to appreciate it fully. The Midrash, however, explains that we can sense the connection and presents us with a parable to illustrate this. A child observing a sunset may think the sun "goes away" and the moon "comes." In truth, we know that both the sun and the moon are there all the time. However, there are times when we see the light of the sun directly and times in which we see it reflected by the moon.

In the same way, the patriarchs are compared to the luminaries. The brilliance of the Shechinah illuminates the world through the lives they lived. The light that we, who are compared to the moon, can radiate is ultimately their light. Our ability to act as reflectors is dependent on our ability to "turn off" the self, so that their light is not blocked by our egos and desires.

When Yaakov blessed Yosef's sons, Efraim and Menasheh, he created a connection that would give them the ability to find the Shechinah that accompanied them (and all of us) and bring it into their lives, which is, of course, the ultimate blessing. This blessing is given to all Jews at all times. Tapping into it is at times difficult even for an individual. But what is even more difficult in our times is to observe the spiritual agony that leaves our people groping in every direction, trying to find the Shechinah once more. How did the connection wither? Let us look further.

Exile and the Thinning of the Connection

The Ramban correlates the descent to Egypt that takes place in *Parashas Vayechi* with the fourth animal that Daniel the prophet saw in his famous prophecy. In his vision, he saw four animals rising from the river. The fourth animal was so horrifying that it could not be compared to any other animal and is not given a name. Each animal represents exile; the first three represent Babylon, Persia and Media, and Greece, and the fourth and final one, the most formidable of all, represents the Roman exile in which the spiritual, emotional, and physical characteristics of Esav have almost redefined us and divorced us from our essence.

The Ramban points out the many similarities between the Egyptian exile and the Roman exile. The immediate event that preceded both exiles was hunger. The famine that stalked Yerushalayim during the Roman siege was the collective reliving of the famine that brought Yaakov and his family to Egypt. In both cases, no one in his worst nightmare could have seen how much longer their sojourn would be.

In the case of Yaakov and the tribes, their final request was that their bones not be buried in Egypt but taken to the Land of Israel. Yechezkel had a prophetic vision in which he saw a valley of dry bones, indicating that in this Roman exile we will be reduced to a degree of spiritual lifelessness that can barely be imagined.

In both cases, the exile was brought about by their own free will. In the case of the tribes, living in Goshen under Yosef's protection seemed to be a choice that was more than just acceptable. In the case of our contemporary exile, the direct involvement of the Romans in our national life came about by Agripas requesting their intervention and presence.

The recurrence of events with such fearful symmetry must teach us a lesson. The lesson learned isn't dry history. It is that exile is a result of our choosing a path that leads away from Hashem until we reach out to Him from a new position, from a place where the definition of who we are has changed. One of the most central lessons of exile, Ramban tells us, is to understand that the restoration of our nation is dependent on rulership being restored to Yehudah. This is not a matter of civics but of national self-definition. When Yaakov blessed Yehudah with the right to rule, he was redefining rulership. Yehudah's single-minded humility in living only for Hashem is the only kind of rulership that opens the Jewish people to rediscovering their ability to reflect the light.

There were many experiments in the past, attempts to form a different kind of monarchy. The first king, Shaul, was all we deserved at the time. Since the underlying reason for our requesting a monarch at that time was to redefine our nationhood and endeavor to be more "normal," to be more like the nations, Hashem allowed us to do so. As He told the prophet Shmuel, "They have not rejected you; they have rejected Me."

It was only after the failure of the experiment, as epitomized by Shaul's failure to annihilate the Amalekites because of misplaced compassion (and possibly even a misdirected attempt at sanctifying Hashem's Name) that we were ready for David. However, when our level diminished further, Achiyah HaShiloni anointed Yeravam ben Nevat, who was not of the House of David. We deserved to have the monarchy torn in half. This, too, was a reflection of failure to establish and idealize an uncompromised relationship to Hashem.

The tragic fate shared by all the Hasmonean kings was a further reflection of this; even holy tzaddikim such as they must serve Hashem on the terms He sets forth. By making them *kohanim* rather than descendants of Yehudah, Hashem was giving them direction concerning the specific path their lives were meant to take. Since they retained the monarchy, their house died out.

Live and Reflect the Light

What does this tell us? We are already in an exile of such duration that we can barely imagine ourselves truly alive. Ironically, sometimes we are blinded to the possibility of living until we find ourselves at a funeral.

When I take myself back to that courtyard and see the faces of the women who stood there with me, I see in the midst of the raw grief an appreciation of life that is rare and precious. It tells us that we should be more ready to be ourselves. Like Yehudah, and David after him, it is within our deepest natural yearnings to find Hashem, without compromise, without "normalization," without misinterpretation of the direction our lives must move.

The Kli Yakar tells us that we must learn to be honest. We must find the place within ourselves that yearns to see the face of Hashem and the face of David as will be reflected in the face of Mashiach. Do we truly long for Mashiach, he asks, when we build ourselves imposing homes that are built for duration? As we entrench ourselves more and more deeply in whatever "Goshen" we find ourselves, are we not recreating a situation of *vayeishev*, "dwelling" there?

If we yearn for Hashem, we must not deny ourselves anything that will draw us closer to Him. Is our conscious or subconscious decision to spend so much emotional energy on "life in Goshen" in every area of our lives, drawing us closer? Is it giving us the ability to reflect light by celebrating every moment or is our pursuit of the pleasures of Goshen resulting in lifestyles that make our lives so full of stress that we can barely stop for breath?

There is a part of each of us that can reflect the light of Yaakov. It says about him that *"lo mes,"* he didn't die. Yes, he is buried in Me'aras HaMachpelah. What is meant by this phrase is that he reached a place in his own development that, rather than impeding him, expressed his light. The body must return to the earth from which it came to allow it to disintegrate and almost "disappear." This allows the limitations and blockages that are so much a part of its nature to similarly disintegrate so that the person can rise in absolute purity when the time comes for the revival of the dead. In Yaakov's case, no disintegration was necessary.

His life encompassed the true lifestyle so fully that there were no blockages. The aspect of ourselves that is similar to Yaakov in a certain sense is also undying. As we rediscover the part of us that no longer wants to live in Goshen, we will discover that part of ourselves that rejects the alienation from ourselves, from Hashem, and from others that invariably comes from breaking the threads that bind us to the Shechinah. We must commit ourselves to living lives in which we build homes to Hashem that will endure forever.

CHAPTER TWENTY
the freedom to be ourselves

THE LOOK THAT passed between us was totally uninterpretable to my children who were watching. A friend of mine, Ellen, had come by to tell me that her daughter was a *kallah*, bride. This was a scene that had been played many times before in their presence. The warm embrace, the laughter, and the bone-breaking handshake are familiar and delightful. The depth of the gaze and the tears that mixed freely with the laughter in this instance were not. "What a success you are!" I found myself saying to her again and again.

To my children, Ellen's daughter was just a chum from school like many others. She wore basic Bais Yaakov blue, jumped rope in the early grades, studied for tests and went to Shabbos groups in the middle grades, and worried about which seminary would accept her in the later ones. When the family moved, the tie between her family and mine was frazzled by distance and schoolgirl preoccupations. Her emergence as a young woman of warm and charming personality enveloped in unpretentious modesty and expressed with delightful individualism was no surprise given her parents.

What I knew that my children didn't was that there could have been several endings to this story, all of them very different from the one playing itself out in my kitchen. I knew the tragedy that had encircled the *kallah* and her family. Suffice it to say that although tragedy leaves many victims behind, the main victim of this particular tragedy was a child too young to understand its dimensions.

Ellen had been a dear friend for years. Her honesty and kindness were bywords. She had built herself brick by brick until she had become almost an institution. The little girl she took in was almost completely silent. The most basic structures of interaction were completely unfamiliar to her, and trust was an almost unattainable objective. So the only word I could utter at Ellen's moment of triumph was *success*.

Success is such a relative term. It has become banal through misuse. It is, in our society, a synonym for material achievement. In the vocabulary the Torah uses, success is totally different. In Egypt, we were successful. Let us look at *Parashas Shemos* to see the nature of the success we were granted.

From Bitter to Sweet

The Ramban points out that the Egyptian exile was the prototype of future exiles. The nature of the exile was that it choked us to the point of forcing us to rediscover our deepest self-definition. What were the stages on the way? How did we come to know ourselves not only as individuals, or a family defined by its relationship to Hashem, but as a nation with no other reason for existence?

During Yaakov's lifetime, the Egyptians had no capacity to gain a hold over us. His spiritual level was so towering that the influence of Egyptian society could leave no imprint. The servitude that commenced with his death became a constant factor only after the last of Yaakov's sons, Levi, died. Yet it was only with the departure of the original seventy "souls" that descended to Egypt that the full force of oppression crashed down on us. It was then that observable change began to occur within us. The change was the blessing Hashem gave us by which we would multiply in direct proportion to our infliction. Why was this *berachah* dependent on our suffering?

The Maharal explains that as long as the original seventy souls lived there was a perceived sense of *sheleimus*, of being whole. It is only from living out the realization that we are not truly whole that yearning is born, and it is only from the midst of this kind of yearning that genuine *berachah* can take hold.

The kind of nation that Hashem envisioned was far more than an extended family of seventy souls complete in themselves. He foresaw a nation of six hundred thousand who would be defined by the Torah they would receive from Him. The condition under which this could occur depended on our developing a unique sense of our nationhood. This was to come about by experiencing our physical vulnerability and fragility. Far from leaving us with no identity, the physical degradation we suffered forced us into redefining ourselves spiritually. How did this occur?

If a person were, God forbid, to lose a limb, he would be forced into recognizing that the limb is not what made him who he is. While his sense of self would be altered, his essential identity would not. He would be forced into acknowledging that his body does not define his essence.

The same moment of collective self-definition resulted from the servitude in Egypt. The more we felt embittered by enslavement, the more eloquent was our quest for spiritual self-expression. Hashem opened doors we could never have opened — as soon as we had the inner surety to enter them.

Thus the birth of Miriam, which paved the way for the redemption, took place when the bitterness had reached its peak. Bitterness was so definitive of life there that it was chosen by loving parents as a name for their only daughter. The strength that is only unleashed through opposition was epitomized by Miriam throughout every episode of her life, from her singing to the doomed children of Egypt to her refusal to allow Pharaoh's decrees to define the future of the Jewish people. Imagine the spiritual fortitude required for her and her mother, Yocheved, to embroider baby clothes (as the Midrash tells us) for doomed infants!

What sustained her and the other women in Egypt was a longing to allow Hashem into their lives. They realized that any other form of definition was worse than foolish; it was dishonest. The word *emunah*, faith, is related linguistically to the word *oman*, craftsman. When a person lives his life with the cognizance of the hidden Hand of the Craftsman behind very facet of His handiwork, he will never allow himself the convenience of playing the game of spiritual hide-and-seek we find so engaging at times.

Miriam wanted Hashem to be the defining factor in her life. In her merit we were given the well that supplied us with drinking water during our sojourn in the desert. What is the connection between Miriam, whose name denotes bitterness, and the well? What is the connection between the well and her limitless faith?

Voiceless Waters, Women's Choices

When we look at *Shemos*, we see that water takes a central role. Water by its nature assumes the form of whatever container it is in. Its formlessness is very much part of its essence. In fact, in this *parashah*, Hashem uses the medium of water to bring us from a state of formlessness to a state of national redefinition. The Midrash tells the following parable to give us a sense of what transpired:

Once there was a king who built a palace and hired mute servants as his entourage. Whenever he entered the palace, he would gesture toward them, and they would return his gesture in sign language. One day the king said to himself, *How much more glorious it would be if only my court was composed of retainers who could speak.* He dismissed the mute retinue and replaced them with a staff of attendants who could speak. His new courtiers, however, soon began to discuss politics and policy and came to the conclusion that having a king was redundant for the continuance of the state and that from then on the palace belonged to them. The king decided at that point to discharge the speaking servants and employ the mute ones once more.

When the world was created, the waters were voiceless. Hashem created man to use his capacity for expression to affirm the King's grandeur. What happened, however, was that we instead used our collective voice in the generations of the Flood and the dispersion to credit ourselves. We looked in the mirror, and our physical mastery of the world allowed us to indulge in the ever-present fantasy of divinity. What we said, in essence, was that the palace does not belong to the King.

What returned us to reality was that in Egypt we were reduced to being mute; we had no more words, no more ideas, no more plans. The final decree, that of murdering the babies, touched the Jewish people in a place where they could feel pain more acutely than any other. When this decree was enacted, we were ready for a new beginning. We were ready to recognize our utter dependency on Hashem in the midst of our vulnerability. We recognized that life's only meaning lies within our relationship and connection to Him. Nothing else has any power or significance.

Why did we find ourselves defined by Hashem's presence in

the freedom to be ourselves

our lives rather than reject Him in anger? Even in the midst of our descent to the forty-ninth level of impurity, we still retained a connection to the patriarchs. Our language reflected a longing for the sort of self-expression that was theirs; our retaining their clothes similarly reflected an affinity toward maintaining a physical tie with them. Deepest of all, our retaining the names they used reflected the most essential tie of all. Our connection to Hashem through the patriarchs could never be broken or permanently rejected.

Miriam, Yocheved, and the other women of that generation brought that bond with Hashem into their daily lives and let it give them their only definition. For them there was no rebellion of mind or speech. They accepted Hashem's will as completely as water assumes the form of the vessel that contains it. The well was more than the reward of Miriam; it was her portrait.

The Sefas Emes tells us that not only was the Egyptian exile the paradigm of all future exiles, but that the same is true of the liberation. Thus a certain amount of the freedom of the redemption stays with us even until today. The potential we have to find ourselves through the Torah, Hashem's will, is the spark of freedom we still retain. The more we choose to let that be our defining self-statement, rather than allowing the material world to hold us captive, the freer we are and the closer we are to our true identity.

We make choices every day. Every day we choose freedom or enslavement. When Ellen received the telephone call in which she was asked to take in a small child who had been deprived and neglected, her response was the kind of response that one should expect from a daughter of Yocheved and Miriam.

Her friends questioned the wisdom of her decision. "You will be stuck in the house," they warned her. "How can you give up your freedom — with no end in sight — for the child of a stranger?" Ellen always knew the truth: she would find a more genuine freedom than she had ever known. She would have the freedom to be herself, her best and most authentic self.

She succeeded beyond her highest hopes. Like Yocheved and Miriam before her, she was rewarded by Hashem giving her the merit to build a house. What a success she is!

CHAPTER TWENTY-ONE
regaining sensitivity

MIRACLES OCCUR WITH surprising frequency in Jerusalem. A miracle is, in essence, a flagpole. The function of a flagpole is, of course, to raise the flag high enough to be seen in the midst of the crowded and distracting stimuli that fill our field of vision. What is then seen is the flag.

Any flag is by definition a symbol by which one's identity is articulated, making it less abstract. Who we are as members of Hashem's people and Who He is to us is at times vague and relegated to a distant part of our inner lives. At such times, Hashem will often raise a *nes*, a flag, to help us find our identity once more. The flag is not taken out, dusted off, and raised on the flagpole only when a situation arouses within us such desperation that we cast our eyes upward. We should not need to be terrorized out of complacency. The flag waves high for us to see whenever our hearts open up enough to look.

Flag Raised at the Kotel

The Tuesday the miracle occurred did not start out different from any other Tuesday. It was so arid that the Kotel plaza was luminescent, creating an unusual bonding of physical and spiritual light. A group of tourists descended the stairs from the Jewish Quarter. They were looking for something they would not find in the barren, shallow spiritless portrayal of the Kotel given by their guide. His words parched their spirits and left them not knowing whether they had been searching at all, and if so, for what.

As he stood in the center of the group drowning their souls with wave after wave of chokingly enervating facts, my heart ached. The usual photos were taken and were followed by a short

regaining sensitivity

interval for offering prayers. After being duly warned that the bus would be leaving in fifteen minutes, the group shifted its attention from the guide to the Kotel.

I noticed one of the group, a girl of about fifteen. She was conspicuous not only because she was about half a century younger than the rest (the granddaughter of one of them), but because her longing to address the One Whose presence never leaves this place was almost tangible.

I did not know whether or not I should approach her. It seemed to me, after a few minutes had elapsed, that all there was for me to lose was my dignity if I was rebuffed, and my dignity had suffered far worse in its time. As I drew closer, she suddenly and visibly gained a grip on the direction she wanted to take. I decided to give her the opportunity to pray without interruption. I could not help but hear her recite the blessings that are said on the Haftarah from their beginning until she concluded with the words *mekadesh haShabbos*. No doubt her misplaced trust in whoever had been her bas mitzvah instructor had given her no tools better than the ones she had. The only tool to which I can compare it is that of the *alef-beis* that was recited with such devotion by the uneducated orphan in the time of the Baal Shem Tov. (The utter sincerity of his supplication was able to avert the terrible decrees.)

I joined my prayers to her pure and simple act of devotion. She had no doubt that her prayers were heard. Her standing before the Kotel that day had awakened her awareness. A flag had been lifted for her, and she could see it waving on its pole by the unfailing light of her inner eye.

How had she succeeded in preserving her vision? Let us look at *Parashas Va'eira* to see more closely the true nature of *nisim*, miracles, Hashem's revelations to Moshe and to the patriarchs, and ultimately to us.

Seeing beyond the Clouds

The Sefas Emes tells us that the clouds that prevent us from seeing the flag are the ten statements Hashem used in creating the world (the ten times in which the Torah states, "Let there be..."). Each statement brought into being another specific and unique form of "otherness." Each one potentially distracts our inner vision. We see only the object itself, rather than its Source.

These ten forms of divine concealment were penetrated by Avraham. With each challenge he faced, another veil was removed until he penetrated each type of the illusion. Layer after layer of concealment unfolded before him. He saw Hashem, the Source of all nature, from the nature of energy to the nature of man. Avraham's clarity of vision was so great that we, his descendants, are still able to retain at least a glimpse of it. It may be dimmed by our varying degrees of ignorance, ego, or materialism, but it is never completely and permanently blocked.

Our access to the world of miracles is through the Torah itself, which is purely spiritual and is not in any way confined by the rules of nature. It came into existence before the ten statements of Creation. When Moshe rose to Heaven to receive the Torah, all the rules that seem to us to be so completely binding were of no relevance. He did not eat or sleep or perform any physical functions. The light of Torah is so bright, however, that at times we block it out; it is painful to our eyes. We seek to confine it to the limits of our experiences in life or to our emotional agendas. We want it to fit conveniently into our lifestyles. While this may not happen consciously, we certainly allow ourselves to be so distracted and engaged by material reality that we fail to respond to the challenges Hashem presents us. In a certain sense, it is as though we are rejecting the role of Avraham.

While our view of the "flag" may be dimmed, we nonetheless always see it when it is lifted high. The spark of divinity Hashem brought to each of His creations is never quite completely hidden. As children of the patriarchs, we find ourselves compelled to look when the flag is held high. Therefore, Eretz Yisrael, which was given in the merit of the patriarchs, is the place in which the light hidden within the very earth is most easily observed. It has often been a catalyst for rediscovering one's capacity to see. How tragic it is that all that could be seen by my anonymous friend was the minuscule spark of Torah to which she had been exposed.

How Can We Recognize Miracles?

The Ramban similarly points out that there are two types of miracles. In one type, we can see Hashem within the rules of nature He created. An example would be Avraham experiencing a famine when he entered the Land of Israel. While the purpose of the famine was to test Avraham's faith, both the need to eat and the possibility of famine are well within natural law. How easy it would be to dismiss the famine as a consequence of poor weather or bad agricultural decisions.

Avraham was well aware that each physical phenomenon has its *mazal*, an intermediary force which serves Hashem by making sure that a phenomenon occurs. He was equally aware that the Ruler Himself is above rules, which are in fact only creations. A person with vision such as Avraham's would not relegate a hidden *nes* to material cause and effect. He would ask himself, *What exactly is being displayed on the flagpole?*

The second type of miracle includes those in which the rules themselves are redefined by the events at hand. We come to see Hashem not only as the Master of nature, but as the Creator of nature. The choice is taken almost out of our hands. Who could choose disbelief in God when He is so obviously running things?

So why do we fail to see what Hashem shows us? In *Va'eira*, we observe the obstinate rigidity of Pharaoh. How could he miss the mark so consistently? The Torah tells us that Hashem hardened Pharaoh's heart. Why would He do this?

Just as there are two forms in which revelation takes place, there are two forms of denial. One form of denial is the end result of many previous denials. For example, a lifetime of involvement in *lashon hara*, slander, can create an inability to believe in anyone or anything. The warped skepticism so inherent in continual defamation of others is disguised, of course, as sophistication. A person thus cursed may eventually lose the ability to see Godliness in others, in themselves, and ultimately in the world. The free choice of whether to observe a given phenomenon as Hashem's Hand or chance may have been extinguished by years of self-taught cynicism. Hashem is only sealing the doors the person himself has chosen to shut.

The other form of denial is refusing to see what is threatening to oneself (even though it may be very apparent to everyone else). Pharaoh refused to see the first five miracles for what they were. It was only after such persistent denial that his heart was closed.

The Message of the Plagues

Hashem will never close our hearts completely. The merit of the patriarchs was concretely brought into our collective memory through the ten plagues. Each plague left an indelible imprint on us. We are commanded to remember the Exodus daily in order to awaken the dormant memories that can never be fully erased.

The Maharal points out that the three divisions of the plagues memorialized by Rabbi Yehudah immutably etched within our souls three realizations: Hashem is the Creator of the earth itself (group one, all of which took place on the earth); He is aware and involved and responsive to every movement on the earth (group two, which took place above the earth's surface); and, finally, He is the unifying Force that caused everything to come into being, the Creator of nature, and is above the earth (group three).

Let us look at one plague from each of the first two groups (most of the third group is in *Parashas Bo*), and let ourselves be moved by their message.

Blood. The *Midrash Ne'elam* points out that the natural function of water is to nurture life. Human blood is water with the addition of other properties that give it the ability to sustain our lives physically. The main property, though, remains water. When water is transformed to blood, the life force that comes forth from that transformation is called *nefesh*. It is the bond between the spiritual soul, which is called *neshamah*, and the body. We have the capacity to choose to view the *nefesh* as an emanation of Hashem or to let the sense of mastery which its vitality provides us, corrupt us.

We can see ourselves so vividly that we deny Hashem. The choice the Egyptians made was to see their own mastery until, in a certain sense, they deified themselves. When Hashem forced them into drinking blood, it was a physical manifestation of the way they were denying the fact of Hashem being the true source of everything nurturing. They had lost contact with Hashem and had only their own *nefesh* power to rely on. When we observed this phenomenon, we, who had never completely broken the bonds between ourselves and Hashem, experienced water and its nurturing power, where they had death and destruction.

We must look beyond ourselves, even if that requires breaking through years of the pursuit of self-reliance. We may have looked only in the mirror to find answers and resolutions. Our successes may have blinded us far more completely than our failures ever could. We must stop saying only "I can do it if I want to" and add the phrase *b'ezras Hashem*, with God's help.

Wild animals. The Shem MiShmuel relates that confrontation with various wild beasts was reflective of the mixture of good and evil to the point of utter confusion that characterized life in Egypt. The *sefer Aroch* brings a midrash that this plague, *arov*, was in fact a human-like animal that was attached to the earth by its umbilicus. When we are defined through our attachment to the physical world, all good and evil become both confused and relative. He points out that it was at this time that the request was made by Moshe that the Jews journey three days from Egypt. The three days hint at the three forces that create the kind of confusion that makes reality negotiable — jealousy, desire, and pursuit of honor.

When a person is beset by jealousy, his own mission and the tools he is given by Hashem to accomplish that mission pale before his emotional attachment to another person's mission and tools. He is glued in place and has lost contact with the only reality that is truly significant in his life: Hashem's plan. Similarly, physical desire misdirects the yearning for the pleasure that can only come from *netzach* — connection to that which is enduring — to the pursuit of that which gives pleasure that is transient and leaves a bitter taste. Pursuit of honor allows a person to escape from his own intellectual integrity into the never-never land of approval-seeking. This plague gave us the opportunity to redefine ourselves. We reentered reality and will always have the capacity to do so.

When I recall that almost-forgotten Tuesday, I see in the girl deep recognition of the Source of all nurturing; I see within her the will to find herself as a human being in a world that is desensitized to everything that is human. I do not know what became of her, but I feel close to her and share her journey.

CHAPTER TWENTY-TWO
silencing the voice of pharaoh

IF NOTHING ELSE, Jewish history is replete with moments of astounding confrontations between darkness and light. From the time of Avraham when he faced down Nimrod with the roaring fires of the furnace, till the generation that would not be broken by the Nazis, it has been part of the landscape of our souls. It is the backdrop to the daily encounters we ourselves have with the forces of evil.

At times we despair. We feel trapped. The Egyptian exile and redemption is a story not only of the liberation of a nation, but the key to the personal redemption of every Jew.

The evil force of Pharaoh is unprecedented. Even the descendants of Haman converted and became judges in the *Sanhedrin*, but we have no such tradition concerning Pharaoh's progeny. The reason for this is that the power of evil represented by Pharaoh was created to be resisted rather than rechanneled. The confrontation was absolute.

The Shem MiShmuel explains that the fact that the letters of the word *paroh* are identical to the word *oref*, the nape of the neck, is not coincidental. The human body is a metaphor for the soul. When the spiritual connection between the body and the heart to the mind is broken, spiritual death is the inevitable result. The body reflects this truth. If the neck is severed, death of the body is a forgone conclusion. When the connection between the mind and the body and heart is spiritually healthy, the mind will determine the direction of the heart's passions and the body's actions. However, if the connection is real but is working in reverse, if the desires of the heart and body determine the mind's choices, then there is spiritual sickness.

The word *paroh* in its reversed form, *oref*, symbolizes a type of spiritual sickness more insidious than any other. The mind at times negotiates its own submission to the body and the emotions. Nothing is more depraved. Let us look at the experience of the confrontation between Moshe and Pharaoh to understand the heart of evil. Let us know it in order to conquer it and render it powerless.

The Sickness of Egypt

In Egypt, the sickness was part of the atmosphere. Every step we took, every breath we breathed was influenced to one degree or another by Pharaoh.

The *Midrash Ne'elam* tells us that wherever the Torah uses the phrase *melech Mitzrayim*, "the king of Egypt," the text is referring to the spiritual force of Egypt, which is the ability to use the mind to gain access to the world of *tumah*, spiritual blockage, rather than the world of sanctity. Pharaoh epitomized that force. When Moshe confronted Pharaoh, he was facing ultimate corruption, intellect gone awry.

Moshe is not alone in having to meet this challenge. The Egyptian exile is the prototype of all exiles, including the one in which we now live. We, too, breathe the air of Egypt. We, too, confront Pharaoh. The desire to explore every facet of reality and then to reduce it to physical sensation is very much a part of the social climate of today's world. Few words have associations as negative as the word *suppression*. Self-control is vilified as suppression and is suspected of being not only a symptom of insanity but its cause. Enlightenment and intellectual honesty have become synonymous with the form of liberalism in which the word *conscience* is not heard. Any form of self-censorship in thought, deed, or action is viewed as coercion.

It sometimes feels good to let the voice of Pharaoh retain its credibility. Often we refuse to silence it completely. The validation that the lowest part of us feels when the highest part of us is trivialized cannot be ignored. We find it difficult to put this feeling into words. Let us turn to the vocabulary used in the Torah.

"I and No Other"

The root of the word *paroh* is *para*, literally, "unrestraint." It is used by the Torah in various contexts. In several incidents the word is used to describe the act of abandoning moral restraint and describes a very specific implement of war used by the forces of evil — the idealization of breaking down norms. All limitations are suspect in an intellectual "enlightenment" that has been redefined. This was Pharaoh. And it is he who Moshe had to confront.

The *Midrash Ne'elam* tells us that the intense intellectual pursuit of enlightenment that was so grotesquely distorted by Pharaoh could be used honestly. The fierce battle to know can be turned toward the search for truth. Moshe embodied the earnest search for knowledge by reaching the forty-ninth level of *binah*, insight. His complete intellectual humility allowed him to accomplish this feat. His mind unclouded by ego or desire was Pharaoh's match. Hashem provided Moshe with the ability to perform the final set of plagues that would bring about recognition of the one ultimate truth that redefines the pursuit of knowledge: Hashem's unity. The plagues were performed not for the sake of Pharaoh, but for the sake of redefining us, the Jewish people.

The Maharal points out that the entire last set of plagues — hail, locusts, darkness, and the slaying of the firstborn — reflects not only that Hashem has mastery over nature, but that He is the Creator of nature. Thus the Torah tells us that Hashem did not enact the final and most conclusive of all ten plagues through a *malach* (a spiritual force created to do His will), nor through positive interventions within nature as we know it, nor by a *saraf* (a burning force with which He eliminates evil from the world), nor through a *shaliach* (literally, a messenger; even the forces of nature that give us access to identify Him were not called into play). The text concludes, "I and no other." No other force can be mistaken for the force that was displayed on that night.

In order not to be blinded by the extraordinarily dazzling spiritual light that Hashem displayed and miss seeing it — as happened to those of us who died in the plague of darkness — we needed to be changed. The mitzvos of bris milah and the sacrifice of the *korban Pesach* must be examined closely to give us the ability to remove our own blinders. These two mitzvos define the path

silencing the voice of pharaoh

toward both personal and collective redemption.

With the mitzvah of bris milah, the human body is redefined. Instead of the body taking on its own persona, this mitzvah gives us insight into its truest nature: it is a creation formed to serve its Creator. Hashem's mastery over the flesh of our bodies is engraved on us. The Sefas Emes explains that the result of this is nothing less than liberation from the confinement imposed on us by the laws of nature. In the most genuine sense of the word, we are free. When we are servants of Hashem we can have no other master.

The mitzvah of *korban Pesach* takes us one step further. The Maharal explains that through this mitzvah we not only declare ourselves to be servants only of Hashem, but we act on that decision. Let us look at this offering more closely. Each detail of its numerous halachos deepens and broadens us. Each aspect sharpens our vision.

Sharpening Our Vision

The animal selected was a lamb. The Jewish people are compared to sheep in that our most authentic self-expression as a nation is following Hashem. The demand that only one lamb was offered per group symbolized the truth that the Jewish people have only one self-definition — although we are subdivided into families and each family has its own path and voice, the ultimate road to be taken is toward Hashem.

The lamb was to be roasted and not boiled. The process of boiling leads to the meat becoming soft and falling apart into many pieces. Roasting has the opposite effect. In order for us to experience Hashem's unity, we must ourselves be unified. It is when we serve Hashem in unity that our servitude to Him is vigorous enough to liberate us from every form of servitude to every other force.

Therefore, the slaughtering of the sacrifice is not considered an act of destruction or annihilation, but a preliminary to achieving a higher state of existence. The blood that is shed is immediately taken up and received for this new higher life. This is symbolized by the next step in the process of sacrifice: after the slaughtering comes *kabbalah*, where the lifeblood of the animal is transferred to holy vessels.

We had our moment of truth. We either offered the sacrifice or we didn't. The Egyptians worshiped the sheep as one of the forces that were part of their world. They lived in a world in which every force had to be experienced and submitted to the endless appetite of the human ego. Sacrificing a sheep to Hashem was the ultimate statement of belief in a unifying power beyond all others. Doing so carried a death sentence. We had to choose.

The blood of the sacrifice had to be put on the doorposts. The text records the command from Hashem thus: "And you shall take from the blood and put it on the two side posts and on the lintel." However, when Moshe told the Elders to transmit this commandment to the rest of the Jews, he said, "Make some of the blood that is in the basin touch the lintel and the two side posts." Notice that while Hashem first mentioned the side posts, Moshe mentioned the lintel first.

The Kli Yakar explains that the lintel, which holds the entire form of the door together, is a metaphor for Hashem's Providence. The two side posts symbolize the merit of the patriarchs and matriarchs who are referred to in *Prophets* as *zero'os olam*, "the arms that hold up the world." Hashem turned our inner eye toward the patriarchs and matriarchs. We must know from whom we come; we must take courage and recognize ourselves as tzaddikim who can begin the process of return.

Moshe said, "Touch the lintel first — we have no strength to begin without You." When we despair, we must acknowledge a profound truth. Our confrontations are not necessarily easier when they are not dramatic. We become weary. The voice of Pharaoh is shrill and loud. We cannot silence it by closing the windows; it resonates from within. We must look toward the unending love of Hashem, the lintel, *mashkof* (which also means the One Who observes). We must let our search for Him be earnest and genuine. We must relearn to touch the part of us that is like the patriarchs and the matriarchs. We will then be worthy of the true and lasting redemption that will once more not be performed by a *malach* or a *saraf* or a *shaliach* but by Hashem Himself, when He will once more reveal His unity to us.

CHAPTER TWENTY-THREE
the tenth song

THE ONLY THING more difficult than marrying off a child is not marrying off a child. There are few areas of life in which our choices must be made with such integrity and responsibility. It is easy to simultaneously feel overjoyed and overwhelmed. Yet we must never allow ourselves so much of either emotion that we permit what should be a rare moment of revelation of Hashem's goodness to be hidden by our need to control events.

Our Sages say that making a match is as difficult as splitting the Red Sea. When we are walking through the torrents of the Yam Suf, we must relive the moment when we all recognized the Hand of Hashem. When our children are young, we cannot deceive ourselves into thinking that the mystery of their vitality and sweetness is our own doing. No mother can (in her more honest moments) totally erase her inner knowledge of the narrow escapes.

In *Tehillim*, children are compared to arrows in the bow of an archer. As we draw them close, we set the direction. But they can reach the target only when we let go. Trusting in Hashem to bring them to the destination set for them before they were born is not effortless. In *Parashas Beshalach*, we had to come face to face with our own limitations. It is there that Hashem implanted within us the ability to retain our reliance on His guidance.

The Healing Split

Ramchal succinctly defines exile as brokenness and redemption as rectification. We were broken to various degrees in Egypt. Although some emerged as tzaddikim who reached dizzying heights of piety and strength that are beyond our imagination, they were far from the only ones to leave. There were those who were damaged to one degree or another. Some were even damaged in the most subtle and delicate aspect of their being — their faith. Hashem wanted to heal the wounds of exile, which were far deeper than any physical injury could ever be. How did He go about healing us?

The Sefas Emes tells us that the miracles that took place in Egypt brought about an inner recognition of Hashem's greatness through the outpouring of His compassion. We experienced His goodness through the supernatural occurrences that characterized the plagues. The spark of the patriarchs within us that is never extinguished gave us the ability to experience Hashem's light despite our insensitivities and our partial blindness. However, in order for that dimension of awareness to stay with us throughout eternity, it had to be "earned." The sea did not split as soon as the Jews set foot in it.

When the Jews stepped into the sea, it split only when they were in it up to their nostrils. At that moment, a change was made within us forever. We gained a level of closeness that can never be eroded by future exiles. It is not a gift; it was merited and is therefore indelible.

The Gemara tells us that the sea was split for Rabbi Pinchas ben Yair, a Sage who lived generations later. This tells us that the capacity to split the sea, and thereby break the laws of nature, is within the potential of every Jew of every generation. The source of this power can be seen when the Red Sea split not only for the tzaddikim but also for those who, in their brokenness and despair, said, "Are there no graves in Egypt that You have brought us to the desert to die?" They, too, walked into the sea. They reached within themselves to find a level of trust and faith in Hashem that can withstand any opposition the future may hold.

Impossible Is an Illusion

The Maharal explains that there are two types of opposition that we encounter. One form is of the type symbolized by Pharaoh. He epitomizes the forces of evil as made manifest through human misuse of free choice. When Hashem saved us from Pharaoh, what we learned is that even free choice, which is the most fragile and therefore the most precious of all of the gifts that Hashem presented to mankind, has its limitations. The limitations are not in whether or not a given person can make disastrous choices; the limitation is on the possibility of that person's choices affecting anyone (or anything) else. No heart could have been harder than Pharaoh's. No liberation could have been more undiminished.

The second type of opposition is the fact that we are constrained by natural law. The word *impossible* is learned early on, and very few of us recognize how totally negotiable the word is. While we give the principle of absolute trust in Hashem at least a superficial and intellectual nod, it seldom reaches the heart with the constancy and intensity we covet. The sea's splitting brought home the elasticity of natural law. Thus we gained the ability to meet any opponent.

We all encounter our private sea splitting. Both earning a living and finding one's mate are compared to the splitting of the sea. We encounter various opposing forces. There are times we feel as though we must place our reliance on the impression we make on the *shadchanim*, the matchmakers. We worry about the image we leave with a prospective employer. We experience sleepless nights and stressful days. But we have no right to relinquish to others the absolute trust that belongs exclusively to our relationship with Hashem.

Are their actions irrelevant? Not at all! Their responses have enduring consequences for them. They will have to account to Hashem for any misuse of the opportunities He grants them. Conversely, they will be rewarded by Hashem for their efforts on behalf of others. What is denied them is absolute power over other people's lives.

If we only made this awareness more a part of our inner lives, how much tension would dissipate! How much genuine gratitude we would feel toward those who try their best even though we do not get the results we yearn for.

There is, of course, another form of opposition. For some of us, the word *unrealizable* is the replacement for the word *impossible* that we dare not use when thinking about Hashem's power even in moments of the most candid introspection. We cannot dream of a match such as the one made by our acquaintance because we are not wealthy (or beautiful or well-connected) enough.

While the laws of cause and effect do exist (just as it is natural law that bodies of water do not split), there is no feat beyond Hashem's strength. We must go back to the splitting of the sea to observe with greater care the means through which the wonder we all witnessed occurred.

Breaking the Cycle of Despair

The Or haChaim clarifies the background events that preceded the miracle. Hashem Who wants only our good, expresses Himself at times through *middas hadin*, the attribute of justice. What this means is that just as in the physical nature of the world there are no causeless effects, the same is true with regard to the world's spiritual nature. Hashem allows us to initiate actions that bring about responses from Him. Thus we are active participants in the unfolding act of Creation. No form of reward can equal the pleasure gained by genuine achievement. It is for this reason that Hashem judges us at times with severity. This severity is the tool with which He grants us the gift of challenge and response. It is only through this that our achievements have integrity.

At the moment we stood by the sea, we were burdened by a deadness of spirit that was expressed by some of us who suggested that we return to Egypt. The accusation aroused by this lack of faith was not the exclusive "problem" of the individuals who complained; it was the burden of us all. Therefore, Hashem told Moshe that he must tell us to move.

When we face opposition that is of either category we mentioned, we must break the cycle of blame and despair. We must awaken Hashem's compassion by "stepping into the sea." We can redefine ourselves through using those moments of awareness we all experience. They can inspire us to make consequential movements that will change our lives. We can move in whichever direction we have to. We can generate Hashem's compassion. It can be awakened by deeds of faith and courage. Only deeds can silence the accusation.

Learning How To Sing

There is one question we must ask ourselves regardless of our personal circumstances. Faith must not only be rationally understood, it must also be felt. If we want the splitting of the sea to affect us, we must ask, "Do we know how to sing?" The difference between song and speech is that song comes from the soul, while speech comes from the mind.

We as a people have sung many songs. The Jews sang ten times. Each one reflected a bridge built between the intellect and emotions. At the splitting of the sea, the Midrash tells us that the children who were nurtured by Hashem Himself when their mothers were forced to abandon them in the fields due to Pharoah's harsh decrees looked up and said, "*Zeh Keili* — This is my God." They recognized Him as the One with Whom they had already had contact.

Do we do the same? We have all had moments of deep recognition. Are we able to take those moments and give them voice?

Nine of the ten songs the Jews are destined to sing have been sung. The tenth will be sung in the time of Mashiach. The word that is used for the songs that have already been sung is *shirah*, which is the word for "song" in its feminine form. The song that will be sung in the future is referred to as *shir*, using the masculine form of the word. The feminine element is viewed as responsive, the masculine element as expressive. Throughout the centuries we have discovered Hashem again and again and responded to Him. He expresses Himself using various prisms of His light to give us ever-changing visions of His unknowable essence. He appears to us at times as the Wise Old Scholar, the Man of War, the Faithful Shepherd. We respond to each one with its own song.

In the time of Mashiach we will express them all as one.

I have a friend who knows how to sing. No one in her family is of towering intellectual brilliance or striking beauty, nor is she the scion of a well-known and illustrious family. She is the mistress of a home that is rich with the sound of her children and the Torah of her husband — and nothing else. When her children came of age one after the other, she would go down to the Kotel day after day and read *Shir HaShirim*. She did so with passion and love, with joy and with wonder. I met her there a number of times and yearned to walk the bridge she had built between her mind and her heart.

As time passed, I noticed a fascinating phenomenon. Not only had her children who had come of age married well (each one with his or her own story of sea splitting), but the names of all of her sons- and daughters-in-law have an interesting common denominator. Each one is a name found in *Shir HaShirim*. When I see them together at family simchahs, I can feel the unheard harmony.

We each have our own song. We must only learn to be silent and to walk into the sea, wherever it is, in order to hear it.

CHAPTER TWENTY-FOUR
the third partner

THE END OF the dream was unforeseen. No one anticipated that the edge of agony would cut so close and inflict such unspeakable pain. The neighborhood chatter addicts had, for once, no words. Only a few years earlier they had foreseen (and foretold) an extension of the glitz and glitter of the best engagement of the year. His prospects seemed almost unlimited, what with his impeccable polish, brilliance, and family connections.

The finality of the judge's sentence sent all illusions crashing down with such force that the fragments of the dream could not be put together. By all accounts, two years in prison was a very moderate term considering the gravity of the crimes for which he was convicted. Manipulating stocks, income-tax evasion, and petty fraud are serious offenses. There was nothing to say.

When I saw his wife several weeks after the conviction, only her eyes told the truth. She would never be the same. Neither would he. Externally she maintained a courageous facade. Her family stood by her, as did his. Their friends were loyal and proffered every imaginable form of assistance. The only friend that abandoned them was the companion that had been with them since the day she chose the ring: *chemdah*.

Chemdah, coveting and yearning for that which is not one's own, had been the third partner in their marriage. It was *chemdah* that demanded more and more. Nothing was ever quite enough. They had to have whatever the gaping emptiness in their hearts demanded. As the incessant pursuit of material possessions defined the daily ebb and flow of their lives, their inability to draw lines to mark their moral parameters became more and more permanent in their inner geography. Questions were not asked; answers were not wanted. The line-up of all the externals of Torah lifestyle acted as a visual testimony to what they had wished to be but were no longer.

The restlessness of spirit that had brought them close to the abyss is no stranger to me. I have seen it in its other manifestation countless times.

When Elizabeth came to study in Jerusalem, the dorms at Neve Yerushalayim were full. In the early years of Neve's existence, the problem was usually remedied by ingenious methods (all involving adding just one more bed to a room in spite of the basic physical premise that two objects cannot occupy the same space). However, Elizabeth, in the course of time, became not only part of our household, but she filled the place in my heart that is often filled by a sister. Nothing could be more natural than her coming to stay "for a while," and staying until Hashem's providence brought her back to the States where she eventually married.

Her "room" was an alcove in my living room. There was little space and far less privacy. In the course of time, I saw the photos of her parents' lonely, massive home in the hills of New England. As the daughter of professionals she had lacked nothing that can be paid for in cash. She had the same restlessness of spirit that characterized that man's wife. It took her to Jerusalem. For the other, it led to her husband's downfall.

What is the source of desire? Why do we long for that which eludes us? Where do the paths of these two women diverge? *Parashas Yisro* sheds light on these questions. Let us begin by looking more deeply into the character of Yisro and the search that began with his yearning.

Searching the World of Truth

The Shelah haKodesh tells us that Yisro was an incarnation and rectification of Kayin (Cain). Kayin saw the entire world as a vehicle for the fulfillment of human desire. From his perspective, offering anything to Hashem was not only a waste but in a certain sense a desecration. Yisro was the penultimate searcher. He, too, understood the natural restlessness that is part of the human spirit. But, unlike Kayin, he was unwilling to settle for material fulfillment. Nothing less than finding Hashem would do.

The Maharal points out that Yisro explored every imaginable belief system. Rather than giving allegiance to a particular form of idol worship, his spiritual odyssey reflected his need for absolute truth. He could not content himself with a prism of light and define it as the Source of Light.

Yisro's seven names are statements about his essential being. They reflect that his entire character had within it the potential to discover every manifestation of Hashem's *middos*, attributes, and would content itself with nothing less. The Sefas Emes tells us that we, as Jews who have access to Yisro's discovery at the end of his journey, must be aware of the nature and intensity of his search. Our ability to receive Torah and allow it to complete us is contingent upon our ability to recognize its goodness and want it more than any of the impostors that flood the market.

Chazal's dictum "*Derech eretz kadmah laTorah*" now takes on a new light. The Maharal explains that recognizing truth and valuing it with the profound dedication of Yisro is true *derech eretz*. Rather than awakening within us the illusion of material ambition, we must let our exposure to the world take us closer to what we most ardently desire. When we search the world for its hidden sparks of truth, the search will lead us to Hashem. The *parashah* gives us the landmarks that give us the clarity to move forward.

Parashas Yisro is probably best known for the Ten Commandments. The last commandment is "*Lo sachmod* — You shall not covet." *Midrash Ne'elam* explains the significance of this being the last of the commandments. The Ten Commandments are the essence of the Torah. Every other mitzvah has its root in these ten. The final commandment is, then, in a certain sense the final statement of the Torah about itself.

The *Midrash Ne'elam* says, "That which is last in the lower world is first in the upper world" — the truth of Hashem cannot be seen in a cloud of falsehood. There is nothing more false than envy. It is a denial of the integrity of Hashem's will and wisdom. Let us explore the darker (and sometimes more familiar) recesses of our own hearts to discover why we allow our search for goodness to remove us from the path to truth. Let us begin to understand why we have to be told not to covet.

The Two Faces of Envy

The Maharal attributes the presence of envy in our hearts to two different (and in some ways opposite) motivations. One is the reality of something actually lacking in our lives. It is only natural for someone who is hungry to envy someone who has food. While some of our lacks are illusory, others are real.

Using envy as an escape from actually endeavoring to fulfill that which is lacking is a convenient emotional escape, but it never provides a solution. At times, a solution is not within our grasp, and we must contend with the fact that Hashem may have a different, truer, and more compassionate vision of what our needs are than we ourselves do. Would Rabbi Akiva be Rabbi Akiva if he didn't struggle? Would his wife be worthy of the adornment of Jerusalem if she had made no sacrifices?

There is another, at times deeper, reason for envy. It is the nature of the evil inclination to take one's attention from the search for meaning and goodness by distracting us. Almost anything can provide distraction. The empty space that Hashem places within us for us to fill with Him can be filled with jealousy and assuaged by the quest for everything other than Him. We can be Kayin or we can be Yisro.

Rabbeinu Bachya elucidates the nature of inner distraction. He says that its source is our constraining ourselves to lives of tedium and monotonous indifference. While on the one hand we are drawn to ease and comfort, the attainment of material satisfaction can be spiritually stultifying. The inner emptiness cannot be filled with more of the same, so we try the new and improved possibilities of material fulfillment. We look toward others in order to escape from ourselves.

The Vilna Gaon tells us that the hunger for attractive homes and exquisite clothing are attempts to satisfy the soul. Conversely, desires for physical pleasure are attempts to satisfy the body. Either can lead (when taken beyond their natural borders) to disaster. The first kind of longing can become so constant and definitive that no emotional energy is left for the pursuit of anything of genuine and enduring value. The serenity that the study of Torah requires cannot coexist with unending restlessness. The second kind of misplaced longing causes an almost animalistic addiction to passivity. Almost any mitzvah requires a material or physical trade-off. There is no place for trade-off nor is there any inspiration effective enough to do battle with ennui. The pain of the emptiness, however, doesn't go away. We look toward the lives of others with all the venom of pent-up and frustrated perceived need.

The Vocabulary of Illusion

How do we move forward? We must first of all learn to deglamorize the kind of fulfillment that is paid for by money. Money can buy comfort and a certain degree of freedom. It can't buy more. When we romanticize possessing high-status items, we create drawings in our minds that portray illusion as reality. We respond to the drawings as though they are the reality they only portray. When we use the vocabulary of illusion (for instance, saying that someone with an eye for sharp dressing is "with it" implies that all others are somehow "without it"), we make the illusions that lead to envy and misguided lifestyles more credible.

Second, we must teach ourselves to seek out the mission that Hashem has in mind for us moment by moment and let its achievement give us the only kind of *simchah* that endures.

The last time I saw Elizabeth was brief and joyous. We had only a few moments to share. Her life is by no one's definition easy. Her eyes told me the truth; they were full of the inner contentment that can come with a life in which the only yearning is that for the One who fills the entire world with His glory.

CHAPTER TWENTY-FIVE
an encounter with absolute truth

WHEN I WAS a child, the disparity between the real world and the world that was presented to me as real via the media was astounding. The books I read as a somewhat precocious and lonely only child opened windows to worlds that never existed. I envisioned a world in which children like myself dressed in their national costumes. Of course, they responded to life more or less like the liberal Jewish writers who wrote books with titles like "Children of the World."

One of my most vivid memories is of the time I shared some of my broadened horizons with my grandmother. I showed her a picture of a pilgrim and informed her that this is how "we" dressed when the Mayflower landed. Her incredulity was something to behold.

"You tink ve come on de Mayflower?" she finally blurted out. "Ve are from Bialystok."

After we had a brief discussion about the various places where our family had lived, I came to the realization that Grodna Gubernya was far more part of our forebears' chronicle than Salem, Massachusetts. Considering what the people at Random House seemed to believe, either they were or I was out of touch with reality. In those days gone by, when even the works of Marcus Lehmann had yet to make an indent on the flow of printed matter that is indelibly part of my memory, moments of truth were not that frequent.

Another one hit me with remarkable, and therefore unforgettable, intensity. As I leisurely perused a book describing career opportunities — after all, as a seven year old, and an only child, leisure was a commodity that was unlimited — I had a sudden flash: no one in my family was a cowboy, a gold miner, a moun-

an encounter with absolute truth

tain climber, or a fireman!

A speedy critique of all the adults with whom I had contact revealed that marriage, which in those days was as prestigious and as dignified as any other venture, was by far the most favored career for Jewish women, unless they had to work because of a grave financial situation. The men in our family tended toward various business-oriented careers, with law being a favorite.

I soon lost my taste for the open plains and they faded into the gray area reserved for other centuries. Instead, the "Jewishness" of law became indelibly imprinted on my memory.

A Colossal Eye-Opener

Thus it was with a sense of closing a circle that was never really open, that I accompanied my friend Lori to the *beis din*. I was to act as her translator as she presented a claim against a former employer at the Jewish court. At last I would live out my dormant fantasy of being a barrister.

As we entered the building on Strauss Street and waded through the various layers of bureaucracy, we soon found ourselves standing before the tribunal of distinguished rabbis. I presented my companion's claim with what I assumed to be breathtaking incisiveness and eloquence. One of the judges repeated the claim I had stated. He repeated it with such faithfulness to the original that I was sure that I had persuaded him beyond a shadow of a doubt that Lori's claim was justified.

He then asked her former employer to state his counter-claim. After Mr. Katz (not his real name) had done so, the *dayan* repeated Mr. Katz's response to Lori's claim with the same exactness. My bubble burst. The realization that eloquence and emotional appeal have nothing to do with Jewish law was a colossal eye-opener for me.

Let us look at *Parashas Mishpatim* to gain a clearer perspective of the nature of Divine justice as opposed to human law and order.

Understanding the Concept of Order

The Maharal explains that the concept of order is often misunderstood. Human order comes about by arranging our lives or our possessions in a manner in which there is maximum efficiency and aesthetic harmony. Hashem's order comes about by His presenting us with the most efficient and spiritually balanced approach to Him.

The laws of the Torah, therefore, are inherently different from the laws humans develop to govern their societies. Since the goal is neither efficiency nor the sort of beauty that is limited by our horizons, by necessity the results are vastly different. Let us first examine the nature of law as has been practiced by virtually every society since time immemorial.

Throughout the centuries civilizations have flowered with dazzling brilliance. When the inevitable fading takes place, as it must, *fairness* and *justice* are often redefined beyond recognition. Non-Jews are commanded by Hashem to maintain a system of law. While the specifics of their systems are left to their discretion (and therefore fall before their limitations), the core of their systems is Hashem's unchanging definition of order: the weak must be protected from the strong. Witnesses must be honest. By doing this, they commit themselves to a limited degree of spiritual "order." But when they fail, they doom themselves to a collective spiritual death, and decline and disappearance are inevitable.

The Sefas Emes elucidates the nature of the Torah's system. Our system gives us an attachment to the root of truth, Hashem. Hashem implanted within our souls sparks of hidden light that give us not only the yearning to cleave to Him, but also the knowledge of how this can be accomplished. It is from this hidden sense of truth that we were able to produce a Sanhedrin.

Thus our sensitivity to justice does not come from the outside, as would be the case if we determined justice through external observation alone. The judge is a vessel through which Hashem brings His justice into the world. The clarity of his light is not of his own making. It is a gift from Hashem. It is this *siyatta diShamaya*, this Divine aid, that is the differentiating factor between this and other systems. The human factor is only that of bringing this clarity from the world of potential to the world of actualization.

In a similar sense, our sensitivity to the needs of others, and the powerful force within us that makes us want to give, is a reflection of Hashem's hidden light within us. It is very different from the manifestations of charity and decency that are at times part of the social justice systems created by other societies. As Jews, the need originates in a place that is so deep within us that we ourselves often cannot put our feelings into words.

It is no fluke that *Parashas Mishpatim* coincides with *Parashas Shekalim*, which discusses the Jews' giving a *shekel* coin. Hashem ignites the two deepest lights within us — the light of truth and justice and the light of compassion and generosity. It is up to us to let them burn with incandescent beauty.

We sometimes allow the lights to be extinguished. It never happens as a result of a conscious decision; it happens because we are influenced by the society in which we live, and we define justice by their standards. The prism by which they see light is that of social harmony. Their observations have led them to conclude that this is achieved by maximizing individual freedom.

The unasked questions concerning where the path to freedom ultimately leads, and whether that unknown address opens the gates of light or darkness, are not part of the nature of their search for justice, nor can they be. We seek the truth of *aspaklarya meira*, the clear glass of Hashem's will, without the limitations imposed by the shadings of human search. When the definitions of justice become confused in our minds, we at times close the doors tightly to that light. We seek justice in the civil courts.

Seeking Human Justice over Hashem's

The rationalizations people use when bringing their cases to the secular courts are neither new nor original: "I'll wipe the floor with him." "The punitive damages alone will keep us in clover for years." "I'll get a better settlement." "They will give me full custody." "They will treat me more fairly."

Rabbeinu Bachya discusses the implications of making the decision to seek human justice over Hashem's justice. We all understand the severity of committing murder. A murderer not only diminishes the image of God by removing a soul from the world, but he is also accountable for all the generations that will never exist because of it. It is only when we appreciate that every human being who ever lived is a descendant of Adam that we realize the implication of killing even one person.

However, Rabbeinu Bachya continues, the sins of theft and that of desecrating Hashem's Name are even graver than murder. Kayin was ultimately forgiven for his sin because of the strength of his *teshuvah*, for we find in *Pirkei d'Rav Eliezer* that his recognition that his sin couldn't be forgiven was considered *teshuvah*. However, the sin of theft is not forgiven until the money is restored. And when a person commits the sin of *chillul Hashem*, desecration of God's Name, he is not forgiven as long as he lives. Both theft and desecration of God's Name can take place when opting for secular courts. The overt rejection of Hashem's will as expressed through the law of Torah is a *chillul Hashem* of major proportions.

In addition, in the typical case where the motivation is material gain, the "winner" in the material sense is the loser in the spiritual one. All financial benefits that are awarded above those the Torah mandates are considered stolen from the litigant, who is forced to pay what he does not owe.

We also must contend with the pain of feeling somehow "ripped off" when we forgo what seems to us to be fair. The realities of this world are so vivid and our perspectives so narrow that what we define as reality is a very narrow space indeed.

When we contemplate some of the other mitzvos in the *parashah*, our horizons are pushed back even further. Among other mitzvos, we are commanded not to cook meat and milk together and not to allow a sorceress to live. The *Sefer HaChinuch* points out that all physical realities have a spiritual root. It is only by observing the backdrop that its reason for existing in its world is understood. When Hashem commands us to avoid the "innocent" rearrangement of reality (whether it is by instructing us not to cook milk and meat together or to do any form of sorcery), it is because He is conscious of the implications of our redefining order and we are not.

Lori won her case. We were both elated. The fact that later the check that Mr. Katz gave her turned out to be valueless did put a bit of a cloud over the picnic. But Lori was realistic enough to remember that a person's finances are settled on Rosh HaShanah for *an encounter with absolute truth*

the year, by the Master of the universe.

Our closeness to Him the moment we left the room together with Mr. Katz to allow the judges to deliberate was far greater the moment we reentered. As we heard the sage and erudite *av beis din* lift his eyes toward us and instruct us to accept the word of the Torah, we knew that the moment of close encounter with absolute truth would never completely leave us.

CHAPTER TWENTY-SIX
the soul of the world

WHENEVER I FIND myself with a bit of time that doesn't need to be accounted for, I take a walk through the streets of Jerusalem. The unrivaled victor in the unspoken contest for my heart is the Old City. I find myself drawn to the narrow alleys leading to the remnants of the Churvah Synagogue, rising like a stone phoenix amid the ashes of destruction, silently awaiting the final return. Streets with names like HaTamid pierce through the layers of time until the centuries fall away like dust.

While this is true on even the most ordinary weekday, the added sanctity of the holidays changes the quality of a simple stroll beyond recognition. On *chol hamo'ed*, during Pesach or Sukkos, the streets flow with unshed tears of joy and longing that remain in the hearts of the thousands of people who find their feet taking them to the Kotel. A family tradition that crept up silently upon us is that after *birkas kohanim* of the morning prayers, we all go for a stroll. My children, whose eyes and hearts are, like those of every child, guileless and inquisitive, usually demand a stop at the exhibitions of replicas of the Temple's vessels. It is there that I find the gap between the emotions and the mind most unbridgeable.

While I know far more than the six year old at my side, we both find ourselves equally transfixed when looking at the replicas. We exchange glances that express far more than words. In *Parashas Terumah*, the vessels of the future Temple are described. The Malbim's commentary on this topic opens doors that not only deepened my understanding of what I see when I see the replicas of the vessels, but of what I see when I search within myself.

The invisible self is so elusive. I find myself looking for it in myself and others, and failing at times because of the layers upon

the soul of the world

layers of self-protective armor that camouflage it. Attempting to find that spot of hidden yearning in every Jew we meet is far more of a challenge than exploring our own inner territory. The *parashah* can provide us a map to places uncharted in ways we would never have imagined. To help us read this map and take us to our desired destination, we can follow Malbim's thoughts, step by step.

A Six-Hundred-Thousand Watt Light

Every human has many limbs and organs, all of which have an individual function. Their unification and vitality come from the soul, which gives purpose and direction to the entire body. While at a very early stage of development, a child may say, "I didn't do it — my hand slapped him," no mature adult would try that one. We all know "who did it." It is the soul, the essential self, that gives the body that directive.

Hashem is the soul of the world. His wisdom, which is His essence, gives life to all existence. Every motion and breath, every moment and cycle, come only from Him. Similarly, each individual is compared to a miniature world, where the hidden and invisible self gives directions to the visible body.

To clarify Hashem's relationship to man, Malbim draws on the analogy of a symphony in which the violin plays a melody and the orchestra responds with counterpoint. The rule Hashem uses in governing the world — His response to human actions — works in a similar sense. When we, for instance, act toward each other with compassion, the response from Above is to allow compassion to flow downward back to the world. Conversely, when we close our hearts to Godliness and allow ourselves distance and coldness, He responds to our callousness by concealing His Face from us. Since His desire is to actuate only goodness and kindness, in a certain sense we cause Him to actualize His will. This is what is meant when we use the phrase *"nachas ruach"* to describe Hashem's responses to our movement toward Him.

From the beginning of time, it was His will to have a dwelling place in this, the lowest of all possible worlds. What this means, the Malbim continues, is that each individual must consecrate and purify himself in his own miniature world, until the body falls under the dominion of his soul. At that point, the light he created by virtue of his free choice will illuminate all the worlds. In response, God's blessing settles on His creations.

The patriarchs are compared to a chariot that brings its Rider to His desired destination. Each of them were able to bring the Shechinah, the Divine Presence, down to this world. Few people embark on spiritual journeys of such magnitude. The masses of the Jewish people have a spark of divinity within them that is analogous to particular limbs and organs in a body. Each one has his or her specific "brand" of sanctity that cannot be expressed by anyone else. But no individual since the patriarchs can be compared to a chariot of God. We are at most parts of a process that includes every other Jew. Therefore our Sages tell us that the Shechinah does not rest on fewer people than twenty-two thousand. In their wisdom they concluded that any number smaller than this cannot create the illumination necessary to draw Hashem's Presence down to this world.

In the same way that the light of one candle cannot be compared to that of ten, six hundred thousand is the number that is the manifestation of all the possibilities of spiritual illumination. The dazzling brilliance of radiance created when six hundred thousand Jews together received the Torah has no parallel. Hashem wanted to give us the power to generate illumination on that scale forever. To that purpose, He commanded us to build the *Mishkan*, Tabernacle, in the desert and later the *Beis HaMikdash*, Holy Temple, in Jerusalem. In doing so, He was giving us the notes with which we can begin the symphony to which He will respond.

The *Mikdash* belongs to Jerusalem, for Jerusalem is different from any other metropolis. In the book of *Psalms* it is called a "city that joins them all together." It is here that all the souls of the Jewish people can unite and with all their individual powers form a single body. This is alluded to when the Torah tells us, "Make a sanctuary for Me so that I dwell in you." The text does not say that the purpose of the sanctuary is for Hashem to dwell in it. Rather, the Torah is telling us that the power of the *Mikdash* is so great that it can affect each one of us profoundly by joining us together so that we are truly one. And then the Shechinah can be drawn down to this world and dwell among us.

The Hidden Light within Us

The human body is, in a certain sense, like a garment that clothes the soul. The soul can make use of every potential offered by the body to give it a means of articulation. For example, a person inspired toward generosity would know what to do with his hand. The true nature of the soul is thus revealed to us by the hand, which is, in the final analysis, merely flesh and blood. The *Beis HaMikdash* acted in the same manner. It gave voice to the spiritual nature, not of a specific individual, but of the entire Jewish nation.

The body can be divided into three basic sections: the head, which is the seat of the mind; the trunk, from the neck till the heart, the repository of the life force that vivifies the body; and the lower body, which is the storehouse of the organs that maintain the body's capacity to nurture itself and to propagate. These three sections of the body are echoed in the design of the *Mishkan*. The Ark, which contained the Tablets of the Law, reflected the nature of perfected intellect. The Tablets contained not our wisdom, but the most profound level of prophetic wisdom, the literal word of God. The Menorah represented the perfect heart, blessed with true insight and understanding, and the Table, the perfect use of the physical side of our reality.

When I go back in my mind's eye to the moment I stood before the replica of the Menorah, I now see so much more. The seven branches reflect a distinct direction that the heart takes in interpreting the world. All turn toward the center, symbolizing the Divine wisdom that gives focus and meaning to our search. The form of the Menorah was shown to Moshe by Hashem Himself. The forty-nine parts of the Menorah (seven branches, eleven button-like decorations, nine flower adornments, twenty-two cup ornaments), together with the essence of the Menorah itself, equals the number fifty. We are told by our Sages that there are fifty gates of wisdom, fifty doors we can open by finding the hidden Presence of Hashem in any person (even ourselves) or situation.

The sounds and colors of the Old City are a garment. Within the garment hides our heart. Every stone and alley reflects the light of the hidden Menorah within us. When I turn around and allow myself reentrance to the mundane world in which the buses leaving the area are crowded, the garment seems to cover the collective body of Hashem's nation so impenetrably as to leave only the tiniest shadow of what lies below it.

Yet I can still hear the beat of the heart.

The cacophony of languages, the variance of age and culture, can never drown it out. The vitality of the outdoor market at Machaneh Yehudah, the new neighborhoods that spring into being like magic, with the stone facades connecting the twentieth century to all those that preceded it, cannot hide it. May we learn to see each individual's flame of divinity and join together to actuate only goodness and kindness.

CHAPTER TWENTY-SEVEN
the power within us

THE FIRST TIME I learned the narrative of the sin of the golden calf, where the generation that had experienced the Exodus had turned to idol worship, my feeling was one of unadulterated annoyance. How could we have done anything so absurdly tasteless in its depravity? The worst Jews I knew seemed above worshiping a domesticated animal. With the quick judgment that typified the callow and uninformed responses of preadolescence, there were no words that could have properly expressed my scorn for the generation that I was later to know as the *Dor De'ah*, the Generation of Knowledge.

My main premise in misinterpreting the event was based on the assumption that only a very limited person could confuse something they had made with the Force that had, in fact, made them. How thousands and thousands of people, including those of a stature beyond our ability to even imagine, would miss this very basic flaw in the nature of idolatry was beyond me. In fact, the second commandment seemed to be almost redundant. My vote was placed with the Master of the world against Moshe, who had prayed on Israel's behalf after they sinned, and had I been included in the decision-making forum, we would not be here. The one feeling that was completely absent from my consciousness was guilt. I had no doubt that this particular sin had nothing to do with me and never could.

How wrong I was. For we are today still struggling with many of the same flaws in our collective character as our ancestors and so must come to terms with the actual event. We still suffer the consequences of this grave sin. It is remembered by Hashem whenever He judges us as deserving punishment and is included in the severity of His judgment.

We are thus left with a paradox. A sin to which we cannot relate, a sin incredibly distant from where we see ourselves, occurred. Yet it is this sin that Hashem sees when He looks at us. What does He see in us that we are blinded to when we look at ourselves?

Why Choose a Calf?

The Midrash elucidates the paradox: Why is the ox at the head of all the sacrifices? It answers with a parable: There once lived a king. There was gossip in his realm concerning the queen's relationship with one of the powerful men of the kingdom. When, after investigation, the king determined that the rumors were false, he made a feast and seated the gentleman in question on the dais. This demonstrated that he saw the man as worthy of his friendship, and certainly not as a rival. Similarly, placing the ox as the first of all sacrifices removes any shadow of a doubt that Hashem could be in any way "threatened" by His creation. Obviously, the corruption was deeper than the superficial image making tells us. What exactly went wrong?

Ramban points out that the people were never accused by Hashem of having rejected Him for an idol, for that was the last thing on their minds. What they wanted was a religious symbol to act as an oracle between them and Hashem, much as Moshe had been a diviner of Hashem's will and His instrument in their eyes. They asked for a force that "would go before us."

The animal that manifested as this "mediator" was far from random. When Hashem later presented Yechezkel the prophet with a vision revealing the path by which His Presence moves, so to speak, from infinity to the limitations of this world, the metaphor used was that of a chariot with four different animals, each considered a "king" of its type. The animals symbolized the forces Hashem utilizes to bring us His will and presence. One of the animals was the ox.

As the king of the domesticated animals, the ox is used as a symbol of Hashem's power over nature. Through the vigor and intricacy of the physical environment, we recognize a force outside ourselves. It is with this same power, which simultaneously conceals and reveals Him, that Hashem created a world in which challenges give us opportunities to earn our reward. We can drown in the world or let it vivify our spiritual connection to Him. The ultimate challenge of life lies in knowing Whom to call *Elokim*, God, and learning to attribute force to Him and Him alone. When we fail to meet with sincerity and truth the formidable tasks we face, we are held accountable for not becoming all we might have.

Why Do We Keep Failing?

The Sefas Emes explains that the Jews in the desert felt themselves to be very much in a situation of continual challenge. They were surrounded by the outer desolation of the desert, which is a mirror image of human frailty. The adaptation of the symbol of the calf (the "son" of an ox) embodied their yearning to tap into the awareness of Hashem's power. By actually giving this yearning a physical manifestation, they felt they were grounding it to this world.

Why would anyone judge this as being idolatrous? Don't we all want tangible reminders of who we are and in Whose world we live? What is the nature of this failure, and why do we repeat it again and again?

As the Kuzari points out, their sin was deciding that a human mind operating without the inspiration of prophecy could create a symbol of anything divine. When Hashem forbade the design of any metaphor for spiritual forces, it was to open us to a form of worship not limited by human imagination or intellect. What we observe in this moment of our failure is not a group of people worshiping a calf but worshiping, in a certain sense, themselves. By delineating their relationship to a specific symbol because that is what seemed to them real and needed at the time, even though they were explicitly told on Mount Sinai not to do so, they crossed a line. Although it was only the *erev rav*, the Egyptians who joined the Jewish people at the Exodus, who crossed the line to actually worship the calf in a way that was genuinely idolatrous, the rest of us were trapped by the limitations of our ability to submit our minds and hearts to Hashem and His mitzvos. They felt they needed a physical manifestation of the divine; God said nevertheless they could not do it. Though they were searching for something spiritual, they chose the wrong tack. Only God could decide how they should worship Him.

The Vilna Gaon discusses the significance of the fact that the sin itself was caused (and in its ultimate sense done) by the *erev rav*. The great miracles that surrounded the Exodus from Egypt inspired in them a yearning for Hashem. Yet their inability to find God in His place of hiding in nature caused them to despise the nitty-gritty performance of the mitzvos. The poetry and wisdom they sought seemed, to them, too deeply hidden by the world.

Being Stubborn at the Right Time

We, as Jews, are different. The most earthly part of every Jew, the animal soul, was formed from the earth of Eretz Yisrael. What this means is that every single one of us has the spiritual fortitude not to ever feel completely "lost" in the desert, for the earth itself reflects God as well as hides Him. The key to living a life in which this dimension of discovery is real is mitzvah observance. This is why the generation that worshiped the golden calf was never given the entire Torah, for they could never truly hear it. This episode reflects the influence exerted by those who sincerely long for meaning and spirituality but are unwilling to submit themselves to Hashem's will as manifest in the mitzvos.

The Vilna Gaon says further that we will have to do battle with the *erev rav* until the coming of Mashiach. We will have to prevail over them — and thereby redefine who we truly are — in our final struggle.

By nature, we reject all forms of idolatry. An interesting societal note can be made of the fact that so many of us today are so educationally deprived that we have only the foggiest of notions of what being Jewish is. Nonetheless, the vast majority of assimilated Jews know one thing very well: they are not believers in any of the more prevalent belief systems.

We are a stubborn people. At times that has been our salvation; at other times it has brought us to the very edge of the precipice. Our subconscious recall of the second mitzvah, heard from Hashem's mouth, touches the moment the *yetzer hara*, evil inclination, left us. For those precious moments we wanted no control, no medium. We were not afraid of the world or of ourselves. Hashem's presence was so perceptible that we stubbornly cling to its memory. If we still let its memory move us in the midst of our ignorance, how did we fail in the desert?

Being True to Ourselves

The Maharal cites the *gemara* in *Avodah Zarah* that tells us that Hashem allowed the evil inclination to prevail so as to bring about a situation in which we could find the words to do *teshuvah*, to repent. While Hashem did not decree which specific people would fail (we all have free choice), He created a situation in which invariably the weak would falter. This situation was a consequence of the high level we reached at the giving of the Torah, which created in us an intense need for closeness to Hashem. The choice of how we bring about this closeness is up to us. Either we do it "by the book," though mitzvah performance may at times seem mundane and may be difficult, or we go our own way and do what "feels right."

The corruptibility of a person who is involved in a subtle and sophisticated battle within himself is far greater than that of a person who is doing battle with his coarse desires. This is what our Sages mean when they tell us that the greater the person, the greater is his evil inclination. The ultimate result of this battle will be seen in the not-too-distant future, when the force of our ancestors' *teshuvah* opens our hearts. Their recognition of "*Hashem Hu HaElokim* — Hashem, He is God" is part of us. We, too, can silence the voice of the *erev rav* within and outside us.

CHAPTER TWENTY-EIGHT
why I don't hate pesach cleaning

THE FRESHNESS THAT seems to touch everything and redefine it is part of the story. The other part is the camaraderie that fills the air, as everyone in sight seems to be taken up with the act of renewal. The story to which I am referring is rather confessional. It is the story of why I don't hate Pesach cleaning.

It seems almost ridiculous to publicly proclaim my lack of resentment to the Master of all worlds for having taken us out of the crushing, futureless, painful reality that was ancient Egypt. However, as a homemaker, I find myself at times in splendid isolation. It has become far more socially acceptable to view the holiday with a mixture of comic relief and voiceless despair that lies just below the surface of pre-Pesach bravado.

I welcome the smells of the cleaning products and sweat of work that is, for once, not done to suit myself. The reason is not that the holiday gives me the opportunity to express my natural efficiency. There are those of us whose homes reflect their capacity to create order out of chaos. Since we all take pleasure in our successes, I am sure (only intellectually, not experientially) that seeing their love of order reflected in their surroundings is very gratifying. This is not the source of my gladness.

I often observe the irony of the fact that not all proficient homemakers are happy come Pesach time. For some, the fear of losing a fraction of control over their well-run kingdoms is a threat that goes far deeper than the shine of the silver. It pierces the very heart. It touches their sense of identity as wives, as mothers, as human beings capable of accomplishing meaningful achievements within the framework of their lives.

I am not one of the efficient, and although I maintain a respectable degree of order, I am never comfortably distant from the edge of defeat. The potential for guilt and self-hatred is never too far away. For me, *erev Pesach* could spiral down into an unceasing cacophony of blame drowning out the sweetness of the song of the Exodus as easily as it could for the vigilant perfectionist.

It has, however, the opposite effect. I get high on aluminum foil and bleach, on crowds and kashering. The Sefas Emes puts into words what has been for me an unspoken truth. Let us look at his comments on *Parashas Pekudei* to get a grasp of the physical preparations for Pesach, its work and its joy (yes, joy!). He gives us insight into how the physical actions we perform are part of the liberation — and who can resist freedom?

The Reality of Cleaning House

The Sefas Emes begins by quoting the Torah itself. "These are the accounts of the *Mishkan*, the *Mishkan* of testimony" is how the *parashah* begins. Rashi comments that the *Mishkan* itself is testimony that Hashem has forgiven the Jews for the sin of the golden calf. The *Mishkan* and the golden calf seem at first glance to be very distant from our pre-Pesach reality. Let us look more closely.

While comparing my home to the *Mishkan* seems rather poetic, it somehow seems off target. The disappearance of socks, the indescribable something that is in the oven, seems light-years away from the *Mishkan*. The "real" world seems almost totally divorced from its Source.

The Sefas Emes explains that the connection between the hidden world — the world of Hashem, the world of the *Mishkan* — and the revealed, physical one (the world of the single sock et al.) was bridged by Hashem when He gave us the Torah. His Torah is not an abstraction; there are mitzvos that are part of the physical world. The nitty-gritty of Pesach is part of a way of redefining what the world really is. All the cleaning, cooking, preparing serves to take the physical and make it into something spiritual.

When He gave us the Torah, we responded to his act of spanning infinity by saying, "*Na'aseh v'nishma* — We shall do, and we shall hear." We shall do Your will in the revealed world, and we shall accept the hidden root of the mitzvos. This recognition is an invisible part of our collective self-definition as a people. Yet there are times when we become distracted from the recognition of the preciousness of the tangible actions we perform. When looking at the sin of the golden calf, which preceded the building of the *Mishkan*, we will understand why.

Giving Up Control

The sin of the golden calf was a defilement of the natural world. We refused to see Hashem either in the desert that surrounded us or within our own hearts. We tried to instill divinity into something physical, though the second commandment explicitly tells us not to. Our need to feel a degree of control over external events silenced the voice of *"na'aseh v'nishma"* within us.

Although we, in our fear and despair in the aftermath of the sin, rejected the possibility of crossing the bridge that connects both worlds, Hashem did not respond by allowing our confusion to redefine us; the inner dimension of connection to Hashem was not severed. He gave us a new means of reaching out from the midst of the tangible material world we find both engaging and overwhelming — He commanded us to build the *Mishkan*.

The *Mishkan*, which was physically intricate, required absolute commitment to doing Hashem's will with precision. This absolute submission to Hashem was a rectification that, by its nature, changed our relationship to the physical world. We made the move that transformed us from being self-appointed masters of the universe to being servants of the true Master of the universe. By doing this, we became witnesses to Hashem's truth in the revealed world.

This world is often referred to as *alma di-shikra*, "the world of falsehood." It lends itself to misinterpretation. When we choose to get past the small-mindedness that we fall into so easily, we ourselves change dramatically. We are liberated from the tyranny of the great lie. Everything around us proclaims, "What you see is what you get." The truth is, what you see offers the opportunity to build a bridge. Only we humans can unravel the tangled perplexity of revelation and concealment. This is our greatness and the key to our personal freedom. Let us see how we can make them our own.

Make a Reality Check

What are the ways in which we can change the way we look at the material realities of life? We tend to see that which we are looking for. What direction shall our search take?

Certainly rejection of the material world is not the plan of its Creator. Rather, the Sefas Emes tells us, the world exhibits the key to revelation within the concealment that is an inherent part of its essence. In fact, he says, everything in the world is in a certain sense a portrait of its Creator. There are three primary means by which the pieces of the puzzle come together, thereby giving us the ability to see the portrait.

One is the world itself. The unity that can easily be seen in the intricacy of the creation (which, of course, requires from us a commitment to see what we look at) reflects the Oneness of its Originator.

Another is the way by which Hashem lets Himself be known through His continual imprint over events. Often it takes the passage of time before we can come to grips with Hashem's Providence. The progression of history always brings us back to the same patterns. When the pieces come together, they present us with the indelible image of the Author of history.

The spiritual forces that are reflected by the events that both occur and recur at specific times can be tapped into every year. The holidays give us the directions by which we can encounter the same potentials and actualize them in ways that are completely new. Thus this Pesach is both the same and different from any other Pesach that has taken place over the last thirty-five hundred years. Our putting together the pieces of the puzzles in ways that are unique to our lives and our experiences reveals Hashem's Presence. The door to interpretation can be opened by our choosing to see what this Pesach reveals. Every moment of physical involvement pushes the door open that much more.

The third way by which Hashem's portrait is painted is by the refinement of the soul that He placed within us. Each one of us has within him a spark of timelessness. We lose contact with ourselves through our continual involvement with the continuum of life. We find ourselves looking through a kaleidoscope that is so absorbing that we lose track of the person who is doing the looking.

The way we can do a "reality check" on who we are is to listen to what we say. The direction our speech takes reveals the inner direction of the speaker. When we lose our sensitivity to who we really are — in Whose world we live and Whose Hand guides us — it shows up in our speech. The vocabulary of self-hatred, despair, anger, and ugliness cannot express the thoughts and feelings of a person who sees the image of Hashem before his eyes.

Pesach Potential

The *Mishkan*, and later the *Mikdash*, gave concrete physical imagery by which we could integrate the portrait of Hashem in the world, in ourselves, and within the framework of the holidays. The fact that we have lost the *Mishkan* and the *Mikdash* is, therefore, reflective of our having lost ourselves.

When our sins become part of our self-definition, our definition of the world, and our definition of the meaning of events, we no longer put the pieces of the puzzle together. If this indeed is our objective state of being, how can we expect ourselves to not be defeated?

The answer, the Sefas Emes tells us, is that while we have at times, rejected *"na'aseh,"* and the relationship to the material world that it implies, we have never rejected *"nishma,"* our ability to attune ourselves to the Source of all existence.

One of the keys to opening up the *"nishma"* is Shabbos. It recreates the intimacy of the bond that is described in the text as *"beini u'vein Bnei Yisrael* — between Me and the children of Israel." Shabbos thus creates a new vision of self, time, and history. When we place this as a backdrop to our moment-to-moment interactions, the physical actions we do take on new meaning.

During these pre-Pesach days, as Seder night approaches, let us treasure the potentials that are opened. They broaden us and deepen us. Let us not trivialize the opportunities we have. When we stand on line and see even those of us who seem very distant from any world but the material one buy their "Pesach order," let us feel the bond that connects us. As we bleach our homes and kasher our utensils, let us feel our souls being cleansed as well.

CHAPTER TWENTY-NINE
the joy of finding the source

WHEN LOOKING OVER our neighborhood phone book for the first time, I was moved by both the abundance and variety of *gemachs* listed. From baby carriages to apart-apartments for Shabbos guests, if someone was lacking an item, whether due to financial constraints or closed shops, invariably there was someone out there ready to lend it out. But some of the more arcane selections seemed to me to be at least partially contrived. After all, why would anyone want to avail themselves of the *arbis gemach* for a *shalom zachor*? Surely chickpeas aren't too hard to come by for this Friday night gathering?

What I failed to take into consideration is the fact that some babies make their entrance into the world rather abruptly, moments before Shabbos. I found myself happily making use of the *arbis gemach* after the birth of a relatively recent grandchild.

Yet there is another component I failed to take into consideration. When I found myself face to face with the woman who operates the *gemach*, I experienced vicariously her delight in the mitzvah. It showed in her friendly, direct smile that conveyed the sunshine of her native California and in the intense piercing of her eyes that almost eclipsed their hidden chuckle. When I took the bag of chickpeas from her, we were both brimming with gladness, I for receiving goodness from the Source of all good and she for finding herself unified for the moment with the image of Hashem within her.

The Talmud tells us that since the destruction of the *Beis HaMikdash*, joy has ceased. The type of exultation we can no longer experience is the kind the *gemach* lady and I shared in miniature at that moment. The direct connection to God, the true source of joy, was made in earlier times by offering *korbanos*, sacrifices. That joy is no longer accessible to us. A look at *Parashas Vayikra* can give us a greater grasp of the nature of *korbanos*.

Kayin's Offering

The sacrifices in *Vayikra* are not the first ones mentioned in the Torah. Kayin and Hevel's offerings reflect a human desire to use the world as a means of connection to Hashem. The fact that Hashem responded dramatically differently to each demonstrates that not all means of reaching out to Hashem "work." We may erroneously conclude when reading the narrative of Kayin and Hevel that one sacrifice was accepted and the other rejected because of the external differences in what was offered. It seems clear that compared to fattened sheep, Kayin's offering was meager, to say the least.

The real issue is very different. The fact that Kayin offered only flaxseeds was not the cause of his *korban*'s rejection. Rather, the cause was his mind-set. The holy Alshich points out that the essence of sacrifice from the Torah's perspective is the sacrifice of the self, a far cry from Kayin's offering. Kayin saw life as a gift given to allow us to assume the posture of the eternal taker. That path creates neither connection nor joy. It is that way of thinking that made him offer what he didn't really need or want.

The idolaters also offered sacrifices. These seem, at first glance, to be the same as those we offer. While they, like we, wish to give of themselves and that which is precious to them, the nature of their gift is inherently distancing. Why?

Focusing on the Sun

In *Tehillim*, Hashem is compared to the sun. The image that is created by that metaphor is one in which He is the Source of all reality, which is compared to the sun's rays. From our vantage point in this world, however, we find ourselves dazzled by the splendor and grandeur of the world. More often than not, we focus on the sun's rays with little awareness of their source, the sun itself.

The Maharal points out that the effect of offering a *korban* is returning to the Cause, that which is His. When the idolaters offered sacrifices it was their way of expressing wonder, not at the sun, but

the joy of finding the source

at the luminosity of its rays.

Therefore, throughout the narration of the sacrificial offerings, the divine name that is used is the name *Hashem*, not *Elokim*. The simple meaning of the name *Elokim* is "Master of forces," the God we see through the curtain of His creations. Our focus is to be not on what Hashem does, but on Who He is. What this tells us is that the thrust of the act is uncovering Hashem's unity, bringing us to envision the sun rather than the rays. How does this come about?

Rabbi Shamshon Rafael Hirsch takes us through the various steps in the performance of the offerings and gives us insight into their meaning.

The first step is the selection of the type of animal to be offered. The specific nature of various *korbanos* required different species. We are seeking to uplift the animal spirit that lives within us and give it new connection to its source. The animal soul has varying aspects, and therefore the Torah mandates that various animals be used.

The bull is a strong animal used for work, while the cow has similar strength but is associated with nurturing, as its meat and milk feed us. Thus the sacrifices that rededicate our energy to Hashem will feature the bull or the cow.

The ram is an animal that instinctively takes the lead; therefore it will be used in sacrifices that refine the direction of our leadership instincts. The goat is used in sin offerings. The reason for this, presented by Rabbi Hirsch, is that the goat spends its life exclusively in the pursuit of desire; it cannot be put to useful work.

Conversely, sheep instinctively follow. Therefore, they are selected for use in the Shabbos and Festival offerings in which we reiterate our bond with Hashem and our yearning to pursue His will and let Him lead us through our lives.

The birds that were offered symbolize our willingness to bring Hashem into our lives even at our moments of greatest vulnerability. In a certain sense, we Jews, like the birds, are the eternal prey of the nations, which are compared to predatory animals. Beyond that level of comparison, each of us in the course of life arrives at moments of defenselessness. At those moments, when we can no longer deny our vulnerability, we can draw close to Him.

Thus the selection of the animal gives us focus on the specific area where we are seeking to draw closer to Hashem.

Closing the Door

The next step is walking the animal and putting one's hands upon it. This creates a bond between the person offering the sacrifice and the animal. The next step is the actual slaughter of the animal. The blood would be placed in holy vessels and then poured in a prescribed way that would vary in accordance to the specific *korban* being offered.

The Torah tells us that the blood of an animal contains the essence of its soul. We are therefore instructed not to eat meat until the blood has been removed through kashering. When sacrifices are offered, however, the blood is not rejected but placed in holy vessels. What this tells us symbolically is that our animalistic tendencies do not need to be repudiated. We do not have to deny our frailties. Rather, they have to be rechanneled.

The final step in all sacrifices is that at least some portion of the animal must be burned on the altar. While the specifics vary from offering to offering, ranging from the entire animal to a three-way division between the owner, the *kohanim* (priests), and the *mizbei'ach* (altar), in every case at least some portion of the animal is burned.

The Or haChaim explains that in truth we deserve to be treated in accordance with the way we define ourselves. When we sin, we are redefining ourselves as human beasts. No one sins without falling victim to the instinctive responses of an animal. Translated into human terms, this is a *ruach shtus*, "spirit of folly." When this happens, the logical consequence should be dying the final and meaningless death of an animal.

However, the spiritual power of the *korbanos* was so great that it could turn an "animal" back into a human. Making this happen required at least minimal willingness on the part of the human to make trade-offs that could be difficult. This is reflected by the Torah's demand that at least part of the animal be burned.

In order to have an honest relationship with Hashem, we must close doors as well as open them. For instance, with a person who has a stronger-than-usual need for validation, we can observe how *the joy of finding the source*

the act of offering a *korban* can change him. What the Torah will demand of him is that he acknowledges this weakness. Once it is acknowledged, the next step is finding a "holy vessel." For one person, that may mean taking a public and active role in a *chesed* organization; for another, it may mean finding a channel for a talent or ability that will provide him with a sense of accomplishment and confirmation of his value as a person. While there may be a sense here of a dual agenda, the very act of finding a permitted and desirable channel demonstrates that underneath the *lo li-Shma* lies a powerful passion for *li-Shma*.

There are, however, easily accessible means of self-validation that must be rejected. Making verbal (and unfavorable) comparisons between oneself and others is one of them. Living life as the eternal victim with the usual litany of blaming and complaining is another. Acquiring status by living at a standard above one's means with the inevitable financial game-playing is another.

When we choose to fill the empty space within us by any of these means, the results are inevitably positive in the short term. It is for that very reason that we willingly bury ourselves under the barrage of ego and materialism they entail. In order to free ourselves from the burden they create, we must learn to close the door. We must recognize that this way we are seeing the rays rather than the sun.

The Shelah points out that all sin comes from fragmentation. All these possibilities must be burned on the altar of one's heart. In the time of the *Mishkan* and the *Beis HaMikdash*, the fire within us was met by a fire from Above. The effect was the simultaneous dispersion of evil and the recognition of Hashem. The unification of fire with fire brought light and joy into the world to a degree that we cannot even begin to imagine today.

We can at times sense a waft of the fragrance of the *korbanos*. In our prayers, when we describe the sun itself using the same words usually used to describe only its rays, we are there once more. When we observe the elevation of the physical and the reunification of fire with fire we are there.

Sometimes it pays to borrow a little *arbis*!

CHAPTER THIRTY
breaking through the barriers

SHE HAD NO reason to treasure the memory. The family gathering was just one more of the frequent get-togethers that characterized her warm though not particularly functional extended family.

The apartment was spotlessly clean for Pesach — but that was the norm for the other 364 days of the year, too. Leslie's grandmother would tolerate nothing less. The family pictures on the wall were dwarfed by the testimonial received from the Workman's Circle acknowledging her grandfather's years of activity on behalf of the society. The paean to progress that every immigrant to the United States yearned to hear, as testimony to the upward mobility of their progeny, was simultaneously deafening and silent.

Over half a century had passed since Bailkeh had first set eyes on Ellis Island as a seventeen-year-old refugee from what she perceived as reminiscent of the Egyptian exile. Leslie was the physical embodiment of the fruit of freedom which she and Sol had envisioned and for which they had toiled. Surrounded by children and grandchildren, the opaque illusion of freedom blinded Bailkeh to the fact that Egypt had followed her over the ocean.

Leslie's memories of the Seder were laced with a feeling of boredom. The Maxwell House Haggados lay silently on the table. The fanciful cover illustrations of the splitting of the sea was even further from Leslie's day-to-day life than the continually unfolding biography of Bailkeh's family.

As seats were taken and conversation dimmed, Uncle Max nodded to Leslie's brother, Steve, to begin the Seder by asking the four questions. He did so and looked expectantly at Uncle Max and Grandpa. Neither of them had any idea of what the answers to

breaking through the barriers

the questions were. As cheder boys they had known. That period of their lives had ended before either of them was four feet tall. The meal was the main feature of the evening and was no disappointment. Leslie leaned back in her seat as the Seder concluded with "*Chad Gadya.*"

As the years passed, Leslie, now Leah, noticed her memories of childhood had changed as she changed. One thing was for sure: It is easier to say no to the past, which by its nature is vivid and defined, than it is to say yes to unfolding potential, which is by its nature neither.

In her early years in the *frum* world, she would alternate between distance and denial when recalling her families' celebration of Pesach. When asked, she would vaguely mention that the family was somewhat traditional and had a Seder. The gulf between Grandma Bailkeh's world and that of the religious families Leah had come to know was too unbridgeable for mere words to span. Leslie saw no reason to try to negotiate a path between her past and her present. Rather than seeing herself as a link on an unending chain, she saw herself as a beginning.

The recognition that her view was myopic came through teaching her children. Reiterating the well-known *aggadah* that the Jews were redeemed in the merit of their having retained their language, their clothing, and their names suddenly brought her back to her childhood. The rich Yiddish, the traditional foods, were a reflection of the same yearning that no doubt was part of the collective heart and soul of her ancestors in Egypt. As the Maharal points out, even at the forty-ninth level of *tumah*, when they had shut every door, they still knew who they wished they were and where they had come from. This awareness, no matter how deeply hidden within the recesses of the heart, is always there. Hashem on His side responds to our hidden yearning for Him. Let us look at the Haggadah to see His love for us and let it touch the subtle love we foster for Him within us.

The Nature of Miracles

He loves us far more than we love ourselves. When we had lost the ability to look in the mirror and see beauty, He did miracles. He knew that in order for us to collectively redefine ourselves we had to experience the plagues. They would tell us who we are not, and then we would be free to discover who we are.

The Haggadah narrates a difference of opinion between Rabbi Eliezer and Rabbi Akiva. Rabbi Eliezer maintains that each plague had four components, while Rabbi Akiva contends that each had five. Each scholar supports his view with proofs from the appropriate verse.

The Maharal explains that there is far more to this difference of opinion, as always, than dry scholarly debate. In fact, what they are debating is the nature of miracles and the way they impact on humans.

The function of a miracle is to redefine reality for us by giving us greater access to Hashem's Presence. The beginning of all miracles takes place in a realm that we can scarcely discuss, let alone envision. There are worlds that are higher than the physical world, where space and time limit our horizons. In the world of *nivdal*, transcendence, there is no partition to artificially divide the realm of the Creator from His creations. Once a miracle descends from there to this world, Rabbi Eliezer maintains, it is limited by the conventional restrictions that define this world. Have we not all heard stories of people looking miracles in the face and flinching? This happens when even the force of a miracle is too weak to penetrate a heart that cannot free itself from seeing physical cause and effect as being all that reality has to offer. Therefore, Rabbi Eliezer sees the number four as definitive of a miraculous occurrence that is held back by the limitations of this world.

Throughout the Hagaddah, the number four recurs. There are four sons, four questions, four cups of wine, and four expressions of redemption. What the number represents is limitation. The four directions reflect the possibility of enclosure and restriction on the simplest physical level. It also hints at a more subtle and suffocating form of spiritual limitation. What chokes our inner yearning is what the Maharal calls *ribui*, multiplicity. When we fail to find the relationship between cause and effect, the unfortunate tendency is to either deny or ignore cause.

In Egypt we were subjugated to every possible restriction. Emotionally, physically, and spiritually we were choked. Rabbi

Eliezer therefore maintains that every plague had to break through the barriers of restriction that are inherent to this world. Thus, he would maintain, Hashem was using the multiplicity of the world to create a new definition for us of who we are — and Who He is. He was telling us that He is here, that He cares, and that He can make the rules and break them. He would open our hearts no matter how tightly we had closed them.

Rabbi Akiva sees the definition of miracles as the number five. In order for the number four (which defines the multiplicity and restrictive nature of this world) to have any interpretability, the number five comes into play. By creating a center, the four directions are suddenly defined as a group and not as chaos. Rabbi Akiva, therefore, would maintain that what makes a miraculous event incorruptible is the fact that it shows Hashem's unity with the world. The main message is that He was and is with us all the time. In the midst of the suffering and the emancipation, His Presence is unchanging. He is at the center of all possibilities.

On Pesach we experience the spiritual adventure of living with the recognition of both symbols. We see Hashem breaking the bonds of every form of our servitude and simultaneously having been with us all along within the restrictions of that same servitude. Thus the four cups of wine which hint at the four expressions of redemption tell us what we reject ("I have taken you from," "I have rescued you from") as well as what we can be ("I have redeemed you," "I have taken you"). We find Hashem amid the suffering and love demonstrated by the redemption.

Beauty and Song

The Maharal tells us that the four cups parallel the four matriarchs. Although the matriarchs were four in number, the letter *hey*, which equals five, is the symbol of all things feminine. It is the letter that turns a noun from masculine form into feminine form. It turns *ish* (man) into *ishah* (woman). Let us examine the specific role of the Jewish women in Egypt to see the way in which the symbol of four and that of five come together.

The faith that was demonstrated by the women in Egypt says it all. They saw the Source of life in the midst of death. Where the

Egyptians sought to redefine life in terms of meaninglessness and ugliness, women like Yocheved and Miriam defined life by beauty and song. The image of Hashem and His eternal presence was never eclipsed by the horrors they experienced. For women such as these, the ability to take in both that which is symbolized by four and that which is symbolized by five was a day-to-day living reality.

Our failures are neither as tragic nor as dramatic as Bailkeh's. We never saw the world of exile — where freedom means indulging in the "pursuit of happiness," even in ways that contradict Torah values — as a world of redemption. Perhaps our parents (or grandparents) never choked on the hopes that the Statue of Liberty inspired in the hearts of so many. Perhaps they, too, saw sparks of life in the ashes that covered Europe half a century ago. When we observe our own lives, we must allow ourselves another perhaps. Perhaps we never stood in Bailkeh's shoes. But if we want true and lasting redemption, that is not enough. We must learn to step into the shoes of Miriam and Yocheved. We must break the barriers of our servitude to what is evil and pursue the freedom — the freedom to keep the Torah.

CHAPTER THIRTY-ONE
does too much freedom restrict us?

THE TEMPTATION TO resist freedom is almost irresistible. As I write these words, I find myself facing two blue eyes that fix themselves on mine pleading for release from the confines of her own seven year old consciousness. She has been back from her pre-Pesach playgroup for about ten minutes. In that time, she ate lunch and gave me a brief rundown of Life in Playgroup. Now there is "nothing to do." All eternity looms before her as the eternal cry of "What should I do now?" passes her lips. What she is in need of is structure.

Living with no clear boundaries is complex. The marriage of body and soul is not always an easy one. Since the time of Adam and Chavah, who experienced their bodies and souls as separate and distinct entities, we have lived in a state of disharmony. The soul is compared to a flame that constantly reaches upward. The body is compared to a wick that holds the flame, grounding it to this world, offering the soul tangible means of self-expression. However, it simultaneously holds the flight of the soul down with its never-ending needs and desires. The question we all face is, which one do we choose to be — the flame that ascends or the wick that anchors it?

The only possible resolution is using the body to give the soul the possibility of physical self-expression. When we lack structured means of doing so, we find ourselves face to face with this conflict.

Channels of actualization are opened to us continually by Hashem, but it takes imagination and resolution to make use of them. Otherwise, the question of what to do looms as one of the least comfortable and most significant that we will ever ask. It is also a question that we almost never ask consciously.

When the body is silenced by satiation, the restlessness of the soul is felt rather than understood. An all-absorbing discontent can be as genuine as the discontent felt by the body when it is neglected or hungry. This could have been the reality facing the Jews as they left Egypt.

It wasn't. When we focus on the mitzvah of *sefiras ha'omer*, counting the days of the omer between Pesach and Shavuos, we gain a different perspective on who we are. It throws light onto the nature of our inherent capacity for discontent and the resolution of disharmony by allowing us to walk the path of our forefathers as they left Egypt. We learn the steps that made their journey successful. We learn to engage our bodies and souls simultaneously and thereby make sense of our yearning.

Opening the Fifty Doors to Freedom

The Ba'al HaAkeidah tells us that yearning has two components. One is pain; the other is hope. We felt both as we left Egypt. The recognition of Hashem's involvement with us and His love for us provided us with the hope that the inarticulate "more" would be satisfied in the course of the journey upon which we embarked. It is a journey that is relevant to us today, as it is made by each one of us moment by moment. We are commanded to constantly remember the Exodus. This reflects the fact that we are continually emerging from both the limitations we have created for ourselves and those that are inherent to the nature of living in a world which is defined by its disharmony.

Doors that open the possibility of meaningful integration of all our capacities are constantly being presented to us. We can open them or we can ignore them. The most horrific of all possibilities is that our fear of failure will cause us to close them so tightly that we can begin to believe that there is no meaning to be discovered. We then despair and despise ourselves as we endeavor to retreat from life.

The Shelah haKodesh tells us that the fifty times the Exodus is mentioned in the Torah is meaningful. Each mention is a hint at a door we had closed at one point and later opened.

The number fifty is an allusion to man's capacity to express

does too much freedom restrict us?

himself harmoniously. How so? Let us focus for a moment on the significance of numbers. The Maharal maintains that when something is true, it is by its definition true on every level. Thus if an idea is "true" philosophically but not mathematically, it is not true at all. Therefore, when the Torah gives us a number upon which we can focus, it is never just an interesting diversion. Rather, it is part of a greater truth. In fact, Hashem gives us the ability to use numbers not only to facilitate the physical conquest of the world, but primarily as a tool that allows us to divide massive concepts into digestible fragments. The number fifty, like all numbers, reflects a specific part of the greater whole. It is used to symbolize the ways by which Hashem's image is expressed by Him and mirrored by our souls, which are in His image. What does this mean?

The part of us that is a direct counterpart of the Creator is what we mean when we use the word *soul*. When we emulate Him, when we imitate His attributes, we are expressing this Godly image. These attributes, called *middos* or *sefiros*, were revealed during the seven days of Creation. The word *sefirah* is related to the verb *le-saper*, "to tell." The Creation, in a certain sense, is Hashem's story of Himself to the degree that we humans can grasp it. Each of the seven *middos* He revealed interact with each other and lead us to a picture of reality that is greater than the forty-nine components that result from combining these *middos*. Thus the number fifty symbolizes Godliness. It represents the whole picture. And it is found in miniature within us as well. We discover our souls as we respond to life. When we use our insight to examine the external realities that face us, and act on them in a Godly way, we can give expression to these *middos*.

The fifty mentions of the Exodus hint at fifty ways that Hashem liberates us. He gives us the opportunity to live lives that express our *middos* and use our bodies. This is how we can develop an integrated and harmonious lifestyle.

We can, however, deceive ourselves into wallowing in illusory freedom and silencing the soul into submission. When there are no limitations placed on the body's expression, it takes up the entire stage. The Maharal points out that denying either the body or the soul is not our purpose. Integration and concordant symmetry of the forces within us is the goal. An affirmation of this connection is found in the fact that we count the days between our physical redemption, Pesach, and the ultimate channel by which the soul finds its goal, Shavuos. By counting, we join the two potentially opposing forces.

The Midrash tells us, "If there is no flour, there is no Torah; if there is no Torah, there is no flour." The act of counting elevates the "flour," the physical, and gives the Torah a bond to the physical world. The doors are revealed, and it is now up to us to open them.

The Sefas Emes tells us that the key to opening the doors is rectifying the *middos* we have in common with Hashem. This is the deeper meaning of the *mishnah*, "*Derech eretz* precedes the Torah." Each day of *sefirah* presents us with illumination from Above that gives us the strength to move foreward more than at any other time. Even so, the Shem MiShmuel comments, we cannot hope in one day to rectify a flaw in our *middos* that is so deep and damaging that it may take a lifetime to heal. What we can do is reach a point in which we have enough pain and enough hope that we retain within us the spirit of yearning for direction and clarity. It is then that we can submit ourselves to Hashem and let Him heal us.

The *Sefirah* Connection

The physical and spiritual sides of redemption take place through structure. The mitzvos provide us with this structure and give us the ability to redirect our *middos*. The first *middah* in the order of the *sefiros* is the *middah* of *chesed*, lovingkindness. How can we do the inner work that enables us to move ourselves with greater *sheleimus* to the halachos of *chesed*?

The more we value our ability to become people who are significant and bearers of Hashem's image, the more we will love ourselves and others. This is not the love that is a cause and manifestation of self-indulgence. It is the common link we share with Hashem — a materialization of our love for Him.

The death of the disciples of Rabbi Akiva is a tragic reflection of how any breakage in the process of this linkage affects all its components. They did not honor each other to the degree that their ability to see both the divinity and the Torah within them should have merited.

Their level is so far beyond ours that what we refer to as their lack of mutual respect is far from the way that phrase translates into our daily lives. They did not push each other on the bus nor marginalize each other because of their individuality. Their mistakes were infinitely more subtle, but invariably sourced in the same lack of inner equanimity. The two examples given above of mutual lack of respect in our society are far more extreme but have the same cause as that which affected Rabbi Akiva's disciples: both they and we suffer from disharmony.

The Torah they learned ideally would give them absolute balance within themselves. The natural indication of this balance would be their responding to everyone with the kind of respect that could only be born of integration and harmony.

The Hebrew word for "honor," *kavod*, has the same numerical value as the Hebrew word *lev*, "heart." True recognition of the emotional integrity of our fellow man will ensure that the *kavod* we give them is authentic. The fact that the death of Rabbi Akiva's students took place within the first thirty-two days of the omer brings this truth home to us. Thirty-two is the numerical value of both *kavod* and *lev*.

Let us use the power of the days that are before us to be more alive, more connected, more harmonious. Let us bring this to our relationships with Hashem and with ourselves and with everyone we encounter. Let us teach ourselves to be less afraid of freedom. Let us learn to regard it as an open door. Let us use the time of *sefirah* to find the opportunity to make the kind of connections with others that are selfless and are not reflections of the endless pursuit of our own needs. Let us reach a higher place, to Hashem Himself. Let us never fear the open door.

CHAPTER THIRTY-TWO
recycling our kedushah

RECYCLING NEWSPAPERS MEANS different things to different people. For a brief while, recycling in the Jerusalem neighborhood of Har Nof meant placing papers in a specially designated receptacle. There is another form of recycling. This takes place when everything old is presented once more as new. The repetition of scandals, wars, and the ebb and flow of business life in the secular press that somehow manage to be simultaneously banal and lurid are a form of this type of recycling. I personally have no doubt that replacing the headlines of 2000 with those from 1995 would probably escape the notice of many readers.

The trivialization of life's meaning is the invariable result of allowing one's sense of truth and eternity to be redefined. Everything that is unimportant seems vital, and everything that is fleeting seems everlasting. We end up confusing death with life. As we know, death is the ultimate form of *tumah*, impurity. Hashem is the supreme Source of life. If we cannot discern which is which in our daily lives, we are left with the transience of last year's headlines as our idea of what is truly meaningful.

The Kuzari offers us an interesting take on the nature of *tumah*. He says the possibility of denying the inherent spark of eternity and holiness in any experience is what reduces it to impurity. Thus it is impossible to define impurity without first coming to terms with *kedushah*, true sanctity.

We use the term in many contexts. Let us see how we can sharpen our ability to define and thereby identify *kedushah* when we see it.

Maximizing Our Kedushah

The Ramban tells us in his essay on *emunah* and *bitachon*, faith and trust, that *kedushah* is a state of being that allows a person to receive Hashem's blessing. Before we discuss how *kedushah* can bring us blessing, we must define blessing. Often we confuse blessing with random good wishes. If we approach the word *berachah* from that perspective, we are really lost when we "bless Hashem" by saying, "*Baruch Atah.*"

Berachah is, rather, an act that generates maximization of potential. Thus, when we bless Hashem, we are attuning ourselves to the fact that He is the source of everything that gives us pleasure and meaning. The recognition of this fact maximizes our experience in living. We validate Hashem's plan in creating a world in which we find the joy of discovery and connection with Him. Thus we can bless Hashem. Hashem has given us a world that is full of the potential of *berachah*. Through living lives of *kedushah*, we maximize our potentials as human beings; we put ourselves in a state that enables us to receive blessing.

Ramban gives us practical examples in various places throughout *Chumash*, as well as in his masterful commentary on *Parashas Kedoshim*. One example of *kedushah* is refining the body by eating in a sanctified manner. Few activities are as transient as eating. Anyone who has faced a kitchen after a *simchah* knows how briefly the food was enjoyed. It too, however, can lead to rediscovering one's eternal soul. This requires *kedushah* in both attitude and action.

In our attitude there should be commitment to recognizing Hashem's goodness. By providing us with food that is not only nutritious but beautiful and fragrant, He reveals His compassion. Momentarily feeling the joy of being beloved can change our attitude toward the food. The gift is no longer separate from the Giver. This moment of recognition redefines the entire process. We not only see ourselves in a different light, but our attitude toward the food itself changes. When we observe the nature of the gift, we come to recognize that we are taking a life form that is less "alive" in the ultimate sense than we are and elevating it. By converting the energy, we absorb the food into part of a journey that binds us to Hashem. The food becomes part of the flesh and blood of the person who eats it. Whatever the person does is the ultimate destiny of the food, as well as its purpose. The food in a certain sense is similar to a sacrificial offering.

There are attitudes that are antithetical to *kedushah*. When we eat or otherwise consume anything material, we are filling a lack. We at times seek to fulfill needs that food could never fulfill by letting the pleasure of eating take on its own life. When this happens, rather than experiencing Hashem's love for us, eating degenerates into a parody of self-nurturing, in which His Presence is either clouded or denied. The need for connection is not fulfilled (after all, we want to find that which is lacking within ourselves, not just "find ourselves" again and again). At this point, we are neither elevating ourselves nor the food we consume. This is, in fact, a degradation of the food Hashem created. Like all inanimate creations, its silence is a reflection of awareness and awe of Hashem. We are, in a certain sense, insulting its very essence. Rather than *kedushah*, we are left with *tumah*.

The actions that open up the possibility of blessing include both the positive (saying a *berachah* in a way in which both the one eating and the food itself is maximized) and the negative (not eating foods forbidden by the Torah). The word *asur* means "forbidden" only idiomatically; its literal meaning is "tied down." The channel by which the food at hand is elevated is the change that takes place within us when we exercise self-restraint.

While eating is no doubt a frequent activity, the constancy of our talking is even more incessant. Speech is uplifted not only by refraining from the *asur*, but by using its enormous potential for blessing. Speech has the potential to unveil the moral goodness of both the speaker and the listener. A bond between them is then created that will leave them both far more human than before.

The Ramban uses strong language when presenting us a picture of the consequences of rejecting *kedushah*. Repudiation of eternity takes place in many forms. It can, to quote him directly, involve being a drunkard on kosher wine, a glutton on kosher food, or among those who "soil themselves with luxury." Let us understand the last phrase more deeply.

Kedushah in Attitude and in Action

The opposite of maximization is (sure enough) minimization, becoming less. When a person feels that the part of him that yearns for more can be satisfied with more food or more status or more possessions of beauty and value, there is an inevitable result: the person's humanity has been marginalized. We are made in Hashem's image. It is His Face we yearn to see; settling for anything less is a curse. We are reduced to a level that is far less than that which our humanity and our heritage offer.

People at times confuse *kedushah* with deprivation. The vocabulary used is misleading. The word *deprivation* implies curse, a diminishment of what life holds out for us to take. But rejection of illusion is never deprivation. *Kedushah* is the conduit to *berachah*, to true and enduring abundance. Nothing could be further from deprivation than the rejection of the spiritual anesthesia provided by escapist extravagance, where we lose sight of the Giver and cannot take pleasure in a gift that is illusory.

I recently saw an ad for a watch that cost seventeen thousand dollars. What made it unique is that it was mechanical. It had to be wound. It was handmade without a quartz movement and took six months to produce. It told time almost as well as conventional watches do.

The holy Alshich would see it as the opposite of *kedushah*.

He defines *kedushah* as Hashem's unity. Anything that brings us closer to becoming one with Him is holy; anything that fosters the illusion of separation from Him is *tumah*. The ultimate possibility of separation from Hashem is not one that is motivated by external experience. What creates *tumah* is ego. We are capable of becoming so finely attuned to our feelings and thoughts that there is no room left either for Hashem or for other people. We can even descend to a point of senseless hatred in which we cannot tolerate others simply because they are not us. We blind ourselves to the fact that there is a transcendent unity that binds us together.

Let us use the physical body as a model. In the human body every cell is itself, yet very much part of the entire system, and the entire system is composed of innumerable individual cells. Similarly, Hashem's *middos* when manifest in people are very much "themselves."

We observe that there are people whose inner eyes are directed away from themselves. They will let their vision encompass Hashem's presence in the world and see Him in others. Since their direction is one in which they move away from themselves and toward others, they are identified by us as people of *chesed*.

There are others whose inner eye is directed toward themselves. They are sensitive to every possible imperfection within themselves and correct them with rectitude and honesty. They are able to put their every feeling and every thought to the scrutiny of their conscious mind. Since their direction is inward and requires great self-restraint, we identify them as people of strength. However, both types are defined within the framework of Godliness (these *middos* being the archetypes of all others).

When we become overly focused on the differences, the invariable effect is losing the greater unity that encompasses both. It is this form of egotism, this exquisite awareness of self, that is the ultimate *tumah*.

Only Torah can take us beyond our ego to the greater picture. It moves us toward relinquishing our egotism and adapting the most expanding and maximizing blessing of all: Hashem's truth. We can choose life! We can move beyond the patterns we have adapted. We may have fallen into patterns of response that reflect the mindless and soulless *tumah* of the exile. Their death-bound definition of significance can be eclipsed by the Torah of life. We can use these days to build bridges within ourselves that will reconnect to our higher selves, to our fellow Jews and to Hashem Himself.

CHAPTER THIRTY-THREE
crossing the bridge

THE CORRIDOR OF the hospital was surreal. There is nothing unusual about that. By its very nature, hospital corridors confront us with a sense of our powerlessness in the face of the human body's unreliability. There is nothing that is more our own, yet simultaneously less our own, than our flesh and blood. Medical emergencies force us into the recognition of our own helplessness.

One of the advantages of the emergency room is its pervasively chaotic and at times inefficient atmosphere. The temptation to avoid reality by handing over care and responsibility for our bodies to the attending staff is completely abated by their obvious (and very human) limitations. They are neither all powerful nor all compassionate. Our openness to recognizing that we are not in their hands or at their mercy diminishes, inevitable in a society intent in looking in the mirror and seeing itself and no other. When this occurs, even the brittle layer of civility we hold on to so tenaciously sometimes cracks. Vulnerability and pride ooze out.

"You Must Stop Crying"

I received The Phone Call one early morning. There was nothing unexpected in its contents. Reb Michael had been critically ill for what would be a lifetime in the eyes of a toddler. Medical crises were as much a part of his lifestyle as teething crises are part of the lives of others. Mazal, his wife of half a century, was on the other end of the line. Her cries were unintelligible, which made them all the more articulate. A nurse took the phone from her and told me to come as soon as I could. Almost as an afterthought, she asked, "Are you a relative?"

Since the Hebrew word for "relative" is *karov*, which literally means "near," I unhesitatingly answered *yes*. Indeed, Mazal's life and mine had been intertwined ever since she entered our family as a babysitter over twenty-one years ago. She was with us for joyous and tragic occasions. Until the inevitable process of aging made the gulf between her and our babies unbridgeable, Mazal was there. Even after she stopped babysitting for us she would come. We were the replacements for the children she never had. She would drop by and leave enormous pots of soup. She would be there the day of a *simchah* and patiently teach me how to coax a bit more flavor from the motionless ingredients on the counter.

The only presence that took up more space in her heart was Reb Michael. In his illness, he was simultaneously her husband and her infant. She sat by his bedside from seven in the morning till seven at night. As the cumbersome hand of illness snuffed out his independence, his every wish became her day's work. When the combination of intense closeness and intense suffering caused sparks of friction to surface, the fire never consumed the bonds of loyalty that held them together.

I dreaded the inevitable moment when I would come face to face with her deep sorrow. I knew there was no way I would be able to escape into the sterile diversions provided by the emergency room.

When I arrived, Mazal was standing near the desk. The nurse's relief at my coming was undisguised. She would now be able to resume the more familiar role of trying to control events. I had liberated her from a role I relished no more than she. There was nothing to say; there was no way to "fix" things any longer.

After a few calls and a few minutes, Mazal's sister appeared. Ruchama carried her years with ponderous dignity and was at home with silence. She took Mazal's hand in hers and gently but firmly reminded her, "It is *chol hamo'ed* You must stop crying."

No questions were asked. Her deep sobbing stopped immediately; the mourning was restricted to the recesses of Mazal's heart. Mirrored in her eyes was the heavy closing curtain on what had been the main event of her lifetime. Her tears remained unshed until the holiday had passed and *shiva* could begin.

Connection through Wisdom

I knew from where she had drawn all her resources. Faith in Hashem was what she had breathed in the air of her native Spanish Morocco. The women who inhabited her country in those days had no educational opportunities. The government school only offered them the option of training as ladies' maids or seamstresses; literacy was not part of the curriculum. Mazal's parents taught her by providing her with an example that was as unswerving as the laws of nature. She would have no questions, because the depth of her faith had already provided her with all the answers she needed. Both would remain unspoken, because speech encloses and limits by its very finiteness.

I could not help but wonder what those of us who see the world through the prism of ideas and information would draw upon if we were in her situation. In his introduction to his commentary on *Parashas Emor*, Rabbeinu Bachya elucidates the process of putting ideas into words without losing their depth or integrity.

He brings the verse from *Mishlei* in which Shlomo says that "one whose words are direct [has] lips that kiss." He explains that the simple meaning is that the pleasure of having one's questions answered is so great that it leaves the questioner feeling as though he has been kissed.

On a deeper level, the verse is a parable. The spiritual and intellectual connection between the giver and recipient of wisdom creates a dimension of connection that is analogous to a kiss. The word for "lips," *sefasayim*, also means "seashore." Wisdom is compared in its infinity to the vastness of the ocean. A wise person can simultaneously touch the infinite and find words that bring this wisdom down to the world of the finite, the "shore." Filtering is an inherent part of phrasing. Every word tells us not only what something is but what it isn't. For instance, if I describe an object as a pen, I am also saying that it is nothing other than a pen. I am "outlining" the object and limiting its scope in order to define it tangibly. Thus the true delight of learning intellectually is that it brings about connection to the infinite by using the finite. With speech, one can touch the infinity of wisdom.

Rabbeinu Bachya points out that the absolute nature of our longing for connection to the infinite once we have experienced it is far more profound than our desire for anything that limits or restricts our access to it, such as physical pleasures. This is played out in the manner of death that was experienced by Moshe, Aharon, Miriam, and the patriarchs — Avraham, Yitzchak, and Yaakov. Their unsullied closeness to Hashem finally released them from the confines of material existence. This is in stark contrast to the normal process of dying. Therefore *Emor* begins with the laws by which the *Kohanim*, priests, are instructed to avoid all contact with the dead.

The finality of physical death to most of us generates more yearning for "one more day" in the physical world. Thus death is a blockage for all but the most righteous, who do not have *tumah*, impurity, attached to their bodies, even in death; their connection between the infinite and finite worlds is too absolute for that to happen.

How do we, who are so far from the spiritual level of the true tzaddikim, the most righteous, achieve this connection to the infinite? The answer is, as Rabbeinu Bachya says, in the delight we experience through learning true wisdom. Even though it must be filtered by our limiting need for articulate understanding, it connects to the same infinity Mazal knows without words.

The Spark of Infinity

There are additional means of union with the unfathomable infinity of Hashem. As the *parashah* tells us, it is through finding it in the very midst of the confines of time. We can discover it through keeping Shabbos and the holidays.

The mitzvah of keeping Shabbos is mentioned almost by way of introduction to the holidays. The Maharal points out that there is a definable relationship between Shabbos and the holidays. There are seven holidays — two days of Pesach, one of Shavuos, one of Rosh HaShanah (although there are two days of Rosh HaShanah it is considered one long day rather than two separate ones), one of Yom Kippur, and two days of Sukkos. Shabbos, referred to as the "seventh day," is the source of all that is symbolized by the number seven. Each of the holidays is one aspect of that which is symbolized by that number. What does the number seven hint at?

The limiting, physical side of our reality is illustrated by the number six. Every physical object has six sides (the four directions, plus up and down). Seven is the innermost dimension that is not mere surface. It is the spark of infinity that is hidden even within the constrictions imposed by time and space. In fact, this is a reflection of the physical world having been created in six days. On the seventh, Hashem created the potential for connection to His infinity by building a bridge between the world of restriction to the world of transcendence. Each holiday reveals a particular means by which the connection between Hashem and the Jewish people plays out.

But how do we learn to hear the voice of Shabbos and the holidays, which are often silenced by the blaring, earsplitting sound of self? We must learn to listen. This means, at times, putting an end to the on-again-off-again game of Trivial Pursuit that can fill our lives. We need inspiration to remind us of what it is we really want to hear. We must look until we find it within ourselves.

How can this be done? The Maharal comments on the mitzvah that in *Parashas Emor* precedes that of keeping the holidays: sanctification of Hashem's Name. He quotes Rashi, who says that one who offers his life to sanctify Hashem's Name must do so with the expectation of death and must not rely on miracles to save him. If he does this, miracles happen for him. The reason for this, the Maharal says, is that a person who is willing to sacrifice his life with no expectation of a miracle is already holy; no real change will take place through his death. Since he is already "listening," he hears Hashem's voice. Hashem will make Himself apparent, because the human half of the bridge has already been built.

When we live as Mazal does, with an awareness of the Creator, in the food that she cooks and in every word that comes out of her mouth, then the limitations of what the rest of us can only move aside by listening to the wisdom of Torah fall aside. We must try to find the Mazal in ourselves, as well as the faithful listener.

CHAPTER THIRTY-FOUR
the source of humility

GOING TO MERON on Lag BaOmer is an unforgettable experience. The word *unforgettable* conjures up various images, both positive and negative; the journey to Meron justifies both. The buses are brimming with an exceptional representation of the Jewish people. The music blares, playing the song "Bar Yochai."

Every possible nationality our two-thousand-year struggle has exposed us to finds its articulation in the variations of language and lifestyle represented by my fellow passengers. We are, nonetheless, all making very much the same journey. We are drawn to a destination that is at once esoteric and demystified. We are celebrating the life and death of a man whose story is known, but whose essence eludes us. We are on a pilgrimage that awakens within our collective heart a dormant awareness of the nature of the world.

On Mount Meron, Rabbi Shimon bar Yochai's gravesite, the revealed, rationally accessible world pales before the world of the spirit. The scene at the foot of the hill is an out-of-season Purim; the gaiety and vitality of people who have come to rejoice reveals that which is usually concealed. Amid the combination of a Middle-Eastern bazaar and a sort of Jewish revival there is a spark of genuine exultation in our collective connection to Rabbi Shimon. We are his as much as he is ours.

At times, the ecstasy degenerates into the sort of frivolity that extends the distance between our higher selves and our more accessible selves. The innocence, however, is never far from the surface.

As I climb the hill, the atmosphere changes. It is no longer Purim. The joy of Torah, with its awesome purity, has emerged. Row upon row of dancing Chassidim and Chassidim for the day (or for the moment) experience a level of spiritual exhilaration that takes them beyond time and place.

Finally, children in hand, I enter the gravesite. The profound holiness like that of Yom Kippur at *Ne'ilah*, the closing prayer of that day, is immediately felt. I find the intensity overwhelming. The physical crowding adds to the inescapability of confrontation with sacredness. There is literally nowhere to turn.

I find myself quietly singing "Bar Yochai" and leaving. It is now my job to answer both my children and myself as the question inevitably surfaces: Why are we here? Why is the anniversary of the departure of Rabbi Shimon bar Yochai from this world commemorated so much more universally than that of other great Sages? Let us first examine the way in which we memorialize the anniversary of a death.

Rabbi Shimon's Last Moments

The customs surrounding the celebration of the anniversary of a death are well known. It is almost impossible to explain them to a person with a poor perspective on life. For a person for whom this world is the only one, there is nothing to celebrate in death. It is seen as an enemy to vanquish in a battle that is inevitably lost. From the perspective of one who sees this world as a precious but transient place for meeting challenges, death is liberation. For a tzaddik, it is the moment of final victory over the forces of evil. For him the enemy can indeed be vanquished.

This was true for Rabbi Shimon. The Zohar describes his death in detail. He was aware that the time for his soul to move beyond the restrictions of this world had come. His final hours were spent revealing the inner light of Torah. His moment of death was indeed a moment of triumph and enlightenment. What kind of a life did he live to merit such luminescence? The Nesivos Shalom gives us insight toward grasping the nature of the Rashbi's greatness.

The Zohar tells us that Rabbi Shimon had the soul of Moshe Rabbeinu. What did they both have in common? What characteristic typified the two of them? The most significant of Moshe's virtues was his humility. It is the only one of his virtues explicitly mentioned in the Torah.

The days between Pesach and Shavuos are days of counting called *sefiras ha'omer*, when we are expected to prepare ourselves for receiving the Torah anew. To that end, each day has a *sefirah*, a characteristic of Hashem, with which we are expected to emulate God and attempt to acquire that trait. The day of Rabbi Shimon's death, Lag BaOmer, is the day on which the characteristics of Hashem that we seek to bring forward from within us is *Hod shebaHod*. The word *hod*, splendor, is related to the word *hoda'ah*, confession, and the word *hodayah*, gratitude. The common denominator shared by these words is the recognition of something beyond self. Thus *hod* is the source of humility. It is this that bound and defined both Moshe and the Rashbi more than any other trait. Let us examine the nature of humility more closely.

The Fallacy of False Humility

We often confuse low self-esteem with humility. When one's faults are allowed to define one's characteristics, the result is low self-esteem. Humility comes not from diminishing ourselves, but by expanding our awareness of God.

We sometimes back away from Hashem because of our hypersensitivity to our faults. Since we are created in God's image and before our birth swore an oath to live a life of righteousness, when our desire to live up to our potential fails us (as is inevitable), we sometimes place the spotlight of our conscience on our flaws. When all that occupies the stage is our faults, we feel that the image of Hashem within us is no longer that which defines us. Rather, the flaw becomes the basis of our identity.

The pain this causes has no parallel. In order to escape the agony of self-hatred, the person who is caught up in this trap seeks to escape. Various forms of "compensations" and illusions are the main means by which the person seeks release from the pain caused by his low self-esteem. He is trapped in fallacy.

Nothing could possibly be farther from true humility. True humility comes from the recognition that everything we are or can envision or experience is an emanation of Hashem's will and therefore sacred. The more awe one has for Hashem's wisdom, will, and presence, the more humbled he will be. Thus it is not in spite of Moshe's great enlightenment that he was on the most profound level of humility but because of it.

Enlightenment at the Rashbi's Grave

The more one suffers from low self-esteem, the more self-protective and closed he will be in encounters with others. The feeling that one is blemished prevents relationships from being authentic, as there is always the fear of being "discovered"; the opposite is true with genuine humility.

The more strongly one can "see" Hashem's light, the more one will project that light onto others. In the same way that the sun's light can reach even the darkest corner because of its strength, the light of a truly humble tzaddik can illuminate even someone who is very distant from Hashem.

We are told, therefore, that Mashiach will truly love even the worst Jew. Mashiach's sensitivity to Hashem's light will find the hidden sparks that are concealed within the recesses of a soul that the person himself may not be aware of.

We can now understand one of the more famous stories about the Rashbi. The Gemara tells us that when the Rashbi and his son Rabbi Elazar left the cave in which they had been hiding for twelve years, they saw people planting their fields. Rabbi Shimon said, "How can these people leave eternal life in pursuit of that which is fleeting?"

Wherever he and his son cast their glance, people went up in flames. They were told then that they must return to the cave. Twelve months later they implored Hashem to release them, appealing to Hashem's justice: "Even the wicked people in Gehinnom are judged for only twelve months," at which point they were released from the cave.

We can't help but wonder how they could possibly have compared themselves to such sinners. The answer is that Hashem did not want them to burn the world with the intensity of their holiness, but rather to endure the defects of the people they met. They should have realized that even though the farmers had abandoned the eternity of the future world for the ephemeral endeavors of this one, they were still holy, still Jews.

It was only when Rabbi Shimon and his son had rectified what for them was a blemish in the development of their characters that they were released from the cave. It was then that their ability to love every single Jew was perfected.

It is for this reason that the Rashbi's *yahrtzeit* (anniversary of death) is different from that of the other tzaddikim, for we all are touched by his light. The place itself where he is buried is also possessed of a special quality. It acts, in a certain sense, as a conductor of light. The myriad of Jews who have streamed to Meron throughout the generations have felt the warmth of the Rashbi's light. The ember of longing for Hashem's light is relit.

Whether or not we put it into words or, harder still, into deeds is, of course, another question. The day itself has within it the power to bring forth the part of us that wants to receive the hidden Torah in the way in which Shavuos has the power to bring forth our yearning for the revealed word of Hashem. Whether or not we can physically be in Meron, let us make a journey that will take us there spiritually. The result can be unforgettable.

CHAPTER THIRTY-FIVE
a glimpse of infinity

IT ISN'T DIFFICULT for me to imagine the horror of being lost in the desert. My sense of direction is such that the possibility of making a fateful wrong turn is never far from my mind when I navigate new turf. The usage of the word *lost*, though, needs clarification.

My initial confusion with the word's application took place when I was in grade school. I have very distinct memories of Mrs. Novick. She was endeavoring (rather futilely) to muster up some excitement in our eight-year-old hearts about Columbus Day. She gave a vivid description of the three ships, the perilous journey, and the climactic moment when America was discovered. With rather thespian elocution, the initial meeting between Columbus's men and some Native Americans was depicted in great detail.

"And that," she concluded, "was the most important discovery made in the Age of Exploration."

I raised my hand. "Where was America before?"

"Before what?" she asked.

"Before they found it," I replied. "Where was it when it was lost?"

I found it difficult to envision an entire population of Indians (let alone an entire continent) aimlessly wandering around Prospect Park. I had unwittingly challenged Mrs. Novick's presentation of human history. She was uncomfortable both with my question and the shallow nature of her answer ("It wasn't really lost..."). I realized that this was one of the many moments where the best answer was to say, "Oh," and nod my head.

The question stayed with me for years. The connotation of *lost* being a term that implies that something is as yet unrevealed to Western eyes is both irrational and ethically unacceptable. It was only years later, when I read the Maharal's comments regarding the Torah being given in the desert, that I came to terms with the true meaning of the words *lost* and *discovered*.

He brings this parable from *Yalkut Shimoni*:

Once there was a king. He entered a metropolis and the awestruck population ran away from him. He entered another, and the same thing happened. He entered a desolate city, and the population came out and praised him. He then declared that this was the place where he would live and establish his monarchy. Thus the mountains and the sea retreated before Hashem, while the desert rejoiced in His Presence. He then said, "This is where My kingdom shall be built, and this is where I shall dwell," and the desert burst forth in song.

Truth: The Whole Picture

What is the meaning of this midrash? The Maharal explains that the *Yalkut* is actually describing to us the nature of developing receptivity toward Hashem. The sea is the physical source of all life. It is, by its nature, delineated by the land that surrounds it — the material and, therefore, finite world. Similarly, the mountains are, in both the literal and figurative sense, the "peak" of the physical world. Both are subject to their calculable limits. In contrast, the desert, with its stark desolation and barrenness, is inviting as a place in which Hashem provides us with a glimpse of the infinity that lies beyond our reach. No visible limitations distort His transcendence.

Various serious thinkers (and also various intellectual escape artists) have tried to reduce the Torah to a rule book for success in the material sphere: Shabbos is wonderful; everyone should have a day off. Honesty is terrific; it keeps the social fabric intact and removes paranoia from one's moment-to-moment inner agenda. Kashrus is the key to health.

While none of these ideas is false, neither are they true in the ultimate sense. Truth is, by definition, the whole picture. Reducing the Torah to a self-help guide for the observable phenomena of this world is at best a partial picture, not the truth.

A Venue for Discovery

The original venue of the Torah is the desert. This reflects its purpose: it is not meant to be a book of interactions for maintaining social contact, but rather for changing and elevating the spiritual level of man. Thus the desert was not a place in which we were lost in any sense of the word. It was the place in which we were discovered.

The way in which the Jews encamped in the desert is the main topic of *Parashas Bemidbar*. In order for the atmosphere of the stark wasteland to speak to them, they had to be able to look within themselves to find an interpretation of its bleakness. They no doubt knew themselves as individuals far better than we do. When they said, "We will do and we will hear," that individuality melded into a collective one in which they shared a common heart. What we must begin to understand through our *parashah* is the meaning of the retention of tribal identity.

The Midrash tells us, surprisingly enough, that at the moment of their greatest unity they felt a yearning to express themselves through their tribal identity. Their separateness was expressed by each tribe having its own banner. As Rabbeinu Bachya points out, the purpose of a flag is to create a symbol of sovereignty. When victory is proclaimed, it is the flag that makes a statement that is more eloquent than words. Let us let the Ramban give us insight on the order in which they traveled to understand what they saw both within themselves and beyond.

Banners of Identity

When they traveled, the tribe of Yehudah began the procession, starting from the east. His banner had a picture of a lion on it, which symbolized the leadership with which he was blessed.

Yehudah was accompanied by Yissachar, the tribe that submitted itself to the burden of Torah, as a donkey would to its load. Its symbol, the sun and moon, reflected the wisdom by which they could redefine the world's finite nature, time, in terms of the infinite, Torah.

Zevulun, whose material wealth would be used to give material substance to Yehudah's leadership and support Yissachar's

Torah, was last in this group of three in the east. This combination of human leadership, Torah, and wealth was used to bring Hashem's will to the forefront of our collective life.

Reuven and his group traveled from the south. The most significant moment in Reuven's life was his moment of *teshuvah*, repentance. The warmth of the sun that is felt most intensely in the south is a tangible metaphor for the constancy of Hashem's mercy that brought repentance into being even before the world was created. There would be no place for man on this earth if *teshuvah* had not been part of the Divine plan. Therefore, Reuven's symbol was the *duda'im*, mandrakes. This is the plant that he, as a child, brought to his mother, and represents his sin of moving his mother's bed into his father Yaakov's tent against Yaakov's wishes. The plant was believed to have fertility properties, and in fact the commentaries say that its form is similar to that of a human being. *Teshuvah* is the ultimate statement of coming to terms with one's own frailty and one's own power.

Reuven was accompanied by the tribe of Gad, whose flag portrays a barricade to symbolize his power. What is the connection between repentance and strength? Few experiences require as much strength as the experience of re-beginning.

Between them was Shimon. The city of Shechem was his emblem. Why does a particular city represent the inner nature of an entire tribe? Shechem is a place that is predestined for the enactment of severe judgment. It is from there that Yosef was sold, from there that the kingdom was divided and Dinah abducted.

The Sefas Emes tells us that the word *shechem* is an acrostic for *sham kevod malchuso*, "there is the glory of His kingdom." It is by means of the agony and soul-searching we go through in contending with the tragic consequences of our deeds that true growth takes place. Shimon, the anti-hero of the narrative of the revenge taken against the town of Shechem for Dinah's abduction, is placed between Reuven and Gad to draw on Gad's strength and to follow Reuven's example of repentance.

The image of an ox adorned the flag of Efraim, who led from the west. The ancient (and possibly extinct) animal known as the *re'eim* was on the banner of Menasheh. Strength, reflected by the power of these animals, joins the symbols of *teshuvah* and Torah.

a glimpse of infinity

The strength to which we refer can be tragically expressed, as was in the case of Yeravam ben Nevat of Efraim, who divided the kingdom and brought idolatry into Israel as a substitute for the worship of God. It was similarly misused by the tribe of Menasheh, which allied itself with Efraim.

Their obstinate rejection of every opportunity for *teshuvah* had its match. When used positively — as in the headstrong stubborn determination displayed by Mordechai in refusing to bow before Haman regardless of the stakes — it is holy. Mordechai was a descendant of Binyamin, who traveled in this group and whose sign, the ferocious wolf, is self-understood.

The fourth and final group was led by the tribe of Dan. Coming from the north, the direction of the greatest concealment, we find the tribe that populized the idolatry of Michah and that of Yeravam. His symbol, the snake, tells us of his comfort with the forces of evil. Dan's ability to be almost intimate with the forces of evil allowed Shimshon to enter the heart of darkness and emerge a tzaddik. He is accompanied by Asher, whose emblem, a tree, symbolizes the olive oil that brought spiritual light and joy to the menorah that was lit in the *Beis HaMikdash*.

Naftali had a deer pictured on his standard. The speed and alacrity illustrated reflect the satisfaction in Hashem's blessing that typified the tribe. The joy of Naftali and the illumination of Asher when joined with the willingness of Dan to never withdraw from any challenge complete the final encampment.

What do we learn from seeing the tribes more clearly? We learn to see our collective goals and aspirations in a way that is more three dimensional than we sometimes allow ourselves to see. We learn to see the world through the eyes of other tribes, both within ourselves and outside ourselves. We learn to validate their dreams. We learn that the tree has many branches.

CHAPTER THIRTY-SIX
the light of awareness

NONE OF US know exactly when and how our journey began. In *Megillas Ruth*, we find that the holy Alshich and other major commentators give us insight into a world that is usually (and purposely) hidden from view: the world of reincarnation.

Machlon and Kilyon were not here for the first time. Their known history begins with the lives of Er and Onan, Yehudah's sons. Their return to this world came about through the process of *gilgul*, reincarnation. Let us look at their history to understand our own.

Their unwillingness to have children with Tamar was the catalyst that brought about Tamar's confrontation with Yehudah. The risks she took to do what she knew was her only honest choice were immense. She no doubt could picture herself abandoned, rejected, and humiliated. All the calculations that were part of the decision-making process that brought her to the crossroads of her fateful encounter with Yehudah could have easily been reduced to the dust and ashes that populate the section of our hearts reserved for broken dreams. Tamar's tragically unfulfilled marriages to Er and Onan did not take her to the precipice of despair, an option we may at times find comfortable, but one that is never really honest.

Er and Onan failed to let their capacity for eternal life determine their choices. Quite the opposite: as the holy Alshich points out, the word *er*, which means "awakening," is composed of the same letters as the word *ra*, which means "evil." The definition the Maharal gives for evil is absence of Godliness — contact with every garment the King wears, but no contact with the King Himself. When we face it, we can either choose to see reality as being nothing more than the garment, as did Er and Onan, or we can let it open our hearts to search for the King. This is the choice that was made by Tamar.

Yehudah's confrontation with his all-too-human potential for evil could not have been easy. Few of us feel comfortable admitting blunders even when the stakes are low and the possibility of getting away with a whitewash job is high. The moment he said, "She is more right than I," he revealed his capacity to be the ancestor of an eternal dynasty.

The Path of Light

Our eternal lives are delineated by the brief time we spend here. We don't see the thread of our choices affecting future generations. At times Hashem opens the curtains of time so we can see beyond the limits of our lifetimes. The story of Ruth and Boaz, Machlon and Kilyon, are the next act in the drama of Tamar and Yehudah, Er and Onan. As we read the story in the megillah on Shavuos, we must ask what it is telling us about our own journey and that of the Jewish people.

The specific illumination of Shavuos that we experience is the same one that was experienced by Ruth and Boaz. It, in turn, is the same as the illumination our ancestors encountered at Sinai. The light is compared to the elation that takes place at a wedding. In fact, the moment of closeness we experienced is compared to that of a *chuppah*, a wedding canopy — and it returns to the world every Shavuos. The prism of time, the changes that take place throughout the generations, and the specific qualities of each person's soul give each one a different glimpse of the subtle shadings of this light. It is this light that enables us to navigate our journey.

Our Sages tell us that one of the reasons we read *Megillas Ruth* on Shavuos is that we are compared to converts when we received the Torah. The holy Alshich sheds light on the nature of this comparison.

He says that the soul of a convert clothes the soul of a great *tzaddik*. It was her mother-in-law, Naomi, who inspired Ruth the Moabite to actualize her potential to act for the sake of Heaven. Her ancestress, Lot's daughter, went beyond what even in Sedom was outside the limits of conventional morality. Her intent was for the sake of Heaven. She was endeavoring to keep the world going by having a child in the midst of what she believed was total destruction. She not only achieved the goal she had aimed for, preserving life, but passed on the ability to find light in the midst of darkness to her future generations of daughters. Ruth took that potential and let it become more and more of what she defined as her most authentic self. Let us follow her metamorphosis.

The Willingness to Be Redefined

There are two qualities that are most visible to us when we look at the megillah and try to discover Ruth. One is the physical modesty she displayed in squatting rather than bending to pick up the sheaves left for gleaning. The endless repetition of simultaneously affirming her sensitivity to Hashem's continual presence while remaining very much in this world is reflective of far more than adherence to a code of dress or behavior. It is reflective of never leaving Hashem's presence. In this she had a great deal in common with Tamar.

The second quality is the outpouring of goodness that was the hallmark of Ruth's relationship with Naomi. This was far from a one-sided relationship. What Ruth received from Naomi was the gift of inspiration. She clothed Naomi in a certain sense, and Naomi gave her life. The coin she used was not just kindness; it was rather a willingness to be redefined.

The Shem MiShmuel tells us of the moment Ruth responded to Naomi's entreaties to return to Moav and not suffer the pain that the trade-offs involved in converting to Judaism would invariably demand of her. Naomi told her of the four forms of death penalty a Jew can incur defined in Halachah. Yet Ruth, who was wise enough to recognize that she could not foresee where future generations would find themselves, accepted the death penalty unconditionally and irreversibly. Her *mesirus nefesh* was not only for herself, but for all generations. The inner light she possessed that gave her the ability to make a choice of this nature is the light we all have the capacity to see on Shavuos — as did Ruth, as did Tamar.

Er and Onan, Machlon and Kilyon, were blind — not in the

the light of awareness

physical sense, but in their inability to see beyond the moment. What inner mechanism lets some of us see, while others walk through life with their eyes firmly closed?

Penetrating the Darkness

The Baal HaTanya tells us that, with the exception of the great tzaddikim, we do not totally identify with the holiness within us. Daily, in the morning prayers, we say, "The soul You have given to me is pure." The wording of the sentence is clear: I am not the soul; rather it is something that was given to me. The "real" me is multifaceted and continually evolving. The instinctive, territorial, self-oriented animal self coexists uneasily with the Godly soul. Even when there is external submission, there is rarely deep internal submission. The soul and animal self are compared to two wrestlers, neither of which is strong enough to gain complete victory.

The more one gives articulation to the Godly soul — by letting the dispassionate process of thought "out-shout" that of animalistic instinct — the closer we are to ultimate victory. This, more than anything else, is what differentiated Ruth from Machlon and Tamar, from Er and Onan.

The process of bringing the mind into play does not mean (observably) that geniuses are more Godly than the less gifted, nor does it mean that emotion is corrupt. What it means is that both emotion and intellect must be channeled. We must struggle to remain honest with ourselves.

The days of *sefiras ha'omer* give us the means to pierce through the fogginess and come to awareness. As women, the need to use discernment is matched by the ability to do so.

The Maharal tells us that the command "Thus you shall say to the house of Yaakov and tell the sons of Yisrael" indicates that women were given precedence when the Torah was given. The Gemara tells us that the reason for this is that women approach the mitzvos with greater alacrity than men. The Maharal explains that this is the natural consequence of women being oriented to substance rather than form. We need to find meaning rather than give meaning. It is up to us to determine where we look for it and toward whom we turn to to help us find it.

We can find meaning in light and use it to penetrate even the deepest darkness. We can also create the artificial illumination of calling darkness light. We can become so limited by what surrounds us physically and ideologically that we forget the fact that we never made a choice to be there that came from awareness and discernment. When we choose light, we can align ourselves to Hashem with the truth of Tamar and the conviction that led to the inner redefinition of Ruth.

Ruth lived to see Shlomo rule. We are told that all mentions of Shlomo in *Shir HaShirim* are not references to him alone, but to the ultimate King of peace (the literal meaning of the name *Shlomo*), Hashem. At the time of *mattan Torah*, the divine wedding between Hashem and the Jewish people, may we receive the Torah with the joy Ruth had as Shlomo was crowned on the day of his wedding.

CHAPTER THIRTY-SEVEN
seeing the goodness

COMPLAINING RARELY SOUNDS trite to the person indulging in it; in some ways, it has become our favorite sport. We seem to be addicted to assuring almost any listener that things are hard. And while I impress on others how I find the weather so oppressive that the motionless air has reduced me to absolute indolence, my (often captive) audience also may have noticed that it is rather warm. In fact, the displeasure one risks when contradicting a heartfelt lament (or even not voicing one's absolute agreement with sufficient empathy) has few equals in social interchange. There is always the real possibility of having the glass one has so tidily described as half full thrown in one's face.

Our addiction to negativity must be examined. It colors our lives gray. Worst of all, it silences the inner voice that recognizes Hashem. Yet it is a hard addiction to break. Let us examine its cause.

A Deafening Silence

The simplest reason for our enjoying focusing on the negative is that it is so incredibly effortless. True, our lives are not easy. We often forget, however, that *easy* and *good* are not only not synonyms, but they can often be opposites. Ease and joy are rarely seen together. We find ourselves endlessly repeating our unwillingness to embrace life according to the terms Hashem puts forth.

We are addicted to the pursuit of ease to the exclusion of the pursuit of goodness and meaning. If we were to relent in our constant quest for contentment and comfort, we would be able to see all the goodness and beauty that surround us. Why is it that we must choose between one and the other? The enigma is one that

Hashem designed.

Hashem hides His presence within the "otherness" of the world and thereby allows us to discover Him in the midst of the awesome beauty and vast scope of what in the end is only a creation. This is hinted at by the name *Elokim* used in the act of creation. Two of the letters — the *yud* and the *hey* — are also used in the Name *Hashem*. The other three — *alef, lamed,* and *mem* — are the same letters as the word *ileim,* which means "mute." The letters also form the word *alem,* which means "closely gathered."

We experience both silence and closeness; both carry His signature. The inescapable and intoxicating presence of solid ground simultaneously chokes us and gives us life. We hear Hashem in His silence when we choose to hear. When we don't, we are distracted by the "noise" of life. We can experience His closeness constantly when we are not distracted by the urgency of getting on with our daily chores. We also can be deafened by the silence and mistake the closeness for adversity. There are ways that we can make a choice to see the goodness. One of them is song.

Don't Complain, Sing!

Rebbe Nachman says, in his *Likutei Maharan*, that when we choose to praise Hashem in song, we create garments for the hidden presence, the Shechinah. The inflections of melody touch the fire, water, and wind that lie dormant within us. We can then move beyond the camouflage of "otherness" and see the joy of life.

Far too often we choose not to sing. We allow ourselves to become habituated to Hashem's concealment in the garment of invisibility and silence. We complain.

I once met one of the rare people who has made a definite choice to see and hear. His story began with its central character, a non-Jewish teenager in the rural wine-growing country of Italy. He had never met a Jewish person, nor had he a close acquaintance who had. Undescribable beauty surrounded him daily. Most of us would have learned to reduce the splendor to opacity. He chose to see its translucence.

One day, he found himself standing in his father's vineyard watching the Giver of life vivify each grape with His luminescence and warm the rocky soil with the unending constancy of the sun's rays. The vow he made that day was not one anyone would take lightly: "I want to know You and to serve You, but I don't know Your name."

One of the ways by which Hashem is known is through His creation. In a certain sense, the boy in the vineyard had already began to know Hashem's name. The name that is hidden within the ten statements of creation was one that he knew. The name that was revealed to us when the Torah was given is one that he learned only years later. Let us see how we, too, can learn His name.

There are two narratives in *Parashas Beha'alosecha* that can help us learn to hear and to sing.

Seeing Duality When There Is Unity

We are presented with the commandment to make trumpets. We are also presented with the story of the *misonenim*, the bearers of complaint. Let us examine both narratives.

Moshe was commanded to make two silver trumpets. They were to be used only for Moshe, who in fact hid them in his lifetime. The only other king to use the trumpets was King David; later kings used the shofar. The trumpets were blown together to gather the community and they were blown singly to call the princes of the tribes. The other times they were both used together was to signal that they were on the move again or going to war.

The people recognized the purpose of the trumpets being sounded was by listening to the notes. Gatherings were announced by the long *tekia* sound, while traveling and war were signaled by the broken *terua* notes. Rabbeinu Bachya explains that the long *tekia* sound, by its nature, drew us close to Hashem's attribute of mercy. We would feel ourselves on the deepest possible level, the level of the fire, water, and spirit within us, responding to Hashem's outstretched arm. The broken sound of *terua* would stir us to our very core. *Middas hadin*, Hashem's attribute of justice, is manifested as His concealment and the restraint of His light. Thus the two trumpets hint at the two attributes by which Hashem rules the world: severity and mercy.

The Rekanati unravels a significant detail in the text. The word *chatzotzros*, trumpets, is written without a *vav* before the *tav* at the end of the word, as is normally done when changing a word from singular to plural. Thus the plural nature of the word is limited; the word is "missing" a letter that is usually used. But it is read (unlike the way it is written) in its usual form. This tells us that the most pristine presentation (that of the Torah) differs from our perception (our way of reading it), which renders it irregular. This suggests to us that although there were two trumpets, they were in a certain sense one. How so? They hint at the two "faces" Hashem shows us. They are really, in an essential sense, both dimensions of mercy. It is our inability to move ourselves aside sufficiently to make room for Hashem that makes us see dualism when there is unity.

Moshe's greatness was that he led only to make Hashem's name known. Therefore, the trumpets were made of silver, which symbolizes mercy, rather than gold. The key to his rectitude was his humility. This was also the most primary of the traits that defined King David. Both saw Hashem wherever they looked.

When we heard the trumpets, we were shaken awake! Our dormant yearning and awe were touched. Nothing awakens us the way music does. The resounding intensity of the trumpets would pierce through all the layers. We stood in the same place spiritually as the young man in the above story who stood in his father's vineyard.

Listening to the Right Trumpet

Let us now contrast the awakening in response to the trumpets with the response made by those who ate manna and complained.

The Sefas Emes compares their sin to that of Adam in the Garden of Eden. In neither case was there any conscious intention to sin. Adam wanted to internalize evil into his very deepest level of being in order to have the depth that results from confronting oneself at times as the enemy rather than as an external foe. Through making choices we experience not only our limitations, but our greatest joy.

The manna is described as "white." This symbolizes purity.

seeing the goodness

There was no evil to peel away, no battle to win. In the same way, but in a unique manner, the *nefesh*, which is the lowest aspect of the spiritual soul, draws its strength from the drama of making choices. A truly spiritual person is one who has developed his inner strength through the process of making choices. Avraham after the Akeidah was a far more actualized person than he was on the day before the event. It was only after his potential was actualized that Hashem referred to him as "one who fears God."

The people described themselves as suffering from "dry souls." There was nostalgia for the theater of Egypt. They wanted the challenge of bringing forth bread from the earth by the sweat of their brows in Eretz Yisrael.

What Hashem had in mind for them was to raise them above doing battle with evil, above the most basic level of spiritual awareness. He wanted to give them the opportunity to eat manna for forty years and wean themselves off the need to do battle. They could have become like Adam before he sinned. Instead they chose to see their lives as dry and lacking in meaning; they chose to complain.

We tend to complain about everything: we complain about the times in our lives that are punctuated by drama and the times in our lives that are not. Both trumpets are silent. We are living in times of unprecedented convenience and prosperity. We don't have to struggle for our spiritual or physical survival as our parents did.

Some of our parents faced moments we can never truly envision, but they maintained not only their sanity, but in many cases their piety. Some of our parents grew up in the stultifying atmosphere of an America that still believed in its own dream. They maintained their personal decency and in many cases the ability to pass along to their children the dreams they had never lived.

We who are deep in the forest of our middle age had to build ourselves upon the foundations they set up for us. Who complained more: our generation or theirs?

Our children have it all; they are brought up in the midst of not only material affluence, but its spiritual parallel. They are often discontent, nonetheless. We may have fallen into the trap of the *misonenim*. We hear the trumpet that awakens us to meet the challenge of battle, but we must learn to hear the trumpet that awakens within us a sensitivity to good. We must learn to see the luminescence of Hashem's life force and the goodness and compassion that surround us. When we teach ourselves to listen, we can teach our children not to complain.

CHAPTER THIRTY-EIGHT
the unbreakable bond

WHEN I WALKED into the living room, the sky was opaque and impenetrable, a strange mixture of mauve and gray, mysterious and awesome. Within moments I was required to recite the blessing on thunder and soon that of lightning. As I picked up my siddur to begin praying Shacharis, I took a final look at the violent beauty of the sky, the wind blowing over the hills that were there before my birth and will endure beyond the passing shadow of my life. The power of the day took me by surprise. But the sun , of course, is not its own master; here, in the palace of the King, it must reveal His continually unfolding intimacy with His kingdom.

In the first verse of *Parashas Behar*, Rashi poses a well-known question: "*Mah inyan shemittah l'Har Sinai?*" What is the connection between the mitzvah to cease agricultural work every seventh year in the Land of Israel, the first commandment in the *parashah*, and the fact that Hashem gave the Torah at Mount Sinai? That morning in my living room, the answer was crystal clear: both *shemittah* and Har Sinai attune us to a deeper dimension of reality than we usually see, the reality of our being in a state of continual communication with Hashem. What we heard at Har Sinai and what we experience when we observe *shemittah* is very similar.

The Gift of Seeing below the Surface

What do I mean by inner reality? When we look at any physical object, our focus is on what our eyes show us: the surface of the object, its four sides, its top and its bottom. These dimensions present us with the object's outer reality. This is why six is the number the Maharal uses to convey to us the external and superficial side of reality. The part of the object hidden from the eye, but revealed to the observer by his heart and mind, is symbolized by the number seven.

All of creation emanates from one Source. Nothing exists, even momentarily, without Hashem infusing it with life force. Also, nothing exists without purpose; nothing is random. This is the inner reality that is so often concealed from our vision because of our natural inclination to focus on the surface. Our ability to make contact with inner reality is a gift. We received this gift when we approached Har Sinai.

The Talmud tells us that the mountain was surrounded by a river of fire. The Maharal explains that this symbolizes the concept that our minds can take us only so far. Beyond the ability of human intellect, which is limited to what the mind can grasp and the eye observe, there is a river of fire — holiness that is above the limitation of observation, that takes one beyond the world of six into the world of seven.

The Midrash tells us, "*Chochmah bagoyim ta'amin, Torah bagoyim al ta'amin* — Believe there is wisdom among the nations; do not believe there is Torah among the nations" (*Midrash Eichah*). What is the difference between wisdom and Torah? Wisdom can be gained by human observation; all of the sciences are ultimately limited to what is symbolized by the number six. Torah gives us the ability to penetrate the surface and enter the realm of inner reality, the reality symbolized by the number seven. As the Sefas Emes points out, Shabbos, the seventh day of the week, and *shemittah*, the seventh year, are times when we can awaken within ourselves the ability to penetrate the surface and see what's inside. During these times, it is easier to see who is the true Source of everything in creation.

The Hebrew word for "physicality" is *gashmius*, with the same root as the Hebrew word for *geshem*, "rain." The Hebrew word for "nature" is *teva*, related to the word *toveia*, "drown." In one's day-to-day life, one can at times find oneself drowning in the endless sea of outer reality. The struggle to balance ordinary living with its ups and downs without becoming totally identified with the external is not always easy. We need to maintain order in our lives without becoming loveless, dry, and disparaging; we need to nurture our inner reality and that of our families with joy and the feeling of renewal without allowing neglect or disorder to subtly destroy what we are building. Weekly we have Shabbos to reawaken the Godly spark. The *shemittah* year can accomplish the same. Let us take a look at this mitzvah.

Destination: The King's Palace

In his commentary on *Shir HaShirim*, the Vilna Gaon points out that the nations, in seeking a relationship with God, invariably reject earthly matters. The monastic retreat from life that characterized Christianity in the Dark Ages is echoed in the transcendental cults of the East and in Islam. The reason for this, he says, is that their souls are not strong enough to make themselves heard above the endless din of their bodies. The nations find themselves in irresolvable conflict. Since they cannot have both worlds, they must choose between them.

There are various words used to describe the soul. One is *nefesh*, which literally means "that which comes to rest." In context, this means the aspect of the soul that we experience through the body against whose borders it comes to rest. The *nefesh* of the Jew, continues the Vilna Gaon, is made out of the earth of Eretz Yisrael, while the *nefesh* of the rest of humanity is made out of the earth of the rest of the world. Just as the earth of Eretz Yisrael has an unbreakable bond with its Creator, so do we, although we may not always see it. The mitzvah of *shemittah*, in which we allow the land to lay fallow, with the realization that sustenance actually comes from Hashem and not nature, reawakens our ability to see inner reality as we experience the outer reality of living our lives. As Shabbos relates to time, *shemittah* relates to physicality.

Rashi's question now is more personal. Of course Har Sinai and *shemittah* are intimately connected. Our search for truth and meaning is irrevocably connected to our mundane lives. As Rashi continues, just as the laws of *shemittah* were given at Sinai in full detail, so were all the others. Hashem gave us the means — the *mitzvos* — to cross the river of fire, yet at times we allow ourselves to be distracted or even disengaged. The power of precision in refining is enormous, yet we have to do battle with ourselves to retain a vision of where the road we are walking will lead us.

Rebbe Nachman used to say, "Wherever I am going, I am going to Eretz Yisrael." His feet led him to many destinations in the course of his brief life. His journey to Eretz Yisrael was fraught with danger and sacrifice. He was there only a short time, yet the journey itself was definitive of his life. No matter where he was, the target was revelation. To live in the King's palace and to experience His Presence was something he pursued with joy throughout his life.

The Yearning for Redemption

We must never think even for a moment that we are alone in our search for inner reality. The Creator of that reality is with us every moment. His love for us and belief in us are far greater than our love or trust in ourselves. In the next *parashah, Bechukkosai*, the following promise is made: "I shall remember My covenant with Yaakov, and even My covenant with Yitzchak, and even My covenant with Avraham I shall remember, and I shall remember the land." *Yaakov* here is spelled with the usually omitted letter *vav*; it is spelled this way in only five places in Scripture. Five times the name *Eliyahu* is also written differently from usual, without a *vav*. The Vilna Gaon explains that the vowels (which are not written in a Torah scroll) are compared to the soul, invisible but vocal and life-giving, while the letters themselves, which are written and observable, are compared to the body. What the Torah is telling us is the nature of the bond between the Jewish people's beginning, which hailed from Yaakov, and its ultimate redemption, which will be heralded by Eliyahu. The *vav* is shaped like a finger. A handshake — five fingers — is extended from Eliyahu to Yaakov, a promise by Eliyahu to redeem Yaakov's descendants. This is the message transmitted by the vowels, the soul of the text.

On a deeper level, what this means is that the prophet Eliyahu, who was given the mission of returning the Jewish people to Hashem, unifying them, and ultimately reviving the dead, was created by Hashem for this purpose. Until we are redeemable, he is incomplete. Our ability to be ultimately redeemed is a quality we inherit from Yaakov. Hashem promised him that even when his descendants will sin, they will remain Jews — they will never lose the ability to look beyond the surface. When we penetrate all the layers, what we see at the core is Hashem's will, life force, and goodness. We see the interconnection of all external reality with its Source. This is what we yearn for when we talk of redemption.

Redemption means being able to be oneself, in the most genuine and least superficial way. It means acceptance of one's own goodness and that of everyone else as well. It means being able to stop calling challenge "evil" and see it for what it is. As the Maharal teaches us, the roles of Eliyahu and Mashiach are like the roles of Aharon the peacekeeper of the Jewish people and of Moshe the lawgiver. Aharon, who gave expression to the hidden love that was in his heart and that of all the Jewish people, through his relentless pursuit of peace was a living example of the spiritual self-expression provided by the positive mitzvos. Moshe transmitted the law without fear or hesitation. His humility was far too great to allow him to "second guess" his Creator by placing obstacles in the way of his serving Him. This is expressed by the Jewish people through our observance of the negative mitzvos. Aharon created connection through observing the positive mitzvos and Moshe gave us the ability to slice through illusions and desires with the discipline of the prohibitions of the Torah.

We all have the potential to reach out to the part of ourselves that wants unification with family and friends, and ultimately our fellow Jews, and direction in our lives more than anything else. This may be disguised as many other desires, such as the wish for domestic harmony or the need for a sense of purpose, but the underlying desire is redemption.

"Eternal Life Is Planted within Us"

How do we get in touch with this part of ourselves? The yearning itself is so delicate and elusive, yet so real! A dear friend of mine recently lost her husband. They were not young, yet they had started anew, both learning for the first time in their lives in a formal setting. I was with her when he left us and with her at the funeral, and I did not know what to say. A rabbi, with eyes that projected warmth and empathy mixed with wisdom, spoke and told the following story of his great-uncle, who had the opportunity to spend a Shabbos with the Chafetz Chaim. Though young at the time, the great-uncle was aware he was in the presence of someone very special and he paid careful attention to everything that passed between them that Shabbos.

Shabbos morning found the young scholar and the elderly Sage in shul. After the Torah portion was read, the Chafetz Chaim turned to his guest and asked him a question: "What do you think about when you say the words 'V'chayei olam nata besocheinu — Eternal life is planted within us'?"

The young man, much to his credit, told the truth. "Well, I suppose I think about keeping my finger on the place so that I don't get confused in the middle of the berachah and make a fool of myself," he replied rather inelegantly.

The tzaddik looked at his guest and said, "Do you want to know what I think?"

"Of course," replied the young man.

"Let me ask you another question: Where will I be in twenty-five years?"

The young man, staring at the parchment-like skin and frail body encasing the ageless eyes, remained silent.

"I'll tell you," the Sage continued. "I'll be in Olam Haba. Where will I be in a hundred years, three hundred years, a thousand years, five thousand years, a million years from now? Still in Olam Haba. Now you know the meaning of the words *chayei olam*," concluded the Chafetz Chaim.

If we were to look at our children, at our husbands, at ourselves, and see *chayei olam*, how different our relationships would be. Our days are so busy. Let us look beyond work, dentist appointments, and bar mitzvah plans to find the *siyatta diShemaya* we are given through mitzvos such as Shabbos and *shemittah*. Let us strive toward drawing ourselves a little closer and ultimately relearning to hear Hashem's voice.

CHAPTER THIRTY-NINE
meet kimchis

OVER THE YEARS, in various places — in Meron, at the tomb of Shmuel HaNavi and at Kever Rachel — I have prayed, along with countless other women, words of prayer that have been said by Jews for centuries. While looking about me, I would see not only the faces surrounding me, but also the faces that inhabit the recesses of my memory: Young women, well-dressed, some with infants staring bewildered at the semi-opaque candle-lit setting. They are unaware of the emotions surfacing in their mother's hearts — hope, faith, and yearning. Older women, some with the tragic addition of despair vying for dominance, join them in prayer.

My mind wanders back to my own living room momentarily. I see the photos of tzaddikim hanging on the walls that give our living room a certain similarity to that of our extended family, the rest of the Jewish people. Their mothers, no doubt, uttered the same words. Hot tears of longing welled up in their eyes and poured down their cheeks. I find myself speaking to Hashem, asking Him to draw me close and grant me that my *tefillos* be heard in their merit. "I would do anything ," I plead silently, anything to be like them, to be worthy of having what they had and giving what they gave. And I hear another voice from backstage saying, "Oh, yeah, would you be Kimchis?"

Meet Kimchis

We learn that Kimchis merited to be the ancestress of seven *kohanim gedolim* due to the fact that "the walls of her house never saw the braids of her hair." My first (but by no means last) acquaintance with her was at school, where it seemed that almost every assembly included at least one admonition to strive toward a higher level of *tznius*, with Kimchis often making a brief rhetorical appearance. My teachers' sincerity and integrity were so genuine that the words never failed to affect me emotionally.

Intellectually, however, I never grasped the connection between the mitzvah and its reward. A mixture of adolescent self-consciousness as well as a spiritual generation gap separated me from my instructors, many of whom were students of Sarah Schneirer. Too many questions were relegated to the back recesses of my heart and left unasked and therefore unanswered.

Some of my friends allowed the spiritual gap separating them from their mentors to be definitive of their relationship not only with the teachers, but to *tznius* as well. As soon as they heard Kimchis mentioned, an invisible shield went up. Putting up a facade of not being moved by the gracefulness of *tznius* was "cool." It was a necessity, to be accepted as a *chok*, a statute for which we were given no logical reason. Other mitzvos were inspiring, and those who excelled in them were admired enormously. Excellence in *tznius*, though, was not a topic for discussion. Many girls who were maximalist in their Judaic studies or in the performance of acts of kindness were minimalists in *tznius*. The need to know where the elbow ends (and where the law is cited) was voiced by young women who were willing to sacrifice their future material comfort by marrying young men with learning in their future. Kimchis just didn't make it as an inspirational example, but was kept as distant as emotion and history could make her.

I rediscovered Kimchis relatively late in life. The Maharal redefined *tznius* for me in a way that was so intellectually compelling that my guard completely toppled before him. *Tznius*, he tells us, is the attribute that is expressed by our resisting superficial self-definition. Its opposite is the inability to separate oneself from what is external. When separation is impossible, the tragic result is an identity that has all the stability of cotton candy. The need to please each person encountered leads to having the value system of a chameleon.

True, no one ever gets up in the morning and says, "From now on, I am what I wear, what people describe me as being, and how much money or status I have." But it seems that subconsciously some people fall into this trap and develop a sense of identity so lacking in individuality, not to mention mission, that their sense of self is almost interchangeable with anyone else of similar external realities.

The way out, the Maharal points out is *tznius* — the rediscovery of the hidden self within self. But *tznius* must be developed as a dimension of one's entire identity. It has manifestations that redefine thought and speech as well as action.

Let us reexamine the consequences of the actions of Kimchis in order to grasp the meaning of the deed itself.

The Chamber of Hiddenness

Her children were *kohanim gedolim*, high priests in the Holy Temple. The function of the *kohen* was to bring down Hashem's outpouring of *berachah*, blessing, to this world. His potential to do this is inherent (since the role is passed down through heredity). His personal worthiness to perform the duties connected to this role is contingent upon his obeying a set of rules that constrain his freedom more than the set of mitzvos that are binding upon his fellow Jew. His role is one of a dual nature: that of acting as a conduit for spiritual outpouring and that of restraint. The duality of the role reflects the interdependence of its two defining characteristics. There is no spiritual connection that can flourish without a structure that will first free the person from the limiting side of surface reality. Similarly, the Holy of Holies was the place in the *Beis HaMikdash* that was able to act as a repository for the most intense concentration of Hashem's light. It was, significantly, hidden from any superficial manifestation of glory, entered by the *kohen gadol* in solitude only on Yom Kippur. It was therefore called *devir hamutzneh*, "the chamber of *tznius*," of hiddenness. In order for a human being to acquire this capacity for detachment from superficiality, no doubt many factors come into play. The Gemara, however, cites one as being that which, in this case, was most decisive: the influence of his mother's character.

Am I willing to be her? Being her means far more than the externals of *tznius*, but certainly means that as well. Will I be able to not be moved by every passing wind? Will I refine my speech and sift out the superficial and needlessly critical and banal castigating of others that is so easy to turn to when one feels in need of establishing one's identity? Do I have the capacity and the strength to live her life, now, in the twenty-first century? Do any of us? Are we too depleted by the unending social and inner pressures to even dream such giant dreams?

The Sefas Emes opens some doors in his discussion of the *sotah*.

The Blessing of the Dust

This is a woman who is suspected of committing adultery, and her husband brings her to the *kohen*. The *sotah* is never an "innocent victim," although she is often misunderstood and presented as being one. At best, she is a woman whose behavior gave her husband reason to suspect her of adultery. Her rectification, if not guilty of adultery but of the lesser sin of being behind a locked door with another man, is the ceremony described in the *parashah*. In this rite, the Divine Name is written and then obliterated, mixed with the earth of the floor of the Temple and placed in water. The water is then drunk by the *sotah*. If she is innocent, she is blessed.

The Gemara says that the blessing in the earth comes from her ancestor Avraham, who said about himself, "I am but dust and ashes." Every Jew has the ability to touch this aspect of himself, the part that is willing to be humble, to generate life and goodness. This is the unchanging part of the self that can never be totally eclipsed by the superficial draw of the material world. When that aspect of one's deepest self is touched, anything is possible. That is why we ask, "*V'nafshi ki afar lakol tiheyeh* — May my soul be as dust before all."

Finding the truly *tzanua* person is a rare and precious experience. Let me share the discovery with you.

Carol (not her real name) was from Wyoming. This is not usual for an observant Jew. Her parents were Holocaust survivors and opened their store in a city in which there was no synagogue, *mikveh*, or organized kashrus, for one simple reason: there were no other Jews (and, truth be told, not too many other human beings). They treasured their isolation, interrupted only by Carol's birth. They "spared" her from what to them had become the unspeakable burden of a strong Jewish identity; still, they would not let her grow up thinking that she was one of "them," the gentiles with whom they lived.

Unlike her parents, Carol found the isolation suffocating. Her escape took the form of attending a college in California and entering an early marriage. Her joy in embracing the world was shattered by the death of her young husband in a tragic accident.

From the midst of her grief, Carol acquired a new treasure: an introduction to Judaism initiated by the rabbi to whom she had turned when making the funeral arrangements. Within two years she found herself in Jerusalem studying Torah, and here, for all intents and purposes, our story begins.

Some people come to Torah because of its truth. Carol understood not only the language of truth but also the language of faith. The mitzvos "spoke" to her in the vocabulary of both. Her progress was remarkable by any measure, not just by the quantity of changes that had taken place within her, but with the extraordinary power of integrating those changes into every layer of her personality.

One morning she came and asked to speak to me. As we sat together, what emerged was that a well-meaning Shabbos hostess had told her that Jewish law requires that a divorcée or a widow continue to cover her hair. The idea had not crossed her mind, since she assumed the obligation applied only to women currently married. When she spoke to her roommate, she was told there might be leniencies. She wanted more information.

Conflicting thoughts crossed my mind with lightning rapidity. *She may not be ready* was followed by *And since when are you a halachic authority* and *It's a mitzvah not to say what can't be heard*. I finally fell back on a rule I had discovered years before: when in doubt, tell the truth. Looking her in the eyes, I told Carol that the question was one of sufficient complexity that it should be presented to a *posek*, a halachic authority. When she felt she was ready to listen to his decision, which was for her to determine, I would be happy to accompany her. Her response was to ask whether I knew a store in Har Nof that sold hats.

Carol had no desire to find out about possible leniencies. I asked her why. She told me that she wanted no disparity between what she was in her inner life and what she displayed as her outer image. She wanted her appearance to reflect what she was inside. I warned her that it would be hard. Perhaps she should consider taking it in small steps. She looked me in the eye and said that to her the question was what did Hashem want, not what did she want.

As we exited the store, I imagined a third presence walking with us. It was Kimchis of course, *shepping nachas* once more.

CHAPTER FORTY
eretz yisrael: a beautiful gift

MANY PEOPLE WILL tell you: living in Israel requires the sort of self-sacrifice that is arduous for all but the most dauntless to consider. From the lack of variety of frozen yogurt to the irksome insistence made within the school system that we not change it, life is indeed oppressive. Many of the natives even have the audacity to speak Hebrew! We resolutely write short stories in which we portray ourselves as heroes doing battle against implacable foes disguised as unimaginative bureaucrats in the Ministry of the Interior. The primitive mentality of those who insist that we do things their way — rather than the enlightened recognition that our way is inherently superior (as are all things Western) — is often the contrast used to create the story line.

Even the weather resists the seventy degrees Fahrenheit that heating and air conditioning have made us see as a right almost as inviolable as the right to own a car. While it may be the perfect place for those whose piety will later be written up in the sort of biography of tzaddikim that begins with "Even as a young child, his spiritual refinement and dedication to Torah was recognized as unique," Israel is not for us plebes.

This conclusion is far from original. One look at *Parashas Shelach* will give us insight into our resistance to the land that is so integrally part of our souls. We learn that speaking of it maliciously is no better than speaking ill of one's closest friend.

A Catalyst for Truth

The words of the spies sent by Moshe were true in the rather banal way we use the word *truth*. Rather than meaning mere verbal accuracy, truth by Judaic definition is the ability to verbalize the entire picture, not just that upon which one focuses at the moment. *Lashon hara* is by its halachic definition verbally accurate; what is wrong with it is that it is never the whole picture. It is the picture of another person (or, as in the case at hand, Eretz Yisrael) minus his Godliness. A line is crossed when *lashon hara* causes the speaker not only to blind himself to the obscured presence of Hashem, but to seek validation by sharing this judgment with others. Let us endeavor to broaden our perspective and to learn to come to grips with the awesome sanctity of Eretz Yisrael.

Like the Jewish people, Eretz Yisrael has defined characteristics that are inherent and can be used either for good or for the opposite. The Maharal tells us that our stubbornness, for instance, is a trait meant to be used to bind us to our principles without compromise. This is especially true of Torah scholars, whose allegiance to truth will never give them what lesser persons refer to as flexibility or tolerance.

When this trait is misused, as it is so often, the result is the sort of controversy in which personalities create principles. The Chasam Sofer points out that Eretz Yisrael mirrors our inner lives in this, that our capacity for true greatness or its antithesis comes forth and is maximized by our presence in Eretz Yisrael. Thus we find that the failure of the spies could not have been predicted in the desert. Only Eretz Yisrael was a powerful enough catalyst to give them the ultimate expression of who they could potentially become.

Why, then, is Eretz Yisrael considered a place of blessing? Should everything about us be expressed? Perhaps the combination of temperate affability and the lifeless insipidness of American culture that comprehensively defines our present exile is better than the vigor and passion that is so much a part of life in Eretz Yisrael?

The Land Is Ours — For a Price

Rambam tells us that under specific conditions a recalcitrant husband may undergo physical penalization until he declares that he "wants" to give his wife a bill of divorce. One could argue that he wants no such thing, that all he wants is respite from suffering.

However, the reality is that what he wants more than anything is to give her the divorce as the Jewish court requires. It is only his misguided stubbornness and capacity for sin that prevented him from doing so. His most genuine desire is to do Hashem's will.

Eretz Yisrael brings us closer to our most genuine selves. Not only is this not always easy (did I mention the price of apartments?) but it is not necessarily meant to go smoothly. Three of the most precious gifts Hashem wants to give us can be acquired only through the self-transcendence that is the consequence of suffering. They are never quite ours unless we pay for them. They are Torah, a portion in the Future World, and Eretz Yisrael. All three make demands not only physically, but intellectually and spiritually. Why do these gifts have such an incredibly high price tag?

The Maharal explains that human self-awareness is often a source of inner conflict (in fact, we have probably noticed this on our own). The vitality of our bodies and emotions and minds are very much attached to the world in which we live. Our minds are absorbed by the endless drama of life itself. Whether our primary question is the what and how of the scientist or the why of those who search for meaning, the catalyst of inquiry is the physical world. Our emotions and choices are awakened by the concrete experiences of life. The body finds fulfillment within its own parameters and thereby creates alternative definitions for pleasure and pride. The soul finds itself relegated to lonely exile.

Jews are not meant to be restrained by the bonds of the brief span of a lifetime. There is more to life than just matter and form. If not, we would content ourselves with understanding only that which can be observed. We would allow ourselves to find emotional identity in events in our past. We would see no reason to reframe our emotions and let them give us spiritual depth. We would let our bodies and possessions and those of others inform us of who is "in" and "cool" and who is a "neb." As a matter of fact, we sometimes do.

Hashem, Who breathed within us the breath of eternity, has more in mind for us than we can imagine. Our minds can grasp truth in its most authentic sense. Our feelings can bring us transcendence of time, space, and every other limitation. Our bodies can be used as bridges to Hashem Himself.

However, we cannot embrace simultaneously the bonds that confine us and the eternity and freedom for which we yearn. The conflict is real: we feel ourselves to be torn at times in two different directions. When Hashem provides us with discomfort, the mask is raised and we see reality for what it is.

Our truth is not absolute; only Hashem's truth is. Our emotions, once expressed, fade into oblivion unless we let them move us into real change and growth. Our bodies are mortal and frail; no amount of negotiation will change this. What is "great" today is forgotten tomorrow. None of this is easy. No one learns these truths painlessly. We are not anesthetized. What the struggle brings us is the truth of Torah, the eternity of the Future World, and the redefinition of physicality that characterizes Eretz Yisrael.

Elevating the Material

The Vilna Gaon explains in his commentary on *Shir HaShirim* the reason we Jews were given mitzvos involving the physical world. The seven mitzvos given to the nations of the world do not require positive interaction with the material. Rather than being told what to do, they are told what not to do. There is no requirement for them to elevate the worldly using wine for Kiddush, for instance, or saying blessings on the food they eat. The reason for this is their conflicts do not require the level of integration ours do. They can find contentment not by using both sides of themselves constructively, but by choosing one above the other. They can immerse in the "real" world or deny its significance. They do not pay the price we do for integration.

The Gra attributes this difference between our approaches to life to the fact that the animal soul of the Jews, the aspect of self that we experience through the body, is made from the earth of Eretz Yisrael. We must uplift it, and we pay for it with joy.

The more aware we are of the depth of our conflict, the more we yearn for the land. The Ramban, who longed for Eretz Yisrael with every fiber of his being, came to the land only to find it desolate. We cannot imagine the absolute barrenness he encountered. Yet he compared his joy to that of a child returning to his mother.

We find ourselves repulsed by the ideologies that have arisen.

eretz yisrael: a beautiful gift

The "new Jew" is in fact nothing particularly new, nor particularly Jewish. It is the voice of fear of self. It was borne of seeing ourselves through the eyes of the nations and finding estrangement. We are a stiff-necked people. We will drain swamps and face the barren expanses of desert to find the spirituality within our bodies.

When Rav Yosef Chaim Zonnenfeld passed a group of children, bareheaded and empty-hearted, his students observed his lips moving and drew closer to hear what he was murmuring. No doubt, there was an expectation that at best he was deploring their situation and at worst cursing the adults who had brought it about. However, what they heard were the words from Hallel: *"Yosef Hashem aleichem aleichem ve'al beneichem* — May Hashem give more to you, to you and to your children."

The awkward silence was broken by his explanation that these children, or at worst the children of these children, will come back to Torah. They are far too stiff-necked to do otherwise.

Eretz Yisrael is beautiful as it is; it is austere and harsh, embracing and never still. May we merit to return to her with all our hearts and souls.

CHAPTER FORTY-ONE
the tragedy of envy

THE RAV'S WAITING room was half empty. None of the books and pamphlets lying on the table was arresting enough to hold my attention or that of my companion. She was conspicuous, not merely self-conscious. In the narrowness of the chamber, she and I were the only ones not dressed in the basic black of the *chareidi* male. Liz (not her real name) was not only female, but single. Great anguish is shrouded in the double syllables of that word that for so many is synonymous with *unfulfilled* and *solitary*.

When our turn came, there were no surprises. What did come as a surprise was the vehemence of Liz's response: "It is easy for him to talk about trusting Hashem; he has it all!"

I found myself unable to respond. What shook me to the core was the realization that her ability to face her own destiny was distorted by her envy. The fact that her malice was so overt and so misplaced made the lie she had told herself who-knows-how-many-times all the more pitiable. The fabrication is familiar to the rest of us. We tend to buy into the false belief that other people's good fortune (as we perceive it) somehow diminishes our capacity to live our lives successfully.

Deceitful Self-Images

The name of the illusion is jealousy. Let us examine it through the lens of Korach's inner vision.

How did a man who in our generation would be cosidered a spiritual giant find himself with no reserves of faith? How could a man blessed with enormous wealth, prestige, and family feel he had nothing?

the tragedy of envy

The blame falls not only upon him, but upon his wife. Her harassment brought about their tragedy. It began after the consecration of the Levites. The Torah required the Levites to prepare themselves for their new role serving God in the *Mishkan*, Tabernacle, with a series of actions. One of these was to shave all their head and body hair.

When Korach returned home, his wife berated him for submitting to what she described as the annihilation of his individuality. He looked like any other Levite, not like "himself." The fact that this was exactly who Hashem, Who created Korach, defined as the "real Korach" was irrelevant to her. She tormented him and thus shared with him the "gift" of her fragile faith. This woman destroyed her home while deluding herself that she was building it. She nibbled at the fabric of Korach's sense of self until there was nothing left. She drew him into the web of superficial self-definition that was so much a part of her.

The Maharal points out that a woman is less rigid than a man. She often yearns to find her own significance through her husband. When he provides her with direction (which often happens when she shows him she believes in him), they can move forward together harmoniously. When she believes, not in him, but in the person she feels will give her "more" (whatever that might be), she can destroy them both.

Often what she perceives as "more" is shallow and unreal. Korach should have resisted his wife's attempts to change him and become the man Hashem wanted him to be. His own capacity for envy prevented that from occurring. Thus the tragedy Korach and his wife shared was in fact rooted in both of them. Let us examine the nature of envy and its causes in light of the *parashah*.

Three Incarnations

The Shelah haKodesh points out that in order to understand Korach, we must take ourselves back to the story of Kayin and Hevel. Kayin's name speaks for itself. His view of life was self-centered; he saw the entire world as his. It was, from his perspective, his *kinyan*, acquisition.

In fact, Hashem gave the world and all that is in it to us as a means of reaching Him. Therefore in a certain sense it is ours. But it was given as a means and not as an end. Kayin's view of the world is called *kinah d'subusa*, "possessive envy," which is rooted in impurity, causing distance from God. When a person is poisoned by this type of jealousy, what he believes in his heart of hearts is that there is no justice and no Judge and no world beyond the one he sees. When Hashem is out of the picture, the center is filled immediately by our selves. We feel we can and must "take care of ourselves." That becomes our goal in life. We become envious of those whose lives seem better (because they have shinier tools) to the point of obsession.

To find his rectification, Kayin had to return to this world three times, corresponding to the three aspects of himself — *nefesh*, spiritual being; *ruach*, breath of life; and *neshamah*, soul — that were corrupted through his envy.

He returned as the Egyptian Moshe killed, and thus reached the atonement he needed for murdering his brother Hevel. The Maharal explains that ultimate submission to Hashem takes place at the moment of death. Then our illusion of empowerment is finally reduced to dust and ashes. The envy that brought Kayin into conflict with his brother was recognized for what it really was: rebellion against the Source of creativity and compassion.

Kayin's second incarnation was as Yisro. His need to grab at what the world offered took him to spiritual exploration. He tried everything, worshiped every power, until he found the unifying force of Hashem.

Reincarnation is a difficult concept for us. Our ability to define reality is limited by our imprisonment within the parameters of time and space. A soul is free of the bonds that still confine us. From our perspective, the fact that Yisro, the Egyptian and Korach were contemporaries is incomprehensible. From a less confined perspective, it is not even a question. What we can grasp is that Kayin's final opportunity for rectification came when he was incarnated as Korach. He was given the role of a Levi. His challenge was to treasure the role Hashem had given him. This final, more subtle step was the one that defeated him.

Victory at Any Cost

Kayin/Korach is far from the only one to be defeated by the intensity of spiritual insecurity. The 250 people who joined in his effort to diparage Moshe's authority were similarly affected and similarly doomed. Korach was envious of Elitzafon's appointment as leader of the tribe, since he felt his own seniority gave him the right to claim leadership (if not the priesthood). But what did the others think? Why were Dasan and Aviram involved? They were neither *kohamin*, *levi'im*, nor prospective leaders of their tribe. (Indeed, reason asks how could both be the leader? Does rational thought even make its voice heard when envy has taken over?) And who was On ben Peles, and why was he invloved?

The Maharal explains that the 250 followers were, in fact, jealous of those in one specific role, that of the *kehunah*, the priesthood. While they grasped that Moshe's role in transmitting the Torah was unique, they saw Aharon differently. His selection to be a *kohen* implied that not only in the world of wisdom and study is there superiority and inferiority but that in the world of action, which they wished to see as a democracy, there is similar differentiation. Not every person was permitted to offer sacrifices. They understood this to mean that there was a spiritual hierarchy from which they were excluded.

Dasan and Aviram loved contention for its own sake. The prospect of reaching higher levels of spiritual attainment held no temptation for them. There was another agenda that was far more precious to them. Divisiveness, while universally despised, is addictive. It is easy to feel artificial meaning in one's life when fighting synthetic battles — those which have no genuine basis in anything eternal. In order to maintain the ego at a high level and experience the perceived victory that is the real goal of the one inciting dispute, there is one prerequisite: reducing the worth of one's rival to nonexistence.

The stakes that Dasan and Aviram played with were higher than we can possibly imagine; they placed the credibility of the entire Torah at risk. Their basic emotional equation is fairly familiar to us. Every "victory" we "earn" on the highway, at work, at home, may be tinged with the stain of ego-building.

Cosmic Mosaic

On ben Peles wanted neither the *kehunah* nor the joy of battle. What he wanted was to feel that no man was more than his equal, even Moshe. He was not addicted to controversy; he was addicted to democracy. How many times do we observe people whose relationship to the greatest Sages is corrupted by the idealization of equality that we breathe in the air of the modern Western world! We are willing to stand when they enter a room, but genuine submission of the mind and heart is another, far more complex issue.

When On's wife intervened and showed him he could only destroy himslf by breaking the ties that hold the Jewish people together, she saved him.

Hashem created the world as a mosaic. Each aspect of reality, each group of people, each Jew, has a specific mission. The only way in which the entire picture of reality that Hashem envisioned at the world's creation can ever be complete is when there is willingness to accept His order. It is one in which no piece of the mosaic is identical to another. We must learn to see the integrity and purpose of our own piece of the mosaic on Hashem's terms, not the artificial ones we create to validate our sense of ego gratification or counterfeit equality.

We must recognize that ease and status are not part of the nature of genuine equality. We must learn to cherish our tools and see those of others as unnecessary for us in our lives. We must seek wholeness and despise the cheap thrill of victory. Nothing destroys us as completely as the jealousy that leads to dispute. Nothing builds us as much as the trust in Hashem, which gives us the courage to live our lives without jealousy.

CHAPTER FORTY-TWO
reflections on enigmas

THE VISTA OF the kibbutz was physically majestic and awe-inspiring in a way that cannot have changed much since the land was explored by Avraham. Its dazzling, natural beauty was no doubt created to open our hearts toward its Creator. Yet I could not help but think that somewhere the message had been lost.

I had little in common with the members of the kibbutz. Under almost any other circumstances, I would have regarded them as foreign to me as an extraterrestrial being. However, life in the Galilee in the seventies opened doors for me that otherwise would have been closed forever.

My life on the tiny village my husband and I called home for close to three years was at times lonely. I had little in common with the families with whom I found myself sharing one of the most hidden and beautiful areas in Israel. I lacked the maturity not only to know them, but to treasure them for what they were.

They were, for the most part, closer to my parents' age than to mine. Their generation came face to face with the clash between what was presented to them as progress and modernity and the richness of faith. While I was drawn to their natural and intuitive observance of mitzvos, I longed for the passion that can come only when intellectual search is part of religious experience. Most of all I missed English.

They also missed English. The members of the kibbutz may have had many serious failings, but lack of ability to express themselves in the language of Shakespeare was not one of them. I treasured the snatches of conversation that took place on our rare encounters. It was understood that once we strayed beyond the borders of child care, the weather, and traffic conditions, we would have to confront world views that were irreconcilable. We kept the distance that allowed us the pleasure of affinity.

I will never forget the day the rules were rendered void. The day was like any other, luminescent and prosaic. My husband had returned from Minchah. We sat for a moment enjoying the ever-present unblemished silence. It was broken by a knock on the door. I recognized the man standing before us as a member of the kibbutz. His work clothes, hanging loosely on his thin frame, bespoke intimacy with a world in which tractors and fields were central. It was a world I didn't know.

My husband's warm "Shalom" was greeted with a diffident smile. It was unmistakable that this moment was not a comfortable one for him. He broke the silence by saying, "I heard that Torah is learned here. I also want to learn."

I felt that time had stopped. My mind could not translate that moment into rational terms. What I was watching was a person living out a *chok*. Let us look into *Parashas Chukas* and gain insight into the nature of the category of law that the Torah refers to as *chukim*.

The Need for Order in Our Lives

The Ibn Ezra defines a *chok* as a vehicle by which a person pursues the awareness of Hashem that is implanted in his heart. He himself may not know why he is doing these things, as their reasons are concealed. We tend to be suspicious of behavior that is not the direct consequence of coming to conclusions based on our own logic. Let us explore the difference between mindless superstitious practices that are the fruit of human reason, and *chukim*.

Superstition is always the result of the all-too-human need to control events or feelings that are outside our dominion. The process of living is at times impossible to interpret as well as frightening. When we choose to look away from the majestic presence of Hashem's Providence and seek security in what is within our grasp, we are left with a reality that few people find completely acceptable. Thus, superstition is that ultimate emotional escape from Hashem. We try to feel a level of control that we do not have and will never have without Him.

Conversely, the desire to set forth just laws by which to govern our public and private lives is a reflection of our ability to continually use the intellect Hashem gives us to order our lives. We are too Godly to content ourselves with the law of the jungle. In today's society, the self-described "good person" is in fact manifesting the aspect of his own spiritual nature that yearns for Divine order.

A *chok* is a journey that takes us still further into the depths of our own spiritual character. The word *chok* is related to the word *cheik*, "engraved." It symbolizes that which is deep, that which is hidden yet having meaning and interpretation. When we dig deeply enough within ourselves, when we allow ourselves wordless meditation that draws us toward the pursuit of meaning and connection with God, we have entered the world of *chok*.

In *Parashas Bechukkosai*, we are told that we must "walk" with Hashem's *chukim* in order to merit the blessings He wishes to bestow on us. Rashi comments that learning the Torah with exertion is what is implied by the use of the word *chukas* to describe the struggle to learn. The integration of information by itself is insufficient for the process of engraving to take place. The inner changes that are brought about through struggle open one's heart to that which is far above the human ability to assimilate.

The Pitfalls of Rationalization

There are inner enigmas in the Torah. The ritual of the *parah adumah*, the red heifer, whose ashes have the effect of both purifying those who are impure and bringing ritual impurity upon those who are pure, is one of the most impenetrable ones. The nature of these heavily shrouded secrets is accessible only to the tzaddikim.

We find that Moshe penetrated the layers of mystery surrounding the *parah adumah*, while King Solomon, whose mind was more gifted than that of any other mortal, did not. The Ramchal points out that the reason for this is that when any idea is limited to the parameters of human intellect, it can be corrupted. The very process of search can be doomed by morally fragile inner agendas that the person himself may not be aware of.

Thus we find that the early reformers misused the Rambam's

brilliant discourse on the objectives of mitzvos in the *Guide to the Perplexed*. Their desire to redefine Torah "rationally" in order to fit the spirit of the times reflected the ethical weakness inherent in self-worshiping cerebral pursuit. Conversely, the nobility with which unlearned women approached the challenge of self-definition when faced with the *yes* or *no* choices of the Spanish Inquisition has few parallels in our history.

The Ramchal tells us that exile itself is a *chok*. It can purify those who are impure and defile those who are uncorrupted. When we have approached the threats that the Diaspora has presented with the limited framework our minds provide, we blunder time after time. We endeavored to assimilate because it "made sense" and was "realistic."

Our ability to observe reality, understand it, and draw honest conclusions is the most precious of all of God's gifts to us. It is the means by which our similarity to Him can come into actualization. Nonetheless, it works only to the degree that we don't strain the procedure through the filter of desire and ego. When that occurs, rather than drawing us closer to Hashem, our intellectual process creates greater and greater distances. Thus, the Sefas Emes explains that all the *chukim* have objective meaning. We will never grasp their inner workings until such time as we accept them without rationalizations. When we approach the mitzvos with simplicity, without the need to justify them to ourselves through rationalization, we become worthy of truly understanding their inner life.

The Shem MiShmuel gives a profound insight into this concept by means of a parable: A child who is learning to read will find himself totally absorbed by the letters themselves. Whatever the text, even if it is a fascinating section of Talmud, it will not seem very different to him from his simple reader.

When comparing our experience to that of a genuine scholar, we find that the scholar will not focus on the letters — or even the words — individually. His focus is entirely on the ideas of the text. Similarly, when a person approaches the *chukim* with true devotion to Hashem, and with the kind of passion that is borne of consecration, his focus is not restricted by his own thought processes.

What binds us together in the service of Hashem more than

any other form of observance is the *chukim*. Each person observes the world and understands it somewhat differently from anyone else. The conclusions we draw are, therefore, going to differ. The realm of *chukim* touches the part of us that is focused not on the external world, but on its Root. In this all Jews are one.

We did not open the heart of our visitor to Torah. It was open already. Whatever else he knew, he knew the passion, devotion, and consecration that lay dormant behind the letters he had not yet seen. He felt at home in the world of *chok*.

CHAPTER FORTY-THREE
changing curses to blessings

WHY DO WE dream when we so rarely know what to do with our dreams once morning comes? For the most part, our dreams seem to us insignificant or beyond interpretation. Why should we have to dream again and again only to awaken again and again to the same confusion that may plague us?

In *Parashas Balak*, we enter the world of Bilam's dreams. What can we learn from them about ourselves and our own dreams? Before we look at Bilam's dreams, we must see how the Torah treats other people's dreams.

The Sefas Emes on *Parashas Vayeitzei* focuses on an entirely different type of dream than Bilam's: that of Yaakov. Yaakov saw a ladder that rested on the ground but reached up to the heavens. Angels were descending and ascending this ladder. There are many interpretations of this prophecy, yet regardless of its meaning, we are left with the question of why the communication took place within the framework of a dream. Why did Hashem use this medium to communicate His will to Yaakov?

In order to know Hashem's will, we need to enter a situation in which there are no vision-distorting impediments between Him and us. Some impediments are the result of sin, some the result of circumstance. When Yaakov journeyed from his childhood home to Lavan's house, he found himself far from Eretz Yisrael. Every country has its own *mazal*, its own specific way in which Hashem makes His Presence known. The only place in which the connection is direct is Eretz Yisrael. All other countries are "colored" by their *mazal*. Therefore, when Yaakov left Eretz Yisrael, he experienced Hashem indirectly, through a dream.

Our entire experience in exile is compared to a dream. We are

changing curses to blessings

far too spiritually desensitized to feel the distortions caused by exile, where there is no true prophesy, no direct experience, even in Eretz Yisrael. The same sort of attachment to foreign *mazal* will be seen for what it is in the future with Mashiach's coming and the restoration of a direct connection to Hashem.

Empirical Knowledge

Our dreams are altered by our inner attachments to that which surrounds us. In his book, *Shiurei Da'as*, Rabbi Bloch deepens this idea by focusing on the request we make after *Birkas Kohanim*, that Hashem heal our dreams and turn them about. He questions the use of the word *healing* in connection with dreams. Dreams are ephemeral; they lack the corporeal tangibility of the body. What could be wrong with a dream? And how can it be turned about?

The answer is that our entire grasp of the mental imagery of dreams is erroneous. We think our reverie reveals the future when in fact what is revealed is the present.

Any event that takes place here and now does not actually begin here and now. The source of all the events that transpire constantly is in the higher spiritual spheres, which came into being when Hashem created the world. The only part of reality that is an "open book" for us is the aspect of reality we experience through our five senses. These act as windows that permit particles of light and truth to enter. The *nefesh*, the lowest and most accessible of all the soul's powers of self-expression, is therefore dependent upon the senses.

We would have no sense of Hashem's wisdom and compassion without the ability to see, hear, and interact with the world. All we grasp is a tiny fragment of the entire picture. We see the end result without its beginning. Even what we do pick up is colored by the shadings of interpretation that our senses give it.

When Avraham looked at the world, he searched for its Master. Physically he didn't see more than we do, but his senses followed the direction that was set within him by his yearning for truth. Bilam saw the world with the same sensitivity and depth. Rather than letting himself be moved into searching for the Master, however, he wanted, in a certain sense to assume that role himself.

Both Avraham and Bilam prophesied while asleep. At that time the window that is open to the *nefesh* is not that of the senses. What exactly is it?

What We See in Our Dreams

It is the extension of reality experienced only through dreams. When we sleep, the *nefesh* is no longer completely attached to the body. The senses no longer "speak" to it. At that time, the *nefesh* is no longer held down by the limitations inherent to the senses, and it is possible for a person to glimpse reality from its very core, before it has descended from the higher worlds to play itself out in the physical world.

The conceptions open to a person in dreams, therefore, are completely different than the vision that same person has during the day through the use of actual physical sight. Even the most moving sight seen by day is inherently finite. Whether it be an awesome encounter of spirituality within nature or the even more awesome encounters we have at times when the spiritual beauty of the soul is only barely clothed by the body, we are limited to the vistas of the eye.

However, since we are not totally divorced from our bodies when we sleep, our dreams use actual physical imagery. Thus, our dreams are a fusion of two opposing realities. There is the spark of infinity that is possible to be seen only when the soul isn't totally held down by the body, and there is the use of bodily imagery, which reflects that the soul is also not totally free. It is for this reason that true interpretation of dreams requires real wisdom.

What we see in dreams is not the future, but rather it is the reality of the present. We can ask for healing for the same reasons that we ask for alleviation of illnesses we have already seen through our senses. We request that Hashem "turn over" decrees that have been revealed to us through dreams. The reason for this will give us insight into Bilam's curses being turned over and actually becoming blessings.

Seeing with Our Inner Eye

There is no such thing as pure evil. Since there is only one address from which everything comes — Hashem Himself — there is always a spark of good hidden even within the worst possible situation or person. Without that spark of Hashem's will, nothing could possibly exist.

Whether we see things as good or bad depends on two factors. One is whether we are willing to strengthen ourselves through overcoming difficulties. The other is whether we are willing to use our capacity for internal flexibility. We can adapt a given circumstance to a purpose that is holy and pure rather than the opposite. The first path is called *eskafia*, which means "conquest," the second one is called *eshafchia*, which means "turnabout."

While the root of all reality is good, to discover this goodness we often must use one or the other of these means. It is within Hashem's power to allow His will to manifest either way. We may face formidable tasks that challenge every fiber of our being. We then have no choice but conquest, hardly an ennobling option. Or we may be presented with the far more subtle and gentle challenge of channeling our goodness.

When Bilam blessed us with the words "How goodly are your tents, O Yaakov," he was responding to the visions he had had of our truest selves. He saw that the tents of the Jews in the desert did not face each other. The source of that perception was a truth about the spiritual nature of the Jews determined by Hashem before the world began. This nature can play out in a way that reflects our willingness to demonstrate our belief in our fellow Jew by living lives in which we respect each other's privacy. This in turn opens the door to propriety and chastity, which are the natural offshoots of living with inner reality.

It also can play out by our choosing to not see our friends and neighbors. We can close our hearts and eyes to them. It was this second way of expressing our deepest spiritual nature that Bilam chose. By putting it into words, he began the process of its concrete manifestation.

What he saw was far too subtle to be grasped by our senses. He was a master of dreams. The ordinary eye can be fooled by the layers and layers of disguises we sometimes wear. But the inner eye cannot be fooled. The direction we take is very much determined by the way we apply our inner nature to interpreting this world.

The Sons of Prophets

Hashem saw more than Bilam did. He saw the beauty of the lives of the Patriarchs and Matriarchs. They are the ones who began the process of turning raw material into actual reality. We, too, can turn curses to blessings.

I once was party to a conspiracy of silence. No words were exchanged, even among my co-conspirators. In our tight community of English-speaking *kollel* couples, nothing could remain invisible for very long. When Gail (not her real name) failed to appear on the sunny ledge overlooking the playground that was the afternoon home away from home of the young mothers, I began to wonder.

She had recently given birth to her third child. I had made the usual visit to the hospital and found her willing to talk about anything but her sweet, normal newborn. As the weeks progressed, things did not improve. Her door was firmly closed. Dov Ber, her young husband, looked like a ghost. I decided a visit would be in place. She opened the door for me and let me into the desolation of her heart that was only too apparent when I saw the apartment.

It was only years later, when she felt free to discuss this extremely difficult period of her life, that she told me of the conspiracy. A wall of silence was erected to preserve the cherished core of Gail's being, her honor and dignity.

I took Gail's children out most afternoons. Leah cooked. Chana brought order to chaos. Rebbetzin J. took charge of the present and future of the family. None of us knew about the others.

It could easily have been different. Bilam's blessing had been actualized. Did we know who we were through prophetic dreams? Hardly. But we knew more about Gail's dignity and humanity.

Our Sages say that if we are not prophets, we are the sons of prophets. Let us study this *parashah* to discover the aspects of our collective selves that are more than the eye can see. Let us develop a new sense of possibilities. Then we can move from the dream state of exile to the actualization of redemption.

CHAPTER FORTY-FOUR
what makes a hero?

WE ALL DELIGHT in our private collection of heroes. We measure the caliber of our lives against them continually and empower them to award us success or failure. We are always in their presence, whether we know it or not. Those whom we would like to see ourselves venerate are often our conscious champions.

Subconsciously we are far less discriminating. Who am I modeling myself after when I look in the mirror hoping that what I will see will be younger, thinner, and richer than what is really there. I doubt it is anyone I would particularly want to be like. How did she (and the mysterious owner of many possessions that make my own look homey rather than elegant) enter the roster of role models that clutter my subconscious?

Part of the answer, of course, is the fact that the society in which we live is materialistic. The non-Jewish world defines heroism much as we do: the intrepidity used in overcoming obstacles. Vanquishing enemies that hamper one's ability to prevail makes for a true hero. But there is one major difference between our version of heroism and theirs: the battlefield. Theirs is invariably material.

The enemies may be actual, as in war, where victory goes to the general who can devise a brilliant, daring — and winning — strategy. They may be psychological, as they were, for example, during the civil rights movement, when its celebrated heroes fought to tear down barriers erected by people's hearts and minds. Other heroes, distinguished explorers and (to a certain degree) great athletes, have vanquished the obstacles Hashem made into an integral part of nature.

The common denominator of these admittedly stirring achievements is the amount of self invested in meeting goals that are not necessarily enduring or inherently meaningful. Often the noble and eternal side of the hero's personality is committed to the pursuit of what is trivial.

As Jews we have historically defined heroism differently. The same commitment of self and spirit is made, but the aim is conquest of a different sort. We endeavor to vanquish that which limits our spiritual movement toward making Hashem's will our own. Let us look to *Parashas Pinchas* to develop a greater understanding of the remarkably Jewish versions of heroism it presents.

Spiritual Valor

Pinchas is described in the text as being zealous for the sake of Hashem. His assassination of Kozbi, a Midianite, and Zimri, leader of the tribe of Shimon, who were in the midst of committing a sin, had nothing to do with his need to prove his own courage to himself or to anyone else. He had no personal demon to destroy, no grudge for which to take revenge. His sole motivation was to reawaken within the Jewish people the realization of who they were and what their collective mission was.

Rabbeinu Bachya tells us that Pinchas's deepest motivation was his awareness of and yearning for attachment to Hashem, not only for himself, but for his people. The very idea of there being any sort of union between the Jews and the Midianites was a distortion of spiritual truth. Taking action was his only option. It was an act of heroism of the highest order.

The explicit mention of the type of weapon he used is significant. The word used in the verse is *romach*, which means "spear." Its numerical value is 248, equal to the number of limbs and organs of the body.

Pinchas approached his moment of valor with his entire being, expecting to die. His decision was unconditional. There was no self that he was preserving. He addressed his entire being to Hashem with each limb and organ of his physical body and the spiritual root that gives it life. Denying the imperative of the moment would have been denying his essence.

From whom did Pinchas learn such true heroism?

Pinchas was a descendant of Yosef. The spark of Divinity that burned within Yosef most unwaveringly is called *middas hayesod*. The literal meaning of this phrase is "the attribute of foundation." Rephrased in language closer to contemporary modes of speech, it is the spiritual capacity to bond with another. It is the source of life in its purest sense.

Yosef's spiritual heroism in resisting the temptation set before him by Potifar's wife was an expression of his deepest and most genuine self. He would overcome any obstacle without compromise, nor did he have any illusions about her or her husband responding to his overt rejection with compassion.

Her motives (like those of Kozbi in Pinchas's time) were confused; she, too, had a spiritual as well as a physical agenda. Her flash of true insight into the future revealed to her that Yosef would be the ancestor of her future generations. Her perceptiveness was only partially flawed; Yosef married Osnas, her adopted daughter. Resisting her was therefore the ultimate insult, for it was rejection on every possible level.

Yosef was sold into slavery in Egypt by the Midianites. Here, too, there is similarity between him and Pinchas. The fact that the Midianites were their common antagonist is no coincidence. The Maharal points out that the Midianites were the most immoral of the peoples with whom our ancestors were forced to contend. It was by encountering them that the *middas hayesod* that is part of our spiritual makeup was forced into expression. The heroism of Yosef therefore "gave birth" in a certain sense to his descendant Pinchas.

Yosef's Strange Request

The *parashah* also presents us with the daughters of Tzelafchad, who are descendants of Yosef's son, Menasheh. They, too, were heroic figures, but the choices with which they had to contend required a different sort of heroism. They were able to remain straight and not swerve to the right (the distortion caused by too much outpouring, even of one's better self) or left (the distortion caused by too much restraint).

Knowing what Hashem truly wants for oneself is a test that is both grave and subtle. As we so often find, either wrong choice is far easier than the only right one. Let us look at the resources of Tzelafchad's daughters. The heritage of Yosef's life was there for them, as it was for Pinchas, at their moment of choice. His inner need to bond with Hashem was part of their deepest selves. A look at another incident in Yosef's life can give us insight into theirs.

Dealing with one's own mortality is neither comfortable nor pleasant for most people. It is a topic avoided in our society by polite people even when directly gazing at the angel of death. One of the characteristics of heroism is seeing death for what it is: an opening to eternity. When Yosef faced the fact that his mortal existence in this world was drawing to a close, he made a request that must have seemed abstruse to the Egyptians. He asked that his bones be brought to Israel.

From the perspective of Egyptian society then (and most Western society now) Yosef was a success. He was a hero in the classic Horatio Alger rag-to-riches sense. He came to Egypt as a slave and "made it to the top." Why would he reject the soil of his adopted country as his place of final repose?

But Yosef's heroism was reflected by his winning battles that took place within himself. He knew of the power of the Land of Israel to bring about constant encounters with Hashem's Providence. This manifestation of the inviolability of Yosef's bond with Hashem was another dimension of *middas hayesod*. The aspects of his life that take on heroic proportions in the eyes of the nations were irrelevant to Yosef. What was relevant was his bond and fidelity to Hashem under any circumstance.

This longing for closeness was the reason for what seemed at the time an inexplicable request. It had the effect of changing the awareness of all the other tribes as well. Throughout the enslavement, a significant part of their ability to remember who they were came through the final request Yosef made of them. It told them that the glory of Egyptian civilization was heroic, but by terms that were not their own.

The Egyptians' world was material. The achievements of Egyptian culture that still astound us, from the hieroglyphics to the pyramids, have no enduring spiritual message. It is for this reason that only a Jew may observe Shabbos. It is the means by which we articulate our closeness to Hashem. It is His will that we celebrate His creativity and not our own.

Our Forefathers: Heroes of the Highest Order

Tzelafchad's daughters understood Yosef's love of the land and made it their own. They knew that with Tzelafchad's death their family's portion might be passed to another family, for there was no male heir. But they approached Moshe and asked that the land become theirs.

The daughters of Tzelafchad made no error. They understood the significance of their inheritance. Their motivation was not the material challenge of taming the land and making it their own. They did not seek actualization through making the desert bloom. That would be heroism of another sort, meant for a people of another genus.

They wanted the bonding that could only be theirs in Eretz Yisrael. They approached Moshe with refinement and humility. This was not because they felt that it was a useful tactic or because of their affinity for civility. It was because their heroism was like that of Pinchas. They only wanted to do His will whatever it would be.

Our Sages tell us that Pinchas is Eliyahu. The Or haChaim adds that in the same way that Pinchas brought about atonement in his time, Eliyahu will bring about atonement in his. The Maharal explains that atonement means catharsis from the causes of distance from Hashem and replacing them with closeness.

We must open our minds and hearts toward the heroic images that are indelibly part of our collective soul. We must learn first to not allow contemporary definitions of heroism to choke us. We will then be worthy of Eliyahu restoring our hearts to the purer ones of our children, and the hearts of the children who have strayed (regardless of their ages) to their forefathers.

CHAPTER FORTY-FIVE
regaining our ability to remain unchanging

PLANNING FOR A BAR MITZVAH doesn't seem to need more than a year at most. The preparations for a bar mitzvah that took place not long ago in Jerusalem began several decades earlier. The bar mitzvah boy made a *siyum* on all of Mishnah. This impressive achievement would be significant under any circumstance. Considering the father had recently arrived from the Soviet Union, the guests were awestruck. A friend approached the boy's father and asked him the secret of his incredible success in educating his son in an environment that was lacking in everything except hostility. The father recounted the following story that took place in his early teens.

When he was growing up, his father wanted to avoid the possibility of his children viewing Judaism as a philosophical foible of their family. The environment was so utterly barren spiritually that finding even one other family that still retained a commitment to Torah was almost impossible. Betrayal was not uncommon, and the price for friendship was therefore too high.

When he reached the critical age of early adolescence, when the need for self-discovery can drive a wedge between parents and children under the best of circumstances, the urgency of his need to experience Yiddishkeit in a setting different from that of his home was crucial. Travel was complicated. An internal passport was required and a reason for being anywhere other than one's assigned cubbyhole (be it work or school) was a prerequisite. His father knew what was at stake. The arrangements were somehow made, and Leibel spent his first Shabbos away from his family.

The host was a prominent scion of a Chassidic family. Under normal circumstances, he would have succeeded his father as rebbe. In the reality

regaining our ability to remain unchanging

with which he had to cope, there were no Chassidim.

Friday night proceeded very much as in the guest's own home. The tablecloth had once been white. The holiness of the Kiddush and the self-sacrifice of the participants were the main features of the menu. The aging couple and their two sons relished their roles as hosts.

The next morning was similar to the previous night, with one essential difference: the two sons were absent from the table. When Leibel asked his host about their whereabouts, he was told curtly that they were at work. He let his eyes meet those of his host without wavering. He knew this was a moment he would never be able to forget.

This man was his father's friend. They had studied together under unbelievable circumstances. Taking risks was their lifestyle.

"My father doesn't allow any of us to work on Shabbos. Why are you different?" was out of his mouth before he realized that basic decency and compassion should have silenced him.

"I want you to know something," his host answered. "We will all be caught in the end. I will be caught, your father will be caught, you will be caught. We will be sent to Siberia. The games we play here won't work there. We will all violate Shabbos, even your father."

Leibel replied with utter stillness. There was nothing to say.

The monotony of the train trip gave him time to think. He realized his father's friend was right. The vast, unending panorama reflected a reality too vast to battle. He entered his house committed to surrender. His father listened to his narrative without interruption. Leibel broke into his father's silence with more force than he intended. "He is right, Tatte! Isn't that the truth?"

The answer he received is difficult for people such as ourselves to grasp. We know the evil empire has fallen. Once one sees the end of the story, the middle loses its mystery. To us his reply seems ludicrous, for we know that there was an end in sight.

"We will be caught. He is right. No one can evade them forever. But this Shabbos still has eternal value, regardless of what will happen later."

The willingness to take the challenge of the moment on its own terms is part of what being Jewish is about. If not for this quality, we would have long ago submitted to the influence of powers that seemed almost omnipotent in the ephemeral slice of time in which Hashem granted them dominion.

We have made many journeys in our history as a people. Each one looks less threatening from the perspective gained by twenty-twenty retrospective vision. Each except the one we walk on now, moment by moment. We have not yet completed our journey. We are in exile, which by definition means we have not "arrived" at our destination. This is true on every level — spiritual, geographical, emotional, intellectual, individual and collective. We have survived, but by no stretch of the imagination are we unbroken and unscarred.

Parshiyos Mattos and *Masei* are read at the time of the year in which we must encounter ourselves with honesty and not flinch at our brokenness. During the three weeks called the *yemei bein hametzarim*, when we mourn the loss of our *Beis HaMikdash* and our subsequent exile, we must gain strength and self-knowledge so we have the courage to go on.

Unchanging Words, Unchanging People

Parashas Mattos begins with Moshe addressing the heads of the tribes and telling them, "This is the thing that Hashem has commanded." Rashi comments that only Moshe was able to use the word *zeh*, "this," when describing his prophecy. The meaning of the word *zeh* is very specific. It means "this" in the most precise sense. Other prophets used the word *koh*, which means "thus." The implication of the word *koh* is that the message being conveyed is less fixed.

The Maharal explains that there are two kinds of prophecy. In one case, the prophecy concerns the world and Hashem's interaction with it. An example of this would be Hashem revealing to Yehoshua that the walls of Yericho would fall. This has eternal significance, but the events themselves are transient. The walls would fall, but they could be rebuilt. That is the nature of the world; that is the way Hashem created it.

The second type of prophecy is that of Moshe. His prophecy included the kind of prophecy in the first group with an additional quality: the Torah and mitzvos. Unlike other prophecies that relate to the world, which continually unfolds and changes, the Torah and mitzvos are unchanging. As Jews, we have a certain need to find the part of ourselves that recognizes that which is unchanging.

Am Kadosh vs. Am Keshei Oref

Later in the *parashah*, we are given insight not only into the unchanging nature of the Torah, but into the component of our very nature that is equally enduring. In the course of discussing the laws of ritual purification when coming in contact with the dead (with regard to the commandment to wage war with Midian), Rashi informs us that the laws of purification would be relevant even though "only you are called *adam*."

The Maharal explains that even though the nations of the world are human, their self-definitions emerge from the material realities that surround them. They are referred to as *mishpechos ha'adamah*, "the families of the earth," since this, the earth itself, is the source of their most basic level of identity. It is impossible to conceive of an Englishman without conjuring up England. This is equally true in terms of individual identity. Career and possessions often are the ultimate and at times the only self-statement that can be made with any honesty.

The nations' identity is therefore constantly in flux. What is true for one generation is not true for the next, and what is true in one set of circumstances is viewed as false in another. This unfolding, evolving identity is at times called "progress."

Conversely, we Jews are called *am keshei oref*, "a stiff-necked people." Our lack of internal flexibility can be misused. The people of Ninveh responded to Yonah's rebuke and immediately repented, while the Jews stubbornly resisted the exhortations of the prophets for decades on end. We are not easily moved. Our identity is not developed or maintained by external experience. But the very part of us that at times will tenaciously combat *teshuvah*, the part of us that resists change, is an emanation of our *kedushah*. *Kedushah* is the ability to transcend the limits of external experience; it is the part of us that is above time and place. It is a reflection of the aspect of our collective identity that can only be defined by that which is unchanging

At times we do deeds that seem to redefine our identity either as individuals or as a people. We seem just as capable of wavering as anyone else. We catch ourselves being so caught up in what is going on around us that we stop questioning who we really are and what we really want. When the bus came, was it I who made the decision to push ahead or did I just find myself caught up with the imperative of the moment? Did I mean everything I said in anger, or was I just absorbed by the free-flying emotions created by the drama of the moment?

The Worst-Case Scenario and Its Rectification

Parashas Masei brings us the case of a person who commits a murder through negligence. Negligence is by its nature a consequence of losing sensitivity to the precious nature of human life because of the vivid character of superficial considerations. No one, for instance, leaves home in the morning with the intention of ending the day with their life and that of others changed forever as a result of an accident. Nonetheless, I have never met anyone who drives who was honestly able to tell me that they never took a safety "shortcut." The distance between the perpetrator of a tragedy and ourselves may be less than we would like to think.

Why does someone speed, or commit any other typical error? Usually it is to "save time." But for who's sake? It is God Who is the Master of time. When we make our choices, they need to be based on the internal, on what is Godly, not societal conventions or the drama of the moment.

The Torah tells us that the atonement for the perpetrator of a murder committed through negligence is exile. He must go to a city of refuge and there redefine himself. He can no longer take shelter in familiarity or in instinctive responses. He has lost the option of living a life that is defined exclusively by external experiences.

He remains there until the death of the *kohen gadol*, who is compared to Michael, the angel who offers the souls of the tzaddikim to Hashem on the supernal altar. The *kohen gadol*'s mission is to create closeness between Hashem and His people. By separating the Shechinah within a person from its body, the murderer created a situation where less Godliness, less closeness to Hashem, could *regaining our ability to remain unchanging*

be found in the world. A dead body is not a repository for Hashem's Presence. He is expelled from the presence of the *kohen gadol*, whose death is his atonement.

Hashem provides the murderer with every possibility of *teshuvah* for a reestablishment of his authentic identity. This process is part of the Torah. Every detail has relevance for our lives. Hashem places us in exile in any one of its myriad disguises in order to give us new choices.

The days of *bein hametzarim*, the time of year when our collective exile began, is a time of challenge and concealment. We must use these days as a time of discovering the truest dimension of our identity. We can find the place in ourselves and in others that is permanently and immutably unchanging. We address our truest selves to the world, instead of letting it be defined by the world.

At times, the enticing, enveloping present confronts a person with less drama than the generation of the Holocaust and Soviet oppression, but perhaps with equal force.

When I look at my school journals, I observe not only the natural changes that take place over time, but changes in self-image. What was I thinking at fourteen? What was I thinking at seventeen? I still recall having my hair straightened at the beauty parlor and choosing the picture of a petite blue-eyed native of Iowa or therebouts when Carmen (yes, that was her name) asked how I wanted to look. Who did I want to be? Why?

I must learn to notice the genuine choices that confront me. The choices are narrower and more decisive than they appear to be. The result may be seen immediately, but at times the results can be seen only half a lifetime later.

Let us retain the image of a thirteen year old making a *siyum*. Let us not forget the discussion that took place between his father and his grandfather decades earlier.